GLORY DAYS WITH THE DODGERS

AND OTHER DAYS WITH OTHERS

GLORY DAYS
WITH
THE DODGERS

AND OTHER DAYS
WITH OTHERS

JOHN ROSEBORO
With Bill Libby

New York ATHENEUM 1978

Library of Congress cataloging in publication data

Roseboro, John.
  Glory days with the Dodgers, and other days with
others.

    1. Roseboro, John.   2.   Baseball players—
United States—Biography.   I. Libby, Bill, joint
author. II. Title.
GV865.R66A34   1978   796.357'092'4   [B]
ISBN 0-689-10864-8   77-23679

Published simultaneously in Canada by McClelland and Stewart Ltd.
Composition by Kingsport Press, Inc., Kingsport, Tennessee
Printed and bound by Halliday Lithograph Corporation,
West Hanover and Plympton, Massachusetts
Designed by Harry Ford
First Edition

FOR MY PARENTS, *who meant so much to me*

PREFACE

It is only a number, .249, a batting average, actually, but it represents in part a man's baseball career. It is John Roseboro's career average, not a high one.

I wish it had been a couple of points higher at least. It was, .251, when he left the Dodgers, but it dropped a little the last two or three years, when he played with other teams. For some reason, .251 sounds a lot higher than .249.

However, there is much more to a player than his hitting average and much more to a man than his playing career. I have always said that an author is at the mercy of his subject. His talent, whatever it is, can take him only so far; the subject has to take him the rest of the way. Because John Roseboro gave me so much, this book is more than it might have been. He was an all-star catcher and a championship competitor, but his career alone does not demand a book. It is the life he led that does. It is not all pretty, but he put it down as it was.

You will not find many numbers in this book. Little play-by-play. It is not just a baseball book. It is a book about what it was like to be the boy he was in the place he came from, where he went, what it was like, and what it did to him. It is a book about the people he has known, some of whom are famous and some not. It is a book about how he came to know himself and what he wanted out of life. It is a book about the highs and lows of a man's life.

I don't think Roseboro spared himself much. Because he was willing to reveal himself to the bone, I had the opportunity to do a book that maybe will go beyond most baseball books. I wanted to say this because if I haven't succeeded, blame me, not him.

In my mind, he is some man.

BILL LIBBY

ACKNOWLEDGMENTS

FOR THEIR HELP, the authors wish to thank Marvin Brown of Atheneum, Matt Merola of Mattgo Inc., Fred Claire and Steve Brener of the Dodgers, Frank Finch, the fine sportswriter who suggested the project, and all the photographers whose photos were provided us. Also, Harold Rosenthal, one of the great baseball writers, who helped with the editing, argued against some of the less pleasant passages, won some arguments with us, lost some, but was of great help to us. Also, our transcriber, Jackie Sommers. And finally, and especially, Barbara Fouch.

ILLUSTRATIONS

GLORY DAYS WITH THE DODGERS

AND OTHER DAYS WITH OTHERS

Walking into an office one day, I pushed a door right into an old lady who was coming out. I said, "Lady, I apologize, I'm very sorry." And she looked at me and said, "Son, the world is full of sorry people. Next time don't be sorry, be more goddamn careful." I've never forgotten that. I've decided I'm not sorry for anything I've ever done. I just wish I'd been more goddamn careful.

JOHN ROSEBORO

1.

THE THING I'm remembered best for is the Juan Marichal incident. It's too bad, because a ballplayer would like to be remembered for something better than a bloody brawl, but that's what everyone always remembers, even those who weren't there or who weren't even following baseball back in 1965. There's more to me than baseball and more to my career than this one thing, but it was spectacular. I guess I might as well begin a book about my life by telling my side of that spectacular story.

It grew out of a beanball incident. I want to be completely honest so I have to admit that while I don't believe in beanballs, I do believe in knockdown and brushback pitches. I don't believe in hurting batters, but I also don't believe in being hurt by batters.

When the pitcher is being hurt, when the hitter is standing on top of the plate, fearless and swinging from his ass, you have to move him back, make him nervous, get him thinking by throwing high and tight, under his chin, or maybe low and inside at his knees.

Whatever else it is, that's baseball.

As a catcher, I've called for it many times. With the Dodgers we had a simple signal. I'd flip my index finger, which meant the pitcher was to flip the hitter. Sometimes you'd call for it on a first pitch, but usually you'd use it when you had a count of no balls and two strikes on the batter. And often as not it set the batter up for the third strike. After you loosened him up, he'd back away from one over the outside.

You didn't use it all the time. You used it at the right time, when the situation called for it. Hell, I even taught my own kid to use it when he was pitching in Little League. I told him, "Jaimie, when you go against a team with maybe one good hitter, you throw it by his throat and he won't be very good for a while, unless he's really a real tough kid, in which case you've got to give the devil his due."

It's easy for a guy like Nolan Ryan, who I got to know when I was coaching the California Angels. He's wild anyway, so when he brushes a batter back or knocks a dude down, the guy doesn't know whether Nolan meant it or not. Well, I can tell you that sometimes he means it. He's this nice, angelic kid, baby-faced, soft-spoken, and clean-living, but he's as bad as a bandit. He'll spin you as soon as look at you, and it doesn't bother him if he bangs you in the ribs.

He's got the batters scared to death and it's as big a weapon as his fast ball.

On the Dodgers, Don Drysdale was the meanest and most willing. It was a big weapon for the big guy. Don Sutton and Claude Osteen didn't hesitate to flip them either, but Drysdale was the one who did it most and enjoyed it best.

Sandy Koufax wouldn't do it. Sandy threw harder than anyone else at that time, about as hard as Ryan does now, but Sandy really was a nice guy and afraid of hurting anyone. The Marichal incident happened when Koufax was pitching. I think if it had happened on a day Drysdale was pitching, he would have taken care of Marichal and I never would have gotten my head hit in.

It happened on a Sunday afternoon late in August 1965, when the Dodgers were playing the San Francisco Giants up in Candlestick Park in the fourth and final game of a crucial series between a couple of clubs that were contending for a pennant.

Actually, it had started on Saturday night. Maury Wills had this trick where he faked a bunt and brought his bat back. The catcher, leaning forward to go for the bunt, lots of times hit the bat with his glove. He did it this time. It was interference and Maury was awarded first base. The Giants howled, but Wills wound up scoring.

When Matty Alou led off for them in their half, he tried the same thing. His bat missed my glove, but the ball hit me hard in the chest protector as I moved forward. I let out a howl at Matty, calling him a "weasel bastard," and said if he hurt me again I was going to hurt him. Then I realized that he hadn't done anything different from what Maury had done. Alou was a little guy and as nice a guy as there was in baseball, so I said, "Forget it—I'm sorry."

I figured it hadn't been Matty's idea anyway, but Herman Franks's, the manager of the Giants. I looked over at fat Franks. There he was, standing on the dugout steps, hollering at me, just wolfin' away. He was saying I shouldn't dish it out if I couldn't take it, which was true enough, but worked-up ballplayers have tunnel vision and sometimes only see things the way they want to see them. The shoe was on the other foot now. I was hollering right back at Franks, saying he was too fat to take his chances at the plate and garbage like that.

What ticked me off was that Juan Marichal was wolfin' at me too, standing next to Franks and really letting me have it. The Giants were asking for an interference call and they weren't getting it. But Marichal was no part of the play and I didn't like him laying in to me. I yelled, "You sonofabitch, if you have something to say, come out here and say it to my face!" but he didn't budge.

At Candlestick Park the clubhouses are close to each other, and sometimes the ballplayers leave together. Walking to our bus that night, I happened to fall in alongside Orlando Cepeda of the Giants. I told him to tell Marichal that if he had the guts to tangle with me, fine, but if not, to quit hiding behind fat Franks and wolfin' at me from behind the manager's back. After that I forgot about it. Maybe Marichal got the message and it made him mad.

The next afternoon, Marichal pitched and Wills led off with a bunt hit down the third-base line. Ron Fairly followed with a bloop hit that drove Wills in, and we were ahead. I guess Juan's Latin blood began to boil. Wills was a big part of our offense in those days. He usually got on base one way or another, and when he got on he was good bet to get home. For some reason, pitchers are more embarrassed by the guys who beat out bunts and scratch out hits and steal bases and score than they are by the bigger guys who hit home runs. Wills was making them look bad and the Giants hated him for it.

He was also our leader, and we were mad as hell when Marichal threw one at his knees next time up. Maury had to flop in the dirt to get out of the way. He was my roomie and I was madder than anyone. You know, it's all right for you to do it to them, but not for them to do it to you. Anyway, his body was all beat up from sliding and being banged by pitches, and I felt for him. But Maury took it in stride. He got up, brushed himself off, gave Marichal a long look, and then went right back to bat.

When Juan knocked down the next batter, Ron Fairly, we got really angry and began to really wolf at him. Clearly, he had challenged us. The home-plate umpire, Shag Crawford, wasn't doing anything, so it was up to us to take care of it ourselves. When Willie Mays, their star, came up in their half, I called for Koufax to flip him. It worked a lot against Willie, anyway. But Koufax couldn't do it. He threw the ball so far over Willie's head that Mays would have had to climb a ladder to get hit by the ball. It went all the way to the backstop.

Koufax later called it a "token gesture." He said he meant to come a lot closer but made a lousy pitch. The thing is, that really gets the other guys to wolfin' at you. They figure you're too gutless to throw at their heads, so they really give it to you. Koufax was constitutionally incapable of throwing at anyone's head, so I decided to take matters into my own hands. When Juan came up, I went out to tell Sandy to pitch him low and inside and I'd buzz Marichal from behind the plate.

The second pitch was low and inside. I dropped it, picked it up, and in pegging it back to Sandy I threw it about two inches past Juan's nose. Later he said I'd nicked his ear, but because of the way a right-handed batter stands at the plate, there's no way you can nick his ear without hitting him square in the head. Unless he's turned to look to his left. And Juan wasn't.

I saw it go by his nose. It was intentional all right. I meant for him to feel it. I was so mad I'd made up my mind that if he protested, I was going after him. He protested, so I started out of my crouch.

He screamed, "Why you do that? You better not hit me with that ball."

I went to hit him with a punch and he hit me with his bat. As I came out of my crouch and moved on him, he backed off towards the mound, raised his bat, and started to swing it at me. I raised my left hand to protect my face. I think he swung three times at me. One of the swings hit me flush on the left side of my head and hurt like hell. I had taken karate lessons, but I forgot all the fancy fighting I'd ever learned and went after him as if it was an alley fight.

I dived at him, swinging punches, and felt at least one of them hit somewhere on his head (later, one of my knuckles hurt). But he pulled away, and as I fell to the ground he tore off my catcher's mask and threw it aside. Now I was without any protection from his bat. Tito Fuentes, who had been waiting in the on-deck circle, came over carrying his bat. I looked up and there were Marichal and Fuentes, with their bats raised, ready to hit me in the head.

By this time players from both sides had come running to join the fight from the field and off the bench. Howie Reed had run all the way in from the bullpen to take on Marichal, who kicked him. Later, Reed showed three spike cuts on his left leg. It took half the Giants to hold Howie off Juan. The other half was holding Lou Johnson back. Howie and Lou were throwing punches wildly. Meanwhile, I managed to roll away and regain my feet.

I didn't see anything clearly. It was all confusion. My head didn't hurt too much, but I had blood all over me and could see I was still bleeding. I was mad that he had hit me with a bat, and mad that I'd only gotten in one blow, which I didn't think had hurt him.

As Marichal ran toward his dugout I chased him, but Willie Mays grabbed me and started to plead, "John, stop it, stop fighting, your eye is out." That didn't do my disposition any good.

Later, Walter Alston, our manager, said, "I thought the bat had knocked Roseboro's left eye out. There was nothing but blood where his eye had been."

Most of the forty-two thousand fans in the ball park that day were Giants' fans, of course, and they booed me as I was helped into the dugout. I remember giving them the finger. Willie Mays sat by my side, cradling my head in his hands and crying, while Doc Buhler, our trainer, examined my head.

I guess Mays was more a ballplayer than he was a Giant. He was a sensitive guy, a good buddy, and he didn't like what his teammate had done to me.

Meanwhile, Marichal was standing in the Giants' dugout, waving his bat at me and challenging me to come get some more. One of our coaches, Danny Ozark, who'd been acting as a peacemaker, went at Marichal then, and the whole thing almost broke out again. Ozark, now the Phillies' manager, later said, "I went after Marichal because he was making fun of someone he'd hurt unfairly. A fellow who would do what he did would hit a woman."

Wally Moon, who had a pretty good fight with Orlando Cepeda, apparently, added later, "I'd never seen one human being attack another with a club before." I hadn't either, and I wasn't too happy about being the guy who'd gotten attacked, even if I'd started it.

Doc Buhler said I had to leave the game so I could go to the clubhouse to get my head stitched up. I didn't want to go. I didn't want to give the Giants and their fans the satisfaction. I told him to wipe off the blood and let me go back in the game. But Alston, our manager, wouldn't go for it. "You got to get fixed up," he said. "Shit," I said.

At Candlestick Park you had to walk from the dugout into the outfield to get to the clubhouses, and as we went the fans were wolfin' me, cursing me, and ridiculing me. Fans see things as they want to see them, of course. They don't always show a lot of class. But, then, neither do ballplayers. As I left, I bent over and patted my rear at them meaning "kiss my ass."

I guess sixty people got into the fight, but me and Marichal are all anyone remembers. It took about twenty minutes to restore peace. I got into the clubhouse, and Russ Hodges, the Giants' broadcaster, who's dead now, was saying I was swinging my mask at Marichal and that Juan was only trying to protect himself. Later, Marichal said the same thing. Absolutely untrue. It made me mad on top of mad.

I have some press pictures, in sequence, which I'll use in

this book; they clearly show Marichal pulling my mask off my head long after he hit me.

Koufax was so shook by the whole thing that he walked the next two batters when the game got under way again. Mays may have been shook, too, but he hit his fourth home run of the four-game series and the Giants came from behind to beat us. They won that battle, but we won the war. They split that series, but we won the pennant.

I had a swollen knot the size of a cantaloupe, and the two-inch gash above my left eye, where Juan's bat had hit me above my mask, was starting to throb like a toothache. Doc Buhler wanted to stitch the cut, but there isn't much flesh between skin and bone at that point on a skull and I really didn't want him to go in there with the needle. He said he could maybe put some butterfly bandages on it, which would hold it closed. So I said for him to do that, and he did.

Candlestick Park security guards and the police were worried about protecting me, so they stuck a Giants' cap on my head and hustled me out of the ball park and got me out to the airport with a police escort before the ball game ended. I took my favorite seat in the card-playing section on our plane and was waiting to pick up our regular poker game when the guys got on board more than an hour later for the flight to New York.

When we got there I didn't say a hell of a lot to the press. All I told them was that Marichal had been wrong and had lost his temper and hurt me, but I didn't rip him or anything like that. I knew him as a good guy who had a bad temper and I just figured he'd blown his cool. I just wished to hell he'd fought me like a man, with his fists. Or maybe just accepted my "buzzer" the way we accepted his brushback and beanball pitches.

He made a public apology for having hit me with the bat, but insisted that he was protecting himself from me. A lot of people on the Dodgers were saying that he should be suspended for the season. It came as a shock to all of us when a few days later Warren Giles, then National League president, simply suspended him for eight playing days and fined him $1,750. Giles said that Marichal's actions were "repugnant" and "obnoxious" and had no place in the game and were harmful to sports. But the fine, while the highest ever handed a big leaguer, seemed like peanuts compared to the money he was making, and the suspension seemed insufficient.

Of course, we wanted one of the best pitchers in the game out of our pennant fight. As it was, he missed two starts and we won the pennant by two games. He pitched all right for a while after he returned to action, but then he slumped in the stretch. I think he was hurt much more than I was by the incident. I don't think he ever threw at batters again the way he had done. That was a big part of his game, but, as I have said, it was only a part of the game, period. But Marichal had many good years after that.

The press made a big deal of the incident. The newspapers were full of stories about it for days. And there were a lot of pictures of Marichal banging on me with his bat. *Life* magazine and *Sports Illustrated* ran them, and most of the other major magazines ran some. We were in demand for a lot of radio and television interviews. Marichal was famous and he helped make Roseboro famous. He was a villain and I was a hero. No action was taken against me.

I remember that was the first time I met Howard Cosell. Les Crane had a nighttime TV show out of New York at that time and he brought me on to be interviewed by Cosell. I remember Cosell ranting and raving at Crane before the show, telling him this was the "sports story of the century" or some such nonsense and trying to make sure we got a big buildup when we were brought on. In the interview itself, Howard was sympathetic to me and called Marichal's deed "dastardly."

After we left New York, the Giants followed us in and Cosell brought Marichal on the Crane show and was sympathetic to him. Cosell made a big deal out of how I had provoked the incident. I thought that was pretty funny and decided right then and there that Howard would switch, and was a lot more interested in looking good than telling it like it was. I have seen and heard nothing since to make me change my opinion.

Of course I had provoked the incident, even though in Giles's statement he called it an "unprovoked" incident. But I don't think anything I did justified Marichal hitting me on the head with his bat. I didn't think the punishment was sufficient and so I sued him for $100,000 or so—I think it was $110,000. The lawyers figure out those figures somehow.

I remember Len Gabrielson of the Giants coming to me to tell me how much Marichal had been changed by the incident and how many people were on his ass about it and how hurt he was and how nice I would be to drop the suit. I said I'd think about it, but I had no intention of dropping it.

Then Gabrielson got traded to the Dodgers and he came to me to tell me how Marichal was a horse's ass, an egotistical, selfish bastard, that every player on the Giants hated him, and that he hoped I broke the bastard.

I called him on it. I asked him if he wasn't the same guy who in a different uniform had told me what a good guy Marichal was and how good it would be of me to go easy on him. He got angry and got on his bicycle—but hell, I guess we were never going to be good buddies anyway, even wearing the same uniform.

It was a mess, it caused more commotion than it rated, and it's lasted longer than it should have. In the end, we settled out of court with Marichal. I got seven thousand dollars, I think. I'm not even sure. Seven years later, believe it or not. It took that long.

I'm sorry the whole thing happened. I never talked to him about it directly until about two years ago at an old-timers' game. We shook hands and I said maybe we shouldn't because now they wouldn't have anything to write about.

It's funny, I'd never had a fight on a baseball field, but after that I got into a few and I got in the middle of some others. It was as if I was marked as a fighter. But there's no question that the bit hurt him more than it hurt me. It soiled him. It has stuck to him like a stain. I think some people think of him hitting me with the bat more than they think of him as the great pitcher he was.

I batted against him many times after that night, but he never threw at me. Oddly enough, near the end of his career he wound up with the Dodgers. I was out of the game awhile and I didn't even go to any games, except I went to one of his games to see why he wasn't pitching well anymore. I saw that he wasn't throwing at batters anymore. I thought that he could still pitch, but the batters were digging in and teeing off on him. Later, I told him he couldn't let Los Angeles fans dictate the way he worked if he wanted to go on working. I said he still had his stuff but he had to back up the batters if he wanted to survive. He just smiled. I guess he couldn't do it anymore.

Well, it's long gone now, but it lingers on and everyone remembers it when they think of Marichal or me. It's a hell of a thing to be remembered for. I played pro ball for almost twenty years, fourteen seasons in the majors, ten in Los Angeles. I started in Brooklyn and wound up in Minnesota and Washington. I wasn't a great player but I was a good one. I was the starting catcher for four pennant winners in four World Series, and I was picked to play in six all-star games.

The title I wanted for this book, .249, should tell a lot. I was just a journeyman as a hitter, though I got some big hits, drove in some big runs, and helped win some big games. In the beginning I was a heavy hitter but I wasn't a catcher. When I came in from the outfield to catch, my hitting went to hell. I concentrated on my catching and I became one of the best defensive catchers in the game. The players voted me two "golden gloves" for my fielding.

I was the regular receiver for a couple of the top pitchers— Sandy Koufax and Don Drysdale. They'll tell you I helped them. I caught a couple of Koufax's no-hitters. Near the end of my career I helped make big winners out of a couple of guys who had just been getting by. They're records I achieved simply by playing a long time with a lot of good players, but I still hold a couple of major-league marks for most chances accepted and most putouts by a catcher.

But I'm not terribly interested in numbers. I'm not going to talk about putouts and assists and hits and errors. I'm interested in people, myself included.

I'm going to try to tell what it's like to be a ballplayer, maybe a little bit about what it is like to be a black ballplayer, and what the life is like when you are not a superstar. And something about those ballplayers I played with and against who were or weren't superstars. And about coaching. And about the managers I played for and coached for. And the writers. And the fans. And the ladies.

I'm in my middle forties, there is more to me than my baseball career, and I'm going to try to tell you what there has been and what there is, what's left of the money I made and blew, the marriage I made and blew, what has come between me and my kids, what happens to a ballplayer when he stops being a ballplayer, what has happened on the long road from Ashland, Ohio, to Los Angeles, going from the small time to the big time, and back down again.

There has been a hell of a lot more to me and my life than the Marichal incident.

Roseboro's first Los Angeles Dodgers' team, the 1958 Dodgers, franchise moved from Brooklyn to Los Angeles.

Front row, left to right:
Charlie Neal, Ed Roebuck, Don Demeter, Arnold Tesh, batboy; Larry Sherry, Jackie Collum, Jim Gilliam.

Second row:
Charlie DiGiovanna (equipment manager); Dick Gray, Joe Pignatano, Pee Wee Reese, Joe Becker (coach); Greg Mulleavy (coach); Walt Alston (manager); Charlie Dressen (coach); Roger Craig, Carl Erskine, Geno Cimoli.

Third row:
John Griffin (clubhouse attendant); Lee Scott (traveling secretary); Randy Jackson, Elmer Valo, Norm Larker, Fred Kipp, John Roseboro, Ron Negray, Danny McDevitt, Duke Snider, Dr. Harold Wendler (trainer).

Back row:
Carl Furillo, Sandy Koufax, Clem Labine, Don Zimmer, Al Walker (coach); Gil Hodges, Don Newcombe, Johnny Podres, Don Bessent, Don Drysdale, Bill Buhler (trainer).

The only two black faces in this sea of white—the Ashland, Ohio, high school football team, 1950—belong to John Roseboro (33), third row, and brother Jim (20) bottom.

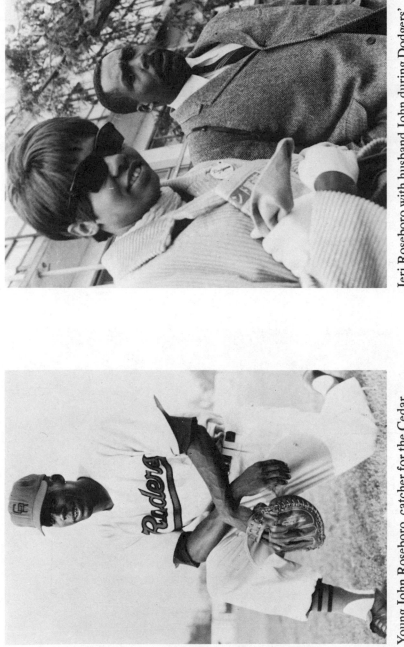

Jeri Roseboro with husband John during Dodgers' tour of Japan, 1965.

Young John Roseboro, catcher for the Cedar Rapids Raiders of Three-I minor league, 1955.

The Incident: Having struck Roseboro with his bat, Juan Marichal is shown pulling mask off John as catcher charges him, contrary to his claim catcher swung mask at him.

Unmasked Roseboro struggles to stop Marichal from hitting him with the bat again as pitcher Sandy Koufax comes on to help. August 1965 incident took place at San Francisco's Candlestick Park in Giants' game with Dodgers.

Roommates John Roseboro and Maury Wills make with the music, 1961. That's a Clavietta Rosey is playing. **Below:** In Brooklyn, 1957, a rookie with the Dodgers, twenty-four-year-old backup catcher John Roseboro sits in the dugout with Roy Campanella, his friend, mentor, and the man he would replace the following season after the tragic auto accident that ended the Hall of Famer's career.

Pitcher Koufax and catcher Roseboro hold up three hands and fifteen fingers representing fifteen strikeouts Sandy threw to John in winning World Series opener against Yankees, 1963. **Below:** Catcher Roseboro, manager Walter Alston, and pitcher Don Drysdale wait for relief pitcher in a sad scene that is part of the baseball picture.

After hitting his first major-league home run, July 19, 1957, to top Chicago, 6–3, Brooklyn Dodger John Roseboro is congratulated by, left to right, Randy Jackson, Gino Cimoli, Gil Hodges, and batboy, while umpire Frank Dascoli remains neutral. **Right:** Looking through glasses he wore to correct an eye problem, Roseboro watches with awe as ball he hit heads for the seats. A three-run home run in the second inning of the first World Series game, October, 1963, it led to a 5–2 triumph in New York and an eventual four-game sweep of the classic. Shocked catcher is Elston Howard. Umpire is Joe Paparella.

Stealing home for winning run in September 1962 crucial contest with Giants before full house in Dodger Stadium, speedy catcher Roseboro slides under tag of Tom Haller while teammate Jim Gilliam and umpire Doug Harvey look on. **Below:** Roseboro receives Golden Glove trophy from representative of Rawlings, after being named catcher on the National League All-Star Fielding Team, 1966.

Sequence shows catcher Roseboro flipping Darryl Spencer, who
goes flying and crashes to ground after trying to knock over Dodger
during home plate meeting.

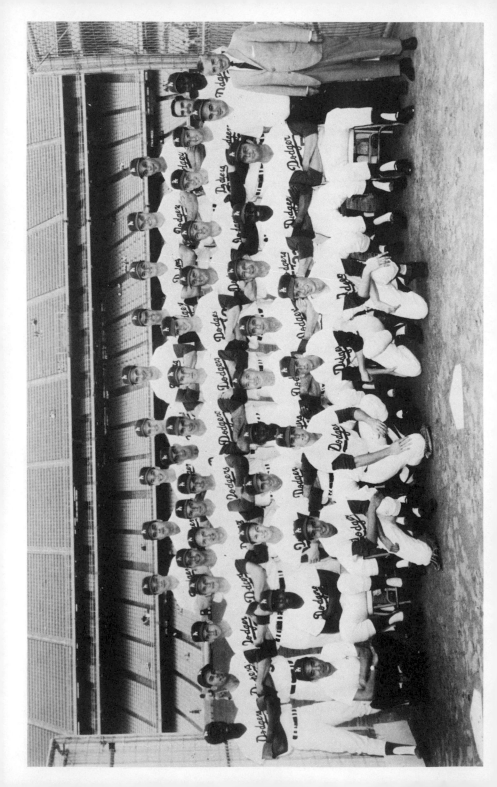

Roseboro's last Dodgers' team, 1967

Back row, left to right:
Al Ferrara, Ron Perranoski, Alan Foster, Tommy Dean, Len Gabrielson, Bob Bailey, Jim Campanis, Jim Lefebvre and Luis Alcaraz.

Middle row:
Lou Johnson, Ron Hunt, Don Sutton, Bob Miller, Jim Hickman, Carroll Beringer (coach), Gene Michael, Jim Brewer, John Duffie, Dick Egan, Phil Regan, Bill Singer, Ron Fairly, Dick Schofield, Jeff Torborg, Claude Osteen, Bill Buhler (trainer), John Mattei (trainer), Willie Crawford and Lee Scott (traveling secretary).

Front row:
Nobe Kawano (equipment manager), John Roseboro, Wes Parker, Lefty Phillips (coach), Jim Gilliam (coach), Walt Alston (manager), Preston Gomez (coach), Danny Clark (coach,) Nate Oliver and Don Drysdale.

Kneeling in front:
Batboys Richard Raya, Richard Aspell, Greg Krakor and John Wernett.

2.

I'M PROUD of my parents. They didn't have a lot, but what they had they made go a long way. They worked hard all their lives and got their two kids off to a good start. They did right by me and my brother, Jim. Mom's gone now, much too soon. She was only in her early fifties. Dad's in his seventies and lives near me in southern California, more or less retired, a long way from Ashland, where he and Mom met.

I'm a junior. John Roseboro, Sr., came out of Atlanta to kick around the country a few years as a young man. He landed in Ashland as a chauffeur for Morris Topping, who owned a Ford dealership. He used to vacation in Florida every year. He'd take the train there and back, while Dad drove the car so that the boss had the use of it in both places.

Ashland was a town of twelve or thirteen thousand people back in the 1930s. It's grown by maybe five or six thousand since. It's about sixty miles southeast of Cleveland and north of Colombus—about halfway between the two.

There are a couple of big businesses and a few factories in Ashland—like the Faultless Rubber Company plant, which makes some pretty good golf balls—but it's not a big-business town, it's really just a small place.

I guess there wasn't too much for a young buck like Dad to do in that town in the early 1930s. There were only a few blacks in the entire town. When he wasn't working, Dad used to drive the car around. Mom's was one of two black families on the south side. They had two houses there. Mom sometimes was sitting on the porch when Dad drove by, and, as the story goes, he'd stop to talk. As I understand it, Mom's family was sort of uppity and not too keen on her taking up with a chauffeur, but Mom and Dad hit it off well and soon were hooked. Mom's maiden name was Cecil Geraldine Lowery, but Dad changed that.

They were married the year I was born, 1933. Dad was in his twenties, mom was only fifteen. Then Jim came along in 1935. Dad was a handsome dude and Mom was a beautiful lady. Jim and I used to love to brush her long hair. She was so young that when she took us shopping, people thought she was our sister. But she was a good mother to us and a good wife to Dad. She had no heart for punishing us. When we did wrong, she threatened to tell Dad. We didn't do wrong too often. Dad took a thick ruler to our bare behinds two or three times, just enough for us to want to do right.

After they got married, Dad worked for a long time in the Ford garage, then he moved to the garage at Montgomery Ward and worked in the tire department. About the time I became a teen-ager he went to work for Harold Hoover's Dodge garage, then got a job with the Ashland school board. When he was with Ford he'd arrange to bring home two or three cars to wash and wax on a Sunday morning for fifteen bucks a car and we'd get to help. And sometimes we'd get to go down to the garage and do a day's work. Dad always worked hard, but he never made a lot of money.

Mom always worked to help out. She took in washing and ironing. Nigger's work in a white town, I guess, but it never seemed like that because it wasn't a bigoted town. It was menial work, but she took pride in her performance. She had to be one of the best laundry ladies ever, because you never saw a crease in her collars or cuffs.

One of the ladies she worked for had bad feet and Mom started to take care of the lady's feet and later to do others. She even did ours. She'd cut toenails and trim bunions and calluses and stuff like that. She was good at that. She had a gentle touch.

Whatever she did, she did with dignity. When she went to work for J. C. Penney's she became the first black in town to work at a downtown department store. She worked there three or four years toward the end of my high-school days, and later when she and Dad moved out to southern California she worked for the Penney's in Pomona. She never minded working. She always found time to keep a clean house and cook good meals.

I guess there wasn't a lot for them to do for fun. Although Dad didn't have to be at work until eight, he'd get up at six and go to the pool room and have breakfast and shoot pool until it was time for him to get to the garage. He'd have lunch and shoot pool at noontime, too. He'd come home right after work, but then he'd go back to the pool room for the evening.

The pool room was his second home. He loved to shoot pool and to this day he's one of the best men you'll ever meet at a table. When we didn't have other things to do, my brother and I passed many a night with Dad down at the pool room and we became pretty sharp shooters, too.

Dad was tough. He had the strongest, hardest hands I ever saw. I guess he got them strong and hard working on cars half his life. He used to put out lit cigarettes in the palm of his hand without blinking an eye. His parents had died young and he had to fend for himself early. I hear he went to war many a time in his early life. I heard of one time when he tore up the pool hall a little.

When Jim was playing for Ohio State and he got burned by Jon Arnett of USC in the Rose Bowl, one of Dad's cronies started needling Dad about it, and my old man knocked him under a table. The cops had come to keep him from hurting him.

I don't think anyone dared sass him. I saw one of his cronies start with Dad one time. I was helping wash cars at Hoover's one Saturday when one of the other workers wanted Dad to wash a newly painted car ahead of others in line. The guy wanted to deliver it early so he might pick up a tip. I guess Dad would have done it another time for another dude, but Dad was mad at this cat because he was screwing around with the wife of one of Dad's buddies. When the dude got demanding, Dad whipped a wet wash mitt out of a bucket of soapy water and whacked the fellow across the face with it. I got between them just as the others came running. Harold Hoover, the boss, and Dad's good buddy to this day, said, "John Junior, you better take John Senior home for the day before he does this dude in." The dude looked happy to see Dad go.

That was the only time I ever saw Dad really lose his temper, but I think he'd have torn that cat apart. Normally, he was a nice, easygoing guy. He believed in the family and he didn't believe in screwing around. Every Friday night after he got paid he brought most of his money home to Mom, but he also brought her a case of beer.

I never saw them drunk and I never saw them do more than sip a little hard liquor or wine, but I saw them drink a lot of beer and Mom drank it the way some people drink soda pop or water. She just loved a bottle of beer, but she never put on weight or got tipsy or anything. Beer was her only vice. Summers she and Dad would sit on the porch and drink beer and talk through the evenings when he wasn't at the pool hall.

While the whites treated us well in Ashland, my folks didn't socialize with any. Sundays we'd drive to towns around the area so the folks could socialize with family or friends. The biggest black event of the year was the Labor Day picnic at Crystal Beach on Lake Erie. It seemed like every black family in Ohio managed to make it. There was so little socializing for some black families out our way that we used to look forward to that holiday all year long. Boy, there always was a mob there, swimming and running races. They played catch and ball and ate more food than you can ever imagine in one place at one time.

The Labor Day on Lake Erie I remember best was when I was very young and Dad took me out in the water on an inner tube. He turned the tube over and told me to swim to shore. He was the strongest swimmer I ever saw. I don't know where he had learned. Lots of blacks never learned to swim because they couldn't get in pools and weren't welcome on beaches. But Dad could swim out so far you couldn't see him anymore and I'd get scared he had drowned. When he dumped me I was scared I'd drown. But he figured I should learn to swim too, and he figured sink or swim was the best way, I guess. I all but walked on the water. I bobbed up and down, thrashing, until he told me to stand up. I thought he was crazy, but when I tried it I found out we were on a sand bar. We were two or three hundred yards out and the water was only up to my knees. He laughed at me and I felt like a fool. As soon as I could, I learned to swim at the Y.

I think we lived in three houses while I was growing up. The first was on Elm Street, but I hardly remember it. Then we moved to Cottage Street, on the outskirts of town, and I remember it because out back there was woods to play in, and alongside the house there was land Dad could farm a little. He loved to garden, and he grew corn, cabbages, tomatoes, onions, and peas, and we got to help. He even had a hog out back. Dirty old thing we had to slop and all. But Jim and I got attached to it.

One day Dad said it was time to slaughter it so we could eat it, and we didn't want any part of that. Dad took a .22 rifle and shot the poor pig between the eyes. When it rolled over, he took a butcher's knife and slashed its throat. Blood was all over the place. I'll never forget it. Mom and Dad made meat to eat out of that poor pig, but Jim and I never took a bite.

About the time I got to junior high school we settled on West Tenth Street. That's the one I remember best, because we lived there the last six to eight years I lived in Ashland. It was a nice house but nothing fancy. We lived well enough. We always got bicycles and boxing gloves and wagons and stuff like that for Christmas, I remember, though I don't think Dad ever made more than seventy-five dollars a week. But Dad didn't buy presents; Mom did. Dad might buy Mom an iron or an electrical appliance, but it was Mom who bought the gifts that had soul in them.

I always worked when I could so I could get things for myself and gifts for Mom and Dad. I remember real early I started to carry a newspaper route. The best thing about it was it got me out of going to church. My brother and I used to go to the Brethren Church and to Sunday school, but when I had to deliver my papers on Sunday I didn't have to go to church. My folks went to church in New London, about sixteen miles away, where Mom had family and where we used to visit on Sundays.

New London had a much larger black community than Ashland and it had two churches the blacks attended—a Methodist church and a Baptist church. I used to like to go to the Baptist church, a sort of a Holy Roller operation, because I used to like to hear them sing those spirituals. At the Methodist church I didn't like the slow way they sang those sedate old hymns like "The Old Rugged Cross." But my parents went to the Methodist church.

My grandmother in New London raised a cousin of mine, Dean Ann Simmons, a big tomboy who played ball with us. She was a great girl and a great singer, and I always wanted her to sing those spirituals with a beat, but the conservative church leaders wouldn't allow it for years. Finally, they hired a factory worker who played the piano as choir director and he put a lot of life into the Methodist church music. He even formed a quartet of singers including my Dad. It was so good it traveled and made appearances around the area. It broke up when they started to make a little money because they started to argue over it. It was a shame, because Dad had a deep bass voice that was really beautiful to hear.

I never got with the church. I think it was because the ministers never made much of an impression on me. But maybe it was because they were too busy trying to impress my grandmother and the other old ladies in town. Those dudes did it to those old ladies until the ladies were fighting among themselves as to which ones were going to do this or that for the minister and which one was going to have him for Sunday dinner. And all those ministers were just dudes like us, working all week and playing minister to make a few extra bucks on Sunday. I didn't see how they'd been set apart so they could tell us how to live our lives. And I wasn't impressed by the people who jumped up in church every Sunday to tell how the Lord had touched them and saved them. The same people jumped up to testify every Sunday and they were all bad actors—the worst drinkers and carousers in the area. I wasn't touched.

We had more relatives in New London than we did in Ashland, all on my mother's side. But the one I remember best was my mother's half-brother, Charles Newsome, who lived with his wife in the other house on the south side of Ashland. He was the first black to graduate from Ashland High School. I was the second, and that was thirty years later. I called him Uncle Doc because he was a dentist. He had been a colonel in the Air Force, but when they wouldn't make him a general he got out and went back to practicing dentistry in Mansfield. He was a good guy who became a sort of second father to me.

His wife, Aunt Bert, was a teacher. She was sort of chintzy. At a big family meal at her big old house she put one little pork chop on every plate. At the end of one meal we were all still hungry and she asked if anyone wanted more. I said I did, and she said I could suck on Uncle Doc's bones. But I remember her as a good old gal.

And he was a good old guy. He always had a bottle of booze with him and he'd go to bed early every night with his bottle, while she would sit and read or write. They're retired now and she has diabetes and is almost blind, but Uncle Doc takes care of her and his garden. I haven't been back to see them for years, but they're a big part of the family I remember from my youth in Ashland.

I did not have a lot of friends, especially when I was young. I wet my bed until I was in the third or fourth grade, and while my parents were wise enough not to make a big thing about it, it hurt me a lot. I don't know why I did it. It may have been more physical than psychological. We lived in a big old house that was heated by coal. The coal didn't heat the house too well and the heat didn't reach upstairs. We slept upstairs and it was always cold all winter. I'd get in bed under a lot of covers and I wouldn't want to get out. I'd dream of going to the bathroom and I'd wake up in a wet bed. When I had to get up early in the morning to deliver my newspapers, I'd have to put a towel over the wet bed so I could get back into it when I got back. You only took a bath once a week in those days, though I took showers at the Y, and while I washed as good as I could I always worried that I smelled bad from my urine. I'd get sweaty on the playground and then sit in class and think everyone smelled me and knew I wet my bed. I just pulled away from people so I wouldn't be embarrassed, until I was nine or ten years old, when I just stopped the wetting.

The only black friends my brother and I had were in New London, where we went Sundays to see family. I recall Junior Caldwell, Cliff Belmer, and Bootsie Evage, whom we used to play ball with. But my brother and I were the only black boys in Ashland. When I started high school I was the only black boy in school. Later, my brother became the second. I have football team pictures in which my brother and I are the only black faces. But, we didn't think about it a lot because we weren't made to think about it. We had plenty of white friends and we weren't treated any different because we were black.

Looking back, it's almost unbelievable, but it was the fairest town I've ever known. We ran into very little racial prejudice when we were boys, and none of it in Ashland. We really didn't run into real prejudice until we began to go out in the world.

Once when I was with the Boy Scouts our troop pedaled on bikes miles out of town to camp, and when we got there the people who conducted the camp wouldn't let me stay because I was black. I pedaled all the way home all alone, but when I told what had happened, our scout master went out there and pulled the entire troop out. Another time, when I was playing football with my high-school team, one of the players on the other team said, "Let's get that nigger." That pissed off all the players on my team. They really banged that bigot the rest of the game. I really felt good about that and it taught me something about playing for a team where your color doesn't count. Still another time, I played semipro baseball for an Ashland team and we went to Cincinnati to play in a tournament, and when we went into a White Castle for a bite, I was handed my hamburger in a sack because they didn't want me eating with the others inside. The others just walked on out with me.

Jim went on to play football for Ohio State and when he went to the Rose Bowl in 1955 a lot of people in Ashland pitched in the money to send Mom and Dad to Pasadena for the game. Ohio State took Southern Cal 20–7. Just getting to go and see Jim play had to be one of the great thrills of their lives. Whenever I think of those people in Ashland I thank them for sending my folks to the Rose Bowl.

Ashland was, and still is, a quiet town. It wasn't a farming town, though we used to go downtown on Saturdays to shop and watch the farm people come in. Watching people come to town was something to do and just having the town fill up on a Saturday was exciting. You'd march up and down Main Street all day. There really was a Main Street and it was the main street in town. Still is.

There was one hotel in town, a two-story job, and it was right next to the town jail. There were two movie houses but we almost never went to the best one, which showed the best movies, because it was on the south side where rich people lived. We went to the Palace, on Main Street. It had bad movies, but it had double features and serials and cartoons and all that. When it closed near the end of my high-school days it left a big gap in entertainment for a lot of us.

Across the street from the Palace was Peppy John's, where you got the best twelve-cent hamburgers and hot dogs with chili, but the bad dudes hung out there so you got your goodies and got out of there if you didn't want trouble. There were a couple of pool halls, but the kids didn't get to go in them much. Dad hung out at the Arcade, so I got to go in there some.

There was a country club, but only the rich played golf. I caddied a couple of times there, but gave it up because those bags were too heavy. Now they have a public course in town. There was a public park, Brookside Park, and we played softball and other games there. They had a good industrial league for the little industry we had there and we used to watch the games some.

Ashland College is there, but it's become much bigger since I left.

It was a nice town and still is. If you could find decent work it was a nice place to bring up kids, a nice place to be a kid, and a person could do worse if he didn't need a lot of excitement. There just never has been a heck of a lot to do there.

When I was a kid, like I said, it didn't seem to matter that my friends were white and I was black. The first friends I remember were Roger and Neil Duffy. They were a little older than Jim and me and we used to watch them dress up in their football uniforms to go to practice or games. We wanted to be like them in the worst way.

When we lived on the outskirts of town the Boyers had a

house near ours, and Harry Boyer became my buddy. His dad had a printing plant in town and we used to pick up some money cleaning up the place.

Harry, Jim, and I used to play in the woods and swim in the pond and the creek. We learned to swim at the YMCA early and never were afraid of water. We built boats and sailed them until they sank. We built clubhouses and tree houses and climbed trees. We hunted snakes, too. We'd catch them with our bare hands, snap their necks, and skin them.

For some reason, I could kill snakes without it bothering me but I never liked killing other animals. Dad used to take my brother and me to hunt rabbits in the woods and he could shoot one and carry it around dead with him all day without it bothering him, but it bothered us.

We had BB guns and shot turtles in the woods, however. And after Dad gave us a .22 rifle we used to ride our bikes to the city dump to shoot rats and cans. One day someone shot back at us. We looked up at a hill across from the dump and there was this guy with a gun. I guess he figured if we were shooting a gun, we should see how it was to have a gun shot at us. I guess he was just having fun with us, but it scared hell out of us. We jumped on our bikes and beat it out of there and never went back.

Anyway, I realized after a while that I really didn't like killing anything, even though for some reason I got to loving guns—the look and the feel of them—and collected them for years.

In town the main place to play was the YMCA. The ladies Mom washed and ironed for paid for memberships for me and my brother from the time we were little kids. It was something they wanted to do for our family and I don't think my folks ever paid dues, which were six dollars a year.

I'm not a social sort, but the Y was one club, if you can call it that, I really liked. I got to socialize with kids who came from all over town and it didn't mean anything to them that I was black. I learned to swim there and took showers there. I learned to play checkers and chess there. I played Ping-Pong and pool there.

Between that place and my pa's place I became a sharp pool

shooter and won a lot of ten-cent contests there. I remember there was a fat kid with thick glasses, Dick Baker, who was a hell of a pool player, but we used to beat him because he couldn't see good and we'd slip balls off the table on him and count them in our score.

I guess that was gamesmanship. I first learned there that anything you can get away with goes in competition.

We had some terrific ten-cent table-tennis games there. I got to where I liked to gamble and became a good gambler. I learned a lot about cards from the dudes in New London and won a lot of money at cards from the guys in Ashland. In fact I've always won a lot of money at cards all my life, including in my career in baseball. At times it's gotten me by some tough times, but I wouldn't want to count on it to make a living.

We played basketball and baseball and softball at the Y. It was our home away from home, and we used it to death when we were growing up. I think the Y also sponsored the Little League football we played at the park, but the park department had a good outdoor program of its own, especially summers, and we played basketball and baseball and softball and football and pitched horseshoes.

My buddies were Gary Averill and Harry Boyer, and also Lennie and Rollie Scott, and George Glaser, and a couple of others, and we went to school and to the Y and played at the park and on the sandlots together. When I think of those good times I miss them.

For all these friends, I was a bit of a loner. I was as much on an introvert as my brother Jim was an extrovert. I had a few friends and he had a hundred. He was eighteen months younger and we really didn't run together, though we played ball together and met coming and going at the house, the Y, or the park.

Still, I was his older brother and I had to look out for him. One time he came running home hollering that this kid had called Mom a bitch. I guess he'd called Jim a sonofabitch, so Jim figured that meant he was calling Mom a bitch. We called the kid Hitler. He was German, I think. He was standing outside our house, taunting Jim, so I took off out of the house and ran him home.

I could run, too. I remember one day we were playing a baseball game in a cow pasture. We were getting beaten bad and I wasn't taking it too well. Our pitcher was taking a lot of time throwing the ball and I had little patience left and was hollering at him from the outfield and throwing clods of dirt at the infield. This big kid hit a double and I hit him with a clod of dirt at second. He said if I did it again he'd bust my butt. I did and he came at me. I had to jump up to reach his mouth, but I hit him in the mouth and took off. It was a couple hundred yards home, but I jumped the creek, went through the woods, across the highway, and got home without him catching me. I had to duck him for weeks before he cooled off.

But if a guy wasn't too much bigger than me, I could give him a battle. My dad had given us boxing gloves when we were little and taught us to box and defend ourselves. I became pretty handy with my fists. I learned early that the guy who gets in the first punch has a hell of an advantage. I was a smart fighter and tried to take the other guy by surprise and get him off balance and really lay into him before he could get organized. I won most of my fights and took care of Jim until the time came along pretty soon when he could take care of himself and maybe me, too.

I never really liked fighting, but I always figured you had to be able to take care of yourself. Later in my life I took karate lessons for that very reason, but then, of course, when the fight with Juan Marichal came along I was lucky to get in one wild punch, and not a very good one at that.

Actually, I was kind of a straight kid. I belonged to the Boy Scouts and loved those uniforms. I learned to tie knots and pitch tents, build campfires and cook food, and I really loved it. When I got a little older I wanted to belong to the Hi-Y club, but at the initiation when they blindfolded me and beat my butt with a paddle and made me eat raw oysters without my knowing what they were and stuffed my mouth with soap flakes, which burned like crazy, I lost interest. I didn't see any sense in letting people beat on you without being able to beat back and having that stuff shoved down your throat. I never wanted to be in those kind of clubs after that, not in college or anywhere else.

There were things I wanted. Whatever I wanted, Mom and Dad tried to get for me. Even before I started school I wanted to learn to tap dance. They paid for lessons for me, but I didn't do too well, didn't last too long, and don't remember many steps. A few years into school I started to take piano lessons, but I wasn't finished with the first song when the rest of the class was finishing the first book. I can remember that first tune but I still can't play it. I started free violin lessons at school, but I never learned one string from another. I started drum classes and I went around smacking my sticks on a practice pad until the instructor told me if I couldn't keep two different times with my two feet I might as well give it up. By that time word must have gotten to the music teachers around town and I wasn't welcome anywhere. I have harmonicas and guitars. I've had four saxophones. I'm a freak for music, but I can't play anything good but a hi-fi.

One thing I wanted was a motor scooter. My buddy Harry Boyer had one and I wanted one. I had saved four hundred dollars from delivering newspapers and washing cars and I pleaded with my parents until they gave me permission to blow it all on the newest, fanciest model Salsbury. We had a ball with it, running it out in the country, but I had it maybe a month before I took too sharp a turn and took a spill. I wasn't hurt too bad and the bike wasn't hurt too bad, or didn't seem to be, but the motor never ran after that. No one seemed to be able to fix it, so it just sat in our garage. To his day I don't remember what happened to it. I remember realizing I had wasted a lot of money, but that was just practice. I got good at getting rid of much more money later in my life.

I had dreams. I used to go out to Ashland Airport, a raggedy old one-runway airport, and watch the little planes take off and land and dream of a day when I would fly one. I did learn later on, though I never did a lot of it. I used to get down to the newsstand early to pick up the copies of the *Cleveland Plain-Dealer* I had to deliver so I could have time for a Coke and Clark Bar for breakfast, and I'd read *Esquire* magazine and dream of all the fancy things I'd find in it that I wanted to buy for myself. The owner was a good guy and he'd give me the old magazines. I'd cut 'em up and keep scrapbooks of the things I wanted. Nice cars and nice clothes. Things like that.

Nice-looking ladies, too. Another thing me and my buddies used to do at that newsstand was to go into the basement beneath it and look up through holes we'd cut in the wood ceiling, trying to see up the skirts of ladies passing by. Obviously, I started to "shoot beaver," a favorite pastime of ballplayers, at an early age. I remember back in our first-grade class there was a girl who George Glaser and I both thought was a beauty. She had a way of sitting down in her chair that showed off her pink cotton panties. George and I got there early every day to wait for her to sit down. We thought there wasn't a nicer sight in the world than that little lady sitting down. We were six years old and horny.

Growing up I thought that nice-looking ladies, like fancy clothes and cars and airplanes, were things I would never have, no matter how nice it was to dream of them. I was scared half to death of ladies. I made a fool of myself over them. I remember one summer they had a college girl running the program at our park and I had a crush on her. She was umpiring a softball game one day and needed someone to catch. I volunteered so that I could get close to her. She said I shouldn't because I didn't have a mask, but I showed off by saying I didn't need a mask, I wasn't going to miss any of those slow pitches. They say you should keep your eye on the ball. Well, I watched one right into my right eye. My eye blew up three times its size and I damn near lost it. Never was going to get to first base with that girl anyway.

I used sports as an escape. I got by, but I was a bad student. I wasn't interested in studies. I was only interested in sports. If I got good grades, it was in physical education. I had buck teeth and thought I smelled bad and I told myself I was too busy with sports to have time for girls. Even if there really wasn't any bigotry in that school, I was still a black cat in a world full of white girls and I didn't have the guts to go after any of them.

I remember I was so good at phys. ed. that I acted as an assistant to our gym teacher, Bud Plank. One day we were supposed to go to the girls' gym for a class in dancing. Bud wanted me to go, but I didn't want to. I had never even touched a white girl and was scared of the idea. I begged Bud to let me stay in the boys' gym and shoot baskets that period. I guess he understood, because he gave in. Too bad. Looking back, I think of it as a turning point in my life. It may seem like a little thing, but I think if I'd gone and learned to dance and forced myself to socialize with those girls, I wouldn't have become so withdrawn and shy and might have developed more personality and learned how to handle those situations. I'm in my forties and I'm still learning how to dance. Taking lessons now, as a matter of fact. I'm still haunted by the social failures of my youth.

It doesn't take much of a hurt to leave a big scar. I remember one of the black ballplayers I played with in New London, Junior Caldwell. He had a sister, Barbara, who was a good ballplayer. Because I saw a lot of Junior, I saw a lot of her. Because we were all together a lot, I think some people thought she was my girl friend. But I'd never even taken her out. The movie theater was the place you took a girl in those days. The blacks sat on the right side, the whites on the left. There weren't many black girls, so you were a big guy if you were black and brought a girl. Somehow I got up the courage to ask Barbara to go with me. We'd been friendly and she'd always acted like she liked me. I was a high-school sports star by then, so I figured there was no way she could say no. She said no. I was surprised and embarrassed badly, even though no one knew. I made up my mind I would never again ask a girl for a date, and it was some years before I did. The thought of it still hurts, and to this day it is hard for me to be aggressive with women.

Oh, I used to pretend I was making out here and there. I guess most guys brag a lot about that, especially in school when you're young and frustrated. Dad used to keep a box of rubbers in a drawer by the bed and Jim and I used to sneak a couple out and carry them with us in our wallets so the guys would see them and think that if we had them we must be using them.

One day one of the young guys on the football team, Dave Johnson, a buddy of Jim's, who always seemed to do well with the ladies, told me he had a girl for me and wanted to double date. She turned out to be one of the two or three notorious girls in school who supposedly had slept with all the athletes. Well, not all. Not me, for one. But that just turned me on. I was ready for it to be me. We went to her house on Ohio Street. Her parents were out. Dave took his girl inside, while I took my girl on the porch. She was willing, but I wasn't able. She had bad breath, which turned me off. I got the rubber on but couldn't get it up, and couldn't get in her. It was a farce, humiliating as hell.

A while later Dad asked me if I knew that girl on Ohio Street. Surprised the hell out of me. I asked him why. He said that she said she was going to have my baby. That scared the hell out of me. I had never discussed sex with my dad, but that was the time. The time for honesty. I told him all about what had happened.

He knew I never lied to him, so he believed me. He said, "Well then, you have nothing to worry about. I'll take care of it." And he did. He went to her and got her to admit that some older guy in town had made her pregnant, not me, and got me off the hook. But that also left a scar, because I became afraid of knocking someone up or being blamed for it and having to pay for it or maybe having to marry someone I didn't want to marry. I didn't trust the ladies that came around when I became a ballplayer and never was able to be easy around them the way the other players were.

But I was glad Dad stuck up for me. Mom and Dad always did. They believed in me and they helped. I guess Dad told Mom about it, and it must have made them think I was making out some, because Mom used to tease me about the ladies after that and she'd call me "evil" and laugh, but in a nice way. She used to say, "John, you're too evil to get married." And I'd say, "That's right, Mom, I'm never going to get married." And she'd laugh and say, "Well, not 'til you're maybe twenty-five." And I'd say, "Not 'til I'm thirty-five, if then."

I believed that then, too, though I fell long before that, as it turned out. I thought then I'd never get married.

In that straight, sheltered childhood I lived back in little

Ashland, Ohio, my best friends were Mom and Dad. I'm glad Dad is still around, and I miss Mom like crazy. She let her sons become ballplayers or whatever they wanted to be. She lived through most of my playing career and I had moved her and Dad out to southern California so they could have an easier life. I had moved on to Minnesota near the end of my career when she died in the middle sixties.

She had heart trouble and she never told anyone about it. She had gone to a doctor and gotten medicine, but at one point stopped getting her prescription refilled. I guess she thought she could get by without it, but fluid built up in her lungs and she had some sort of a mild attack that hospitalized her. They said she would be all right, and she was out of the hospital within a week. I was married by then, and my wife, Jeri, flew to California to be with her on a Monday, and by the time Jeri flew back to me in Minnesota on Friday she said Mom was home and feeling good. She even brought back some pictures of Mom looking good, sitting on the couch with Dad.

Sunday night we got a call that Mom had had another attack and been rushed back to the hospital. And then before we could make a move we got another call. She had died. It took a while to accept it. It hit me very hard. We were told a blood clot had gone to her brain. After her first attack they moved her out of the hospital so fast it was hard to believe that they'd seen how serious it was or done all that could have been done. It was as though they hadn't heeded a warning. We were bitter, but we didn't say anything or do anything about it. Maybe we should have sued, but even if we'd won, money wouldn't have brought her back.

We flew back for the funeral, although I hate funerals and had vowed never to go to another one. Sometimes a lot of family gets together for a funeral and there's a lot of hand-shaking and kissing and even laughing, and I don't like that. Then there's a minister saying insincere things about somebody he maybe never even knew very well. Worst of all, there's that dead person laid out in a casket, looking like something other than the living person you remembered. And you're left with the memory of them looking like that.

I had to go to the funeral home with Dad to make arrangements and it was just terrible. It's a real ripoff, and they take advantage of poor people when they're pushed off balance. We didn't have much money, and I suggested to Dad that it would be just as well if he got a minimum-cost casket, but he is proud and wanted the best for Mom even if it couldn't help her, so he went for one of the most expensive. If you count cost, Mom had a fine funeral. But a funeral's a funeral. I used to tell Mom that there was no way I was going to go to her funeral or visit her grave and didn't want anyone going to mine or visiting me after I was gone, and she'd laugh and agree with me. She had understood, but the family didn't. I tried to get out of going, but everyone acted shocked and insisted I had to go, so I gave in.

It was the worst time of my life. Even my kids had to go see their grandma laid out looking like some other lady than the beautiful lady they'd known. I stood there looking at this waxy-looking woman with all the expression gone from her face. The look of her stuck in my mind and I can't get it out. I thought of the good times we'd had and the good she'd done me and what I'd done for her and I thought I hadn't done nearly enough. I thought she was gone too soon and if I only had a little more time I could have done so much more. I guess we all think that way at those times, but that doesn't make it any easier. I got all choked up wishing she'd had more in life and I'd somehow showed her more how much I loved her, and I started to cry.

Because I was a big baseball player, all sorts of bigwigs in Pomona turned out for the funeral. The mayor was there and other executives of the city and people from the police department and the fire department and the schools. I like to think she'd have liked that, but I really don't think she'd have cared. They were there for me, not her, but it was her day, her last one, and it bothered me that there were so many people who didn't even know her, although I know they meant well. If I'd had a choice, I'd have preferred a private ceremony, if any, but the others in the family wanted it the way it was.

One thing I insisted on was a short eulogy. I had a buddy, Bob Haversham, the only minister I've ever really gotten close with, and I brought him in to help the people at Mom's church with the arrangements. I insisted he give the eulogy. He told me he would and he made it short. He knew me much more than he knew Mom and he didn't pretend he knew her and didn't phony it up. He has a feeling for people and he put a lot of feeling into his little talk and let it go at that, and I was grateful to him. But then Jim and his wife and Dad and others started to cry and it became the ordeal I dreaded.

I got through it somehow and went to the cemetery and saw them put her, in that fancy casket, into the ground, and I couldn' help cryin'g. Finally, we left and went back with Dad and sat around and talked about her. It took a long time to end.

Later, I went back by myself once. I stood over her grave and reminded her that I wasn't one of those who could come every Sunday or every anniversary or something and put flowers on her grave, but I would be thinking of her a lot, which is what I think matters most. I think if she heard me she understood and agreed it would be all right that way.

I do think of her a lot. I think of her having me at fifteen and looking like my sister all her life. I think of her maybe not having much fun all her life. I think of her working all her life. But she had dignity and pride and took pleasure in doing for others. And she had a family that loved her. She left a mark on us, which has to matter.

I think of her a lot. I have her pictures and I look at them a lot. But I don't have her.

3.

EVERY Sunday we got in the family car and Dad drove us somewhere. Usually we went to New London to be with family, and I got to play a lot of baseball there. They had kids there like Junior Caldwell and Cliff Belmer and Pete and Eddie Mack, who could really play. I think they could have played pro ball like I did if they'd gotten the chance. A lot of high schools didn't have teams and most small towns weren't scouted. A lot of prospects were overlooked, especially black boys, until the 1960s or so.

In case you've forgotten, it wasn't until 1947 that Jackie Robinson broke the race barrier in baseball. He became a hero to every black boy, but it was ten or fifteen years before baseball went after any but the best blacks and before a lot of blacks got into the game.

Take Eddie Mack. He could hit hell out of a baseball, but all he became was a Sunday player on a black team in Mansfield. He was still playing when I was winding up my major-league career, and he'd come visit me when I'd get to Cleveland and we'd talk over old times. I'd wind up giving him a couple of bats and a glove or something. A professional bat is a lot better than a bat you buy in a store and Eddie was so grateful it was embarrassing. Here I'd been playing twelve, thirteen, or fourteen years for big-league teams and he'd been playing all that time for a black team out in the boondocks at a time when there wasn't even much black baseball left. He may have been a better ballplayer than I ever was. I hate to think of all the good black ballplayers who never got a chance to play on a good field in a good league.

Sometimes Dad would drive us to Mansfield, which wasn't too far away. There were still a lot of black baseball teams in those days, and we liked to watch the semipro team in Mansfield. The blacks had a ball park outside of town and it was a big gathering place for them, with a lot of drinking and gambling going on during games every Sunday through the spring and summer. You'd pull into the parking lot and there'd be a lot of old friends.

Black clubs would come in from all around to play the Mansfield club. I used to try to compare myself to those players, and they had some who were way ahead of me. The player I remember best was a first baseman, Jimbo. I don't remember his last name, but I remember he could really pick it, which is what we called defensing at first base.

The Cleveland Buckeyes had a first baseman who was even better, Archie Ware. He could dig throws out of the dirt better than any first baseman I ever saw. He used to show off by putting on a show of it in practice before games. I think they threw in the dirt deliberately to him just so he could show off. He could defend that bag better than Gil Hodges or Ron Fairly, two of the best I played with later.

Sometimes Dad drove us as a family to Cleveland, but most times, and it wasn't enough times, the black kids would get to go in a group from Ashland and New London and Mansfield to see a ball game in Cleveland, and we'd see the Buckeyes or the Indians.

The Buckeyes were one of the best. They played at old League Park, where the Indians used to play, and they played some of the best black clubs in the business. Besides Archie Ware, the Buckeyes had Sam Jethroe in the outfield and Sad Sam Jones on the mound. Jethroe and Jones made it to the majors, but it was too late for old Archie Ware.

We got to see the Indians play at Municipal Stadium once or twice a year. That was in the late 1940s when they had Bob Lemon, Bob Feller, Mike Garcia, and Early Wynn, but they usually lost the pennant to the Yankees. They had one of the first black big leaguers, Larry Doby, a great player and a hero of mine. And they gave Satchel Paige a chance to pitch in the big leagues even though he was long past his prime. That gave me a chance to see the greatest of the black pitchers, maybe the greatest of all pitchers, period. They had a white catcher, Jim Hegan, who was a hero of mine. He did things smooth, effortlessly. He was a real pro and when I became a catcher I copied him, remembering him.

They also had a black outfielder named Harry "Suitcase" Simpson. I will always remember him because he stole a foul ball from me. It's always a kid's dream to catch a foul ball at a big-league ball game. One time during practice I was standing near the right-field foul pole, watching, when a ball came right to me. Just as I went to catch it, a big glove jumped in front of my face and took it away from me. It turned out Simpson had stolen it. Usually a big-league ballplayer lets a kid catch a foul ball when it's hit into the stands in practice. Sometimes they even threw you one they caught near the stands. But Simpson just threw this ball back to the infield, and it steamed me.

Years later, barnstorming with big leaguers, I landed in Mexico with Simpson and I chewed his ass out. I told him he wouldn't remember me but I remembered him because he wouldn't let me have the big-league baseball that I came closest to catching when I was a kid. He laughed and we became friends, but I never really forgave him.

I made it to the big leagues the hard way. I learned as I went. I had little instruction as a kid, but I played a lot. Dad never played real pro, but he had played pickup games a lot as a kid. He taught my brother and me some things that stuck with me. He bought me my first mitt and I'll never forget it. I think he paid $2.98 for it at a discount store, but that glove got me started. It was a good glove and it lasted me a long time. In those days you played where you were needed, and I played every position with that glove.

The first place I remember playing was in that cow pasture near where I lived. There was also a cow pasture we played in in New London. Plowed-up, bumpy fields. We used dried cow dung for bases. We used beat-up old bats and balls. We'd wrap 'em with black friction tape to make them last as long as possible. A lot of the guys didn't have gloves. We didn't have a full team most of the time. We played with five or six guys to a team, depending on how many showed up. But you got a lot more times at bat than a lot of kids do in Little League today.

The problem in New London was that if you hit the ball too far, you hit it into the creek, and it not only made the ball stink, but it made you stink when you went in after it, and it ruined the ball and your clothes. I was more concerned about the ball, but Mom always was more concerned about my clothes.

Until I got to high school I played more softball than baseball because there was more softball to be played and more places to play. I played a lot at Brookside Park. I was a terror at softball. I batted both right-handed and left-handed, hit hard, and played every position. I even pitched, and to this day I can throw a ball almost as far underhand as I can overhand.

When I got to high school I really got into baseball. My coach, Bud Plank, liked me and helped me. He taught me more about fundamental baseball than anyone else did. He may have been in a little old high school, but I think he knew more about fundamental baseball than anyone I ran into in the big leagues until I coached for Ted Williams.

Bud was a lot like Bobby Winkles, too. He ran a real sharp ball game.

When I first went out, I went out for catcher simply because when they asked for catching candidates no one volunteered. I figured I would get into games sooner than the players at positions where upper-class kids were set, and that's the way it worked out.

However, we didn't get in more than eight to ten games a season. A lot of high schools around there didn't play baseball, there wasn't much money for travel, and we didn't have much good weather before school let out. It was cold until well into April, and rained a lot after that. School let out in June.

Another reason I wanted to catch was that a pal, Lou Petit, was a pitcher. He was a left-hander and he threw pretty good.

Bruce Henderson, a right-hander, was our other star starter. That was our pitching staff. We needed a relief pitcher, so I pitched some, too. I had seven different pitches. Actually, I only had a fast ball, a curve ball, a change up, and a knuckle ball, but I threw the first three both overarm and sidearm so I count them twice.

When you get right down to it, the only pitch that paid off for me was my fast ball. I could throw hard and I tried to blow it by the batters. I got by, but I was no star.

I wasn't a star as a catcher either, but I was the best they had. I could catch and I hung tough on wild pitches and plays at home, which was the most important thing. I wasn't afraid. But I didn't like catching all that much. They only had old, beat-up equipment for me. I had an old chest protector and mask and an old catcher's mitt. Home plate was just a piece of wood laid on the ground.

I preferred playing the outfield. I was a good outfielder. I always was fast, I could go get the ball, and I had a strong arm. I thought of myself as an outfielder who caught because there was no one else to catch, and I went into pro ball later as an outfielder before I was put back behind the plate again.

What I was more than anything else was a hitter. I hit the ball real well in high school. Of course I wasn't facing top pitching, but I hit all pitching. My last two years I hit .450 one year and .530 the next.

Actually, when Jim came along two years behind me he hit a longer ball. He had a lot of power. But he didn't hit as consistently. He wasn't as fast as I was. And he didn't field as well. He played most of the infield positions and a little out-field.

I was voted most valuable player on our team. I was also voted most valuable player on our football team, but when Jim came along he became a better player and was voted most valuable player after I had moved on. I think Jim was voted most valuable player in basketball too. I never played basketball in high school. I had played at the Y, and I was okay, but not outstanding. Jim played with a group from the Y right through high school and they were outstanding and became a top team.

Jim and I had skinny legs and when we used to play basketball at the Y, Mom would put Vaseline on our legs so they'd lose that ashy look. I guess we were ashamed of our legs. We were the only blacks on any team we ever played on at the Y and in school and we were aware we looked different than the others. We weren't tough enough to say the hell with it or that black was beautiful.

Actually, football and basketball were the big games in high school. Only some family and friends came out to see a baseball game, but the crowds came to see football and basketball. The girls came to see the guys play football and basketball and you had those cute little cheerleaders at those games. It turned us on. And the town newspaper wrote more about high-school football and basketball than baseball.

Ohio always has been big for schoolboy football and I thought of football as my main game for a long time.

I remember one of Dad's brothers got us some football gear starting us in the game when we were just kids. Dad's parents died before I was born. I only got to meet a few people from his family on trips to the South a couple of times. I remember they had some strange names. There was one set of twin boys named Horace and Forace and a set of twin girls named Sally and Cally. Laughed like hell every time we thought of that. Anyway, Dad's brother Hubert, a big guy, had played football for North Carolina A & T, a black college. He was a career man in the army. He came to visit us one time, and when he saw us playing tackle football without pads, he took us to the hardware store and bought us not only pads but uniforms and helmets. Some of our friends had stuff like that and we used to envy them, but Uncle Hubert took care of that.

Years later when I joined the Dodgers in Brooklyn, Uncle Hubert was living in New York. He used to call up and ask for tickets to the games we played at the Polo Grounds. I could get all the tickets I wanted, so I left him four a lot of times. One time, Lee Scott, our traveling secretary, came to me in the clubhouse and asked if I had an uncle who I gave tickets to. I said I did and he said he didn't know how to tell me but my uncle had been caught scalping the tickets outside the ball park. Lee asked me what I was going to do about it. I said, "I'm not going to do anything about it. He's my uncle and I love him. He was good to me when I was growing up and I'm not going to be bad to 'him now. If he wants tickets, I'm going to get them for him. And if he wants to sell them or give them away, that's his business."

When I got to high school I went out for football. I got hurt right off. I was sweeping right end when I tried to hurdle a group of guys who'd gone down. I caught my right leg. I heard it snap and went down feeling scared. Sure enough, it was broken. I was finished for the season.

It also kept me from going out for basketball. I never did go out for basketball, but I did go back to football the next year. That winter I got around on crutches and coached a kids' football team for the Y. Gary Averill helped me and we taught the kids the kind of stuff we'd just started to get taught and we made up plays and we won and took a title.

By the time I got off crutches and got my leg out of a cast it had shriveled, but I exercised and exercised and the size and strength came back. I don't think I lost much speed. I could always run like the wind. I won the starting job as halfback and I guess I became one of the best running backs that school ever had.

The coach, Cloyce Taylor, was a nice guy. He worked us harder than we wanted to work, but he taught us and helped us a lot. I'm a very lazy athlete, but he got on me and stayed there and made me put out.

It's a tough game. I didn't like getting hit, and I really hated getting hit by my teammates in practice. But I started to live for those Friday nights when everyone in town turned out for our games and always gave them a good show. Later on, I lost my fear of getting hit and really got to like hitting.

I ran so well they always wanted me to go out for track but I was too lazy to run around that cotton-picking track all day and do wind sprints and stuff like that. But I ran for a lot of yards and a lot of touchdowns in my two seasons as varsity football star at Ashland High. I even played quarterback one game. Our regular quarterback, George Glaser, and his sub, Dave Johns, were hurt. I used to throw the halfback pass at times so the coach called on me. I had small hands and couldn't grip the ball too well, and I was awkward dropping back, but I got by.

It was bitter cold for my last game and I wore all the clothes I could get my hands on under my uniform. I was so scared of being banged down on that frozen field that I wouldn't let anyone tackle me. As I remember it, I ran for four touchdowns and threw for a fifth. We won big.

It was a great way to go out. Football for me was my first taste of being an all-star, a trophy winner, a hero, someone who stood out, and I really liked it. Who wouldn't?

But brother Jim was a far better football player. He was two years behind me and the years we played together he mostly blocked for me. After I moved on, he went on to be a lot better than I ever was. I was faster but he was shiftier. He'd find holes in the line and pick his way through a broken field beautifully. He also was good defensively in the backfield. He had a feel for where a pass was going and he was a hard hitter. He made All-Ohio his last two seasons, was recruited by a lot of colleges, and went to Ohio State, the big football school in the Midwest for many years.

He played for Woody Hayes in the backfield with Hopalong Cassady and Bobby Watkins. My first chance to see him there was the homecoming game at Columbus in 1955. I had just gotten out of the service, and I went with Mom, Dad, and Jeri, though we weren't married yet. Jim did it all on offense and defense. He had the best day I ever saw him have. They always make a big deal of the most valuable player in that game, with all the alumni on hand, and when they announced Jim had been voted the MVP that day it just choked me up. There were more than eighty thousand people in that big old Ohio Stadium and it was really something to have them standing and cheering my younger brother. Mom and Dad had tears in their eyes. I really love my brother and it was a moment I'll never forget.

After college Jim was drafted by the Green Bay Packers, but they didn't offer him a fair salary. They didn't have many blacks on their team at that time. Bobby Mann, an end and a kicker, was one. I don't remember if they had any others. They made a big deal of what an honor it would be for Jim as a black to play for the Packers in Green Bay and that turned him off. He went to Canada instead and played a year or two before returning to Ohio. It's too bad because he wasted a lot of ability, but he became a good businessman and made a good life for himself.

We had one other Ashland player that I know of who played professional football, Max Messner, who had played with Jim, gone to Cincinnati University, and gone on to play five or six seasons in the sixties with the Lions, the Giants, and the Steelers. He was a fine linebacker. I don't know of any other Ashland players who made the majors in any other sports.

I guess I lasted the longest in the big leagues of any Ashland player. They tell me I'm the biggest thing in sports ever to come out of my hometown, which maybe doesn't mean much when it's a small town that doesn't turn out a lot of top players. It's funny when you consider that I was so unimportant most of my years there and that it really looked like I wasn't going anywhere when I did leave there. However, I have to say it's nice to have been a hometown hero.

4.

M Y COLLEGE career was shorter than it was sweet.

I was spoiled by my success in football and baseball at Ashland High. I thought the colleges would be coming after me for football and the big-league clubs would be coming after me for baseball. I was disappointed.

A "bird-dog" scout named Chick Skelley, from nearby Shelby, came with a baseball contract, but it was a contract with him, not with a team. He said that if I signed with him, he'd sign me with the Pittsburgh Pirates.

A bird-dog is not a full-fledged scout, but I didn't know that then. A bird-dog is an independent who usually deals with all the teams. He's paid by a team only if he brings them a prospect they want to sign.

He's what we call a ten-percenter. His contract called for him to get ten percent of anything I got. I talked it over with my folks. No one else had come around. So I signed. And he left. I didn't see him again for a while. No contract with the Pirates came through.

It looked like I'd have to look for work, get a job, and forget about baseball or football. Then a scout for Central State College came around and offered a football scholarship. I guess I was low on their list and when some other prospects fell through they got around to me. But they were number one on my list. I grabbed the scholarship. It just paid the basics— tuition and books, room and board—and I had to work for spending money, but it got me out of Ashland and into the world, and it kept me in sports.

I wasn't going far out into the world. Central State is a black college, though it had a few whites, maybe more now than when I went there in 1951. It's a university now, too. It's in Wilberforce, Ohio, which isn't on most maps. It's near Xenia, which is near Dayton, and which is about 140 miles north of Ashland.

When Mom packed my few clothes in an old suitcase, gave me a case to send my laundry home in, and she and Dad put me on a Greyhound, it was the first time I'd been on a bus in my life, much less a train or a plane. I wore my only suit, my Sunday-go-to-church meeting suit. A piddlin' ol' bus ride was an adventure.

Playing for the football team, I took my first train ride, to Baltimore to play Morgan State. That was an adventure! Rockin'-and-rollin'. We went around a curve in Pennsylvania I later found out was the famous Horseshoe Curve. From my seat in about the middle of the train I looked out the window and I could see both the engine and the caboose, curving in front and in back of me. We were leaning so far to the left I thought we were going to fall right off the tracks. It was scary. The others laughed at my fright.

It wasn't until I got into pro baseball that I had my first plane ride. I was scared when we took off and when we landed. In between, I wondered if we were going to fall out of the sky, but I had always wanted to pilot a plane and later I took lessons and lost my fear. By then I was sort of sophisticated by comparison to when I first got to college.

I started after girls in college. I was eighteen and it was time, and I had the feeling for it by then, but I didn't have a lot of luck, and I remained frustrated.

I remember when my first semester was about to start I was sent with some of the other football players to the girls' dorm to help bring in the bags for the freshmen who were arriving. One of them was the most beautiful broad I ever saw. She stepped out of a big black limousine and was wearing a long fur coat. She looked like class, and she looked so good some of the guys were ready to jump her right then and there.

Later, this lady who was from Louisville turned out to be a

soft touch. I never got a feel, but I guess a lot of the other guys got it all. In fact, a couple of guys got her to come to their room at Hallie Q. Brown Hall, our billet. When word got around, the rest of the guys started to pound on the door and demand to be let in. They wanted to run a train on her, which is to say everyone would get his shot in a sort of gang-bang. Half dressed, she hopped out a window and hurried home to her dorm. She was known as "Hallie Q." after that.

I finally did get me a girl friend. She was the first date I ever had. Mary. She had fat jowls so she was called Bubba Cheeks. No beauty, but cute—less than five feet tall, I think—and with a nice personality. A nice girl. I worked with her in the cafeteria and beat off some competition to go with her. Almost got me kicked out of school, though it was no fault of hers.

On Halloween night there was a party in the cafeteria. Those of us that worked in the cafeteria didn't get to go until we'd cleaned up. By then it was nearly nine o'clock and the girls were supposed to be back in their rooms by nine. By the time we got to the party, it was over. We felt frustrated. The cafeteria was in the basement of the girls' dorm, so we stalled to get in a little necking at least.

There were just four of us—Mary and me and another couple—necking and stealing a feel, maybe, when we heard footsteps coming down the stairs. Mary and me ducked into a side room. It was the house mother and she found us there. She looked like Aunt Jemima or something, her hair up in curlers, wearing a bathrobe, but not wearing any smile. I guess she saw Mary smoothing her clothes, because when she reported us she said we had been having sex.

I was called to the dean's office and he was ready to expel me. Times were different. You weren't allowed to have girls in your room or in any room. You weren't supposed to have sex, I guess. I hadn't had any, not really. It would have been a bad deal to have been expelled from school, especially for something you didn't do. I guess I convinced the dean we hadn't done anything, because he let us off the hook. The coach put in a good word for me and that helped.

They had movies in the auditorium and I used to take Mary there. Unlike a movie theater, an auditorium has no side lights and when the only light is from the movie projector it's really dark. The football players used to bring their girls there and try to make out in the back rows. I brought Mary there but I never made out. I'd go back to my room frustrated as hell.

One night I told my roommate, Horace "Sing Sing" White, that my testicles hurt like hell. He said, "Oh, you stupid country nigger, you got the blue balls." Scared hell out of me. I asked him what the hell that was. He said it was what happened when you started to ache from having gotten excited and not having gotten off. Doctors say there's nothing to it, but I believed it. Only trouble was, the girls I told about it didn't. I guess guys have been using that line for years and I guess all the girls have heard it.

I went to Mary's home one day. Right up the road, eight to ten miles away, in Cedarville. Depressed the hell out of me. She was the oldest of thirteen kids, with another on the way, and her mom was all worn out and her pa had no way of earning the money to take care of them right. The poverty scared me away from Mary. I guess she was working her way through college and trying to make something of herself so she could do something for them. I don't know what happened to her. I hope she found something good in life.

It wasn't a bad life at Central State, but it wasn't too good, either. Nothing fancy for the football players like at Ohio State. We lived in dorms that were like army barracks. Old wooden buildings broken up into rooms, two or three players to a room. Ours was called Hallie Q. Brown Cottage, but it wasn't any cottage. I think Hallie Q. Brown was a lady who'd done something for the college.

My roommates were Horace White and John Brooks. White was a fullback and Brooks was a guard. White was a helluva player, but Brooks was only a reserve. We called White "Sing Sing" because he was from Ossining, New York, where the prison is. He was a track star as well as a football star and a terrific runner. He was a talented individual—an artist and a musician, a top student, and a captain in the ROTC.

He was personable and outgoing and he helped me a lot because he brought me out of my shell some. He could really "Bogart" the broads. When a guy was smooth and laid on a good line and held himself apart from people, we called it Bogartin', a tribute to the late movie star we all saw in old movies. Sing Sing could really Bogart the broads into the bushes. He had a job cleaning up classrooms after school closed for awhile and I guess he kept a couple of girls after school and copped 'em on the desks.

He didn't have any dough. I once caught him cooking a pigeon he'd caught. He'd killed it, plucked it, and put it in a little pan of boiling water on a hotplate we kept in our room. I couldn't believe what I was seeing. I said, "Sing Sing, how can you eat that bird?" He said, "Hey, Rosey, I'd eat shit if I was hungry enough and could figure a way to take the stink out of it." I guess he was hungry. He was a big guy and I guess he didn't get enough to eat in the cafeteria when they fed the football team.

They fed us about five in the evening and there wasn't anything to eat after that unless you went across the street to The Grill, a sandwich joint, or to the school canteen, where you could get sandwiches, but most of us football players couldn't afford it. A lot of the students socialized in the canteen, but I felt out-of-place in that scene and didn't sit there more than a couple of times.

Some of us were saved from starvation by a cat called the Pie Man, who used to come around evenings selling cheap apple pies, peach pies, and potato pies. I was saved by working in the cafeteria, where I could steal some toast or cake after we finished cleaning up the leftovers and dishes. And then Mom used to visit on weekends and bring my favorite apple pie, but by the time Sing Sing and Brooksie and others got into it, I didn't always get a lot.

The basketball billet next to ours burned down one night and a lot of those cats lost most of what they had with them. After that, Mom used to collect clothes and stuff in Ashland and bring it to Central State to help out the basketball players, but Sing Sing always got to it first and got what he wanted and could use before the basketball players got to it. I worried about our rickety old wooden barracks burning after that, but it didn't happen.

Mom and Dad came most weekends—every weekend during

football season when we were playing at home. They were thrilled that I was in college. But I hadn't prepared properly for it. I hadn't studied much in high school and what I had studied hadn't been college-type courses. I had taken wood-working and printing and typing and music and stuff I liked, but I didn't like studying and I didn't do well in my classes. I got by in high school and I got into college, but I had a hard time getting by there.

Biology was hardest for me. I had to dissect cats and frogs and learn the strangest terms. I hated it and cheated like mad to get by, but the teacher turned out to be the baseball coach, Cap Lane, and I guess he didn't grade me too hard. The class I liked the most was psychology. I found it fascinating, but I also found it hard. The teacher, a lady, Dr. Anderson, did grade me hard.

I recall in speech class every speech I ever gave was about baseball or football or some other sport, because that was all I really knew. I used to sit by a window overlooking the campus and daydream, and when the teacher called on me for a five-minute talk off the top of my head I'd get up and get into football and baseball. About halfway through she'd say "That's all right, Mr. Roseboro, you can sit down," with a sigh that said she was sick of my sports.

Sports was my life, the only thing I knew, and I was only prepared for a life in sports, and didn't prepare properly for the rest of my life. I guess I had a good chance in college to make something of myself outside of sports, but no one made me see that then and I didn't stay long enough to find out for myself. I guess it was a turning point when I didn't take advantage of an opportunity to become more than just a jock.

It wasn't that I wasn't willing to work, but I didn't study. I didn't have a lot of time to study. It didn't seem fair to me, because sports, with practice and games and all, takes up a lot of an athlete's time. The sports teams bring in the bucks, but even athletes on scholarships had to work part time. The top athletes got the soft touches. Our star quarterback took tickets at the auditorium movies, for example. And I worked in the cafeteria. I went back for a second year, to stay out of service, after I'd gone into pro ball, and worked at the Frigidaire plant in Dayton nights. But I never went back to college after that.

There was a sort of caste system at college, maybe in all colleges for all I know. The kids whose parents had dough and who had all the spending money they needed stuck to their own crowd, the "in crowd." They acted like they were on a higher plateau than those who had to work or scrounge around for a buck, even the athletes, though we were set apart from the rest, too. As an athlete I could have pledged one of the poorer fraternities, but I couldn't afford the sixty-bucks initiation fee and my Hi-Y experience in high school had turned me off. I knew I was right when a buddy came back from initiation with his butt beaten red raw. I didn't mix much. I worked and stuck to sports.

On the bus ride to school we passed right by the football field where the players were working out. I had never seen more than two black cats on a football team and few players of any real size. I remember being awed by seeing a field full of black guys, all of them bigger than any players I'd ever seen, and I was scared to death. "Rosey," I thought, "what have you gotten into?"

Practice had started before the school semester began because the playing schedule started right with the semester. I got my scholarship a little late and got there a little late. When I turned out, I got pants and pads that were too big. I had my own shoes, but they were beat-up. I looked funny and felt like a fool.

The coach was Guy "Country" Lewis and he was a smart, touch cat. If you fucked up on the practice field, he used to say, "Back it up here, boy, and let me kick it." And, by God, you turned around and let him boot you in the butt. It was a way he had of making you cut down on mistakes. His main assistant was a former All-America from Iowa, Big Jim Walker, and Big Jim was stern too.

They had a pretty fair team. Lorenzo Clark was a great all-around athlete who as our running back made All-Black All-America. Nip Parker, the other running back, also made All-America. Sing Sing, our regular fullback, was ferocious. The quarterback, "Stump" Baylor, who was well under six feet, but had big hands, could throw the ball really well. And his backup, Doc Robertson, was the best ball-handling quarterback, the finest faker I ever saw. They had dudes with size and strength along the lines. They had dudes who could play on that team. None of them went anywhere because no one was scouting black football too much in those days.

I took a beating from some of those bad dudes when I first went out for the team. I was one of the freshmen without a big reputation and we were just meat for the regulars while they were building themselves up for their regular foes on Saturdays. I found out I didn't have a reputation beyond Ashland, no matter what I had done there, and no one knew what I could do. I never really got a chance at running back. I never really had a position. They put me where they needed me.

I won a place for myself on one play. I was playing defensive back against the regulars when a cat who was competing with me for Mary Walker's affections went out for a pass. As he went up in the air for it, I went at him. He caught it, but I hit him before he came down. I had Mary in my eyes when I drew a bead on him and I gave it a little extra on her behalf. I hit him a hell of a lick and turned him end over end in the air. I almost killed him.

Everyone noticed. The coach took particular notice. Country Lewis took me off the scrub club, got me good gear that fit, and put me on his first team as linebacker. The position was new to me and it wasn't the one I wanted, but I wanted a position. I made mistakes, but I hit like hell every chance I got and I kept my position.

I learned a lot. I remember one day when a guy came through a big hole off tackle at me. I moved up into the hole and right into the guy, thinking, "God, I'm going to cream him." I was standing up, waiting, and he ran right over me. Next thing I knew I was lying on the ground and our All-America, Clark, was kneeling next to me and laughing. "Hey, motherfucker, you'll lay into him low next time, won't you?" he said. I mumbled maybe I would.

I learned my lesson. After that I went at them rather than waiting for them to get to me, and I got low and got my shoulder into them and drove through them, and maybe flipped them right over my back. It was something I was able to use years later as a catcher, blocking the plate. If I had to stand up to take the throw I wasn't afraid to get knocked over, but if I could duck down and put a shoulder into them and throw them, I did.

I only weighed 180 or 185 as a linebacker in college and as a catcher when I broke into baseball, but I lost my fear of a collision. I wasn't afraid to hit someone before he hit me. I always hit hard and I often threw the other guy hard.

Freshmen were eligible to start and as a freshman I played regularly and won my letter. I really got turned on by the pep rallies before big games at home. I loved the bonfires and the crowds of excited students and the shouting and singing and cheering. We'd had pep rallies in high school, but nothing like that.

We played black colleges like Morgan State, Tennessee State, Kentucky State, Youngstown State, Morris Brown, Lincoln, and others. We were not, as I remember, the best of them, but we beat some of them. The games were rough, but I did well enough to enjoy them.

One home game I remember, I intercepted a pass and had fifty yards in front of me for a touchdown. I was so excited, so anxious to make a touchdown, I just took off without looking for any blockers. I flew down that field and the only guy between me and the goal line was a fellow on the five. I figured I could take this one guy. I threw him a fake and flew past. But as he went off balance he reached out and tipped my toe. I went off balance and went down on the one. They rushed in the offensive squad, I went out, and my only college touchdown went down the drain.

I don't know how well I'd have done if I had played four years. I might have made a real good linebacker, but I'd never have the size to make the pros. I might have made a good defensive back, but I don't know that. I might have made a good running back, but I don't know that either. I don't know if I'd ever have gotten the chance to play in the offensive.

Anyway, brother Jim was a better back than I ever was and he didn't last long in the pros. He didn't get a lot of opportunity. I might not have, either.

It turned out to be baseball for me, but in a way I never expected. After my first semester in college, my grade average was 1.7. It took a 2.0 to be eligible, so I found myself ineligible for baseball. I guess Cap Lane, the coach, didn't expect that much of me, so he didn't make that much of a fuss about it. He let me work out with the team. I warmed up the pitchers, pitched batting practice, even cleaned out the clubhouse.

One afternoon a fellow came up to me on the practice field and introduced himself to me as Cliff Alexander, a Dodger scout whose territory was Ohio. I have no idea how he knew about me. I never thought to ask. Maybe Chick Skelley had turned him onto me. Anyway, Alexander said he'd heard I could play and invited me to work out with the Dodgers, who were in Cincinnati for the weekend. I was flabbergasted.

I put on that one suit—a brown tweed that was really baggy. I had a yellow and brown tie that went with it. I packed a few other things in my little bag and drove to Cincinnati with Cliff. He put me up at the Netherlands Plaza Hotel, introduced me to Roy Campanella and Joe Black, and asked them to see me through the weekend. They and Jackie Robinson were the only blacks on that team. Don Newcombe was in service. Anyway, I was awed just meeting them.

They invited me to have dinner with them in their room. I had never stayed in a hotel before, much less had room service. Hell, that hotel must have been twenty stories tall and I'd never even been in one that was more than two stories. And when this uniformed cat came through the door pushin' in this great big tray full of food I was stunned. I'd never had a shrimp cocktail. I'd never had a big steak all my own. It was the first time I'd seen sour cream on a baked potato. We had vegetables and strawberry shortcake and Coke and ice tea. And to top it off, when the guy finished laying it all out for us, Campy just signed the tab.

I said, "Man, is this how you handle things in the big leagues?"

Campy laughed and said, "Oh yeah, you don't pay for your food on the road, the club does."

And Black said, "Anything you want to eat, just sign your John Hancock."

And I said, "Hey, if this is the way you guys live, this is the way I want to live."

Campy said, "All you got to do is play a little ball."

So after an evening of fine food and fast talk with my new friends, I went out the next afternoon to old Crosley Field to prove I could play ball. I was scared to death. They gave me a Dodger uniform and I got dressed and went out on the field early, before most of the regulars were there.

Chuck Dressen was the manager and he and Alexander watched me work out. I remember I didn't get too many swings. I had to lay bunts down both baselines and then I got five swings. I hit a couple hard, as I remember. Then I caught batting practice and caught infield practice. I had to field the bunts and throw to first and to second. I could throw a ball through a brick wall, but I was slow getting the throw off, and I might miss the brick wall. I recall one of the coaches, Jake Pitler, yellin' at me, "Throw the ball, let it go, let it go." And I threw a couple of what we call "frozen ropes" right over the second baseman's head into centerfield.

I felt terrible because I thought I looked terrible. But they must have thought I looked all right. I guess I had good moves and a good swing and I showed them I could throw hard and run well. I guess they thought I could develop.

They had a lot of minor-league teams in those days and signed a lot of players on the chance they could develop. They offered me a contract and I grabbed it before they could change their mind. They offered me a five-thousand-dollar bonus. It may not seem much now, but it was more than I ever dreamed of getting. Hell, I'd have signed for nothing. Anyway, I wound up with only half of it. The contract I had signed with ten-percenter Skelley called for him to get half of any bonus I got, as it turned out.

That was a pennant-winning Dodger team I signed with in '52, though it went on to lose the World Series in seven games to the Yankees. I wondered how long it would take me to make the majors. As awed as I was by those guys, I think I just thought I'd make it, sooner or later, else why would they have signed me? That's the way I thought, anyway. They said I could finish my school year before starting my pro-baseball career.

Alexander said they had a lot of places in the minors they could put me and I didn't have to go to the South if I didn't want. I said I didn't want to; no way. I'd heard too much of the KKK and lynchings. I said I didn't think that much of the southern people. So they settled on Sheboygan, Wisconsin, in the Wisconsin State League, to start me when my school year ended.

When I got back to Central State, word got around that I was going to go pro with the Dodgers. All of a sudden people there figured if the Dodgers were interested in me, they should be. All of a sudden Cap Lane wanted me to play on his team. He figured if I wasn't turning pro until June, I could play on his team until then. He tried to get my grades raised so I could get the three-tenths of a point I needed to be eligible. He might have gotten a couple of other teachers to raise my grades, but he couldn't get Dr. Anderson to raise my psychology grade just so I could play baseball. So I still fell short, I still wasn't eligible, and I still couldn't play.

I'm sorry I never even got to play a single season of baseball at my college, Central State, but I figured I was on my way to the big time, where you could order food you'd never even heard of before and didn't even have to pay for it. Only thing, it took a little longer than I thought it would.

5.

I REPORTED to Sheboygan in the Wisconsin State League in June 1952. I had just turned nineteen and I was still wet behind the ears. It was a lot longer way from home than Central State.

It wasn't just going away to school. It was starting a career I naturally hoped would be a good one for me. I was scared, but it turned out to be a nice town, a good team, and a good experience.

Sheboygan was a city of about forty thousand at that time, not too small, but not too much to do either. We used to sleep until noon, mess around downtown afternoons, get to the ball park about five, get out about eleven, and go home to sleep. Milwaukee wasn't too far away, but we didn't go.

There were blacks on the ball club, but no others in town. I have a letter I wrote home in which I told the folks, "There isn't a nigger in Sheboygan." I also wrote, "Dad, send your old clippers to me. The peckers don't know how to cut a nigger's hair, so we'll cut our own."

Actually, there was one black in town. He shined shoes.

Four of us—two blacks and two Cubans—lived at a rooming house run by a Mrs. Leffin. She was white, and she bragged about us as "her boys" and mothered us half to death. She fed us fine so we didn't have to go out to eat when we were at home. Sometimes we'd have backyard cookouts in which she'd stuff us with all the knockwurst, steaks, and hamburgers we could eat.

She had a son, Dennis, who was about seven or eight when I was there. When I was with the Dodgers, I invited him to visit us and he stayed at our house and we took him to Disneyland, Knotts' Berry Farm, Farmers' Market, and the other tourist places. He had a ball. When it was time to put him on the bus for the trip home, he said he'd never been treated better in his life and started to cry. It really got to me.

I know he's married now, but I don't know what's happened to him or to his mom. She was getting on in years last time I saw them, which was when I was coaching with the Angels and we played in Milwaukee. They'd come to the games and come down to the seats by the field and we'd hug and kiss so much that people must have thought we were crazy.

I met a girl there, Gwen, who lived around the corner. She hung around the house a lot and we used to sit on the porch swing and chat and neck a little, but no more than that. I didn't have the guts to try to go further and don't know if she'd have let me if I tried. I just didn't ever take her out in the town. She was a white girl, the first one I ever romanced.

On the road we didn't live it up. It was a bus league—small towns like Wassau, Oshkosh, Green Bay, and Fond du Lac, which we could get to on short bus rides, and we didn't stay over at a small hotel or rooming house unless we had to. The major-league teams that operated these minor-league clubs tried to keep expenses down. The contract I'd signed called for me to make $150 a month through the baseball season, so I wasn't saving anything. I was lucky I wasn't the sort to spend much, either.

The only bad experience I had was at Wassau. I was catching and a white cat sitting in the seats behind home plate was sassing me with "chocolate drop" and "snowball" and stuff like that. I figured I'd better give that sonofabitch the bad eye so maybe he'd stop mouthing off. I turned around, deliberate-like, and gave him my meanest look. He hollered, "I'll come out and give it to you if you want, nigger." I let it go.

It was Class D ball, but in those days a ballplayer had to work his way up from the low minors and there were some pretty good ballplayers and pretty good ball played in the low minors. I think the only other player who might have made it off our team was Jim Koranda, a fast, hard-hitting outfielder but he fell short. We had some who got to triple-A but no further, like big Pedro Almendares and little Oscar Sardinas, our Mutt and Jeff sluggers, and Connie Grub, a pitcher, who won twenty for Montreal later on.

Some of the ball parks around the league weren't too bad and the one we had in Sheboygan was pretty good. Almost all our games were played at night and the lights could have been better, but that's always the case in the minors.

Joe Hauser, a living legend, was our manager. Joe was a minor-league Babe Ruth. He hit sixty-nine home runs one season in the old American Association for Minneapolis and sixty-seven one season in the old International League for Baltimore, but he only had a few years in the big leagues because of a broken kneecap.

Hauser was a German from Milwaukee. When he hollered, you heard him. He was in his fifties, a little guy for a guy who'd hit all those home runs, but feisty and tough. He used to hit ground balls so hard during infield practice you had to stop 'em or lose your legs. I swear he was trying to skin our shins. But he used to say he hit 'em hard because they wouldn't come easy in the games. If we learned to handle the hard ones, the easy ones would come easy. I guess he had a point.

He drove us to a pennant by twelve or thirteen games and that got us rings. I found out you got a ring anytime you won a pennant in baseball. The higher you went, the better the ring. We got little rings, but they were good enough for me. I was happy to get mine and I figure Joe got it for me, though he was not an easy guy to play for.

I remember in my first game behind the plate I caught a foul tip on the index finger of my right hand, my throwing hand, and chipped a bone. I went to the team doctor in town and he immobilized the finger with an aluminum cast and said I'd have to lay out awhile. When I showed it to Hauser before the next game he wasn't too impressed.

"What the hell is that?" he asked.

I said, "I busted my knuckle and can't catch."

He said, "Well, if you can't catch, you can play the outfield. And take that goddamn cast off."

So I took the cast off and played the outfield. My hand hurt like hell, but I could still catch the ball and I learned to throw it with three fingers. I was able to grip the bat with my left hand and three fingers of my right hand and I got by. I bunted the ball a lot. I could still run. If I got it on the ground it was like writing home for five and getting ten back because I could beat out infield hits.

I remember I was fighting for the batting title with a kid named Richie Patton, who was with Wisconsin Rapids in the White Sox system. He hit like hell and it burned him up when I beat out bunts. I'll never forget one time when I got to first base, and he said, "You don't have any talent at all, you know that? All you got is speed." And I just laughed at him because even then I knew it didn't matter how you got it. A hit was a hit in the box score the next day.

I don't remember for sure but I guess he beat me out because there's no asterisk by my .365 in the record book and an asterisk shows when you led your league in that thing. I'll keep the .365, though, because I never hit anything like that again in my career. It's funny, but I remember in my first game I popped to the third baseman, grounded to the pitcher, and struck out before I had to come out with my injury, and I thought that the hitting might be hard to come by in pro ball, but I hit like hell after that.

I started out swinging from my ass, but Hauser was smart. Even though he had been a hell of a home-run hitter, he believed in hitting the ball where it was pitched. By that I mean that if you were a left-handed hitter, like I was, you hit the outside pitch to left, the inside pitch to right, and you tried to hit the down-the-middle pitch up the middle. He got on me and didn't get off until I got the idea.

I only hit one home run in the sixty-nine games I played, but I got ninety-five hits. I hit a lot of doubles and triples and stole a lot of bases. I drove in forty-nine runs. Maybe I wasn't a home-run hitter, but I was a menace at bat.

After my finger got better, I caught some and even played the infield some, but mostly I played outfield.

The next season I went to Great Falls, Montana, in the

Class C Pioneer League as an outfielder. I played centerfield and learned how to go back and come in on a ball. I had that running speed and I covered a lot of territory. I learned how to charge a hit and make the fast throw to the right base. I threw guys out from deep center.

I had a hell of a throwing arm, but I guess it was erratic. I made twenty-three errors my first two seasons as a pro and I think most of them were in throwing. It was a physical thing I had to learn, grooving my throwing style. I didn't make too many mental mistakes and I was a fast learner. Tell me something once and I'd remember it the next time.

I was getting good experience and needed it. I was getting used to playing every night or every day, sometimes under difficult circumstances, in intense competition, and I was learning and enjoying it. I guess I went back to swinging from my ass some my second season, because I hit eight homers and my average fell off to .310, but that still isn't too bad. In fact, it's the last time I hit .300. I played eighty-two games and got ninety-four hits and scored seventy-eight runs and drove in sixty-three. I got a lot of doubles and triples and stole a lot of bases again, too.

It was a tough league, too. Frank Robinson broke in that year and tore the league up before he moved up.

Ours was a nice town and I was a nice young man. There were about fifty thousand people, but not five things to do. I stayed with the other blacks on the team at a boarding house run by an old couple in the Negro part of town. There weren't too many blacks there, then. I guess there still aren't. With a lot of Indians, it looked like an Old West town, wide open, with dust blowing up all the time.

We played in towns like Billings, Montana, and Pocatello, Idaho, and the toughest part was that everything was spread out and we had to make some bus trips of four hundred miles. Traveling by bus was tough. You never got any good sleep and you got all stiff and sweaty and then you had to get out and go on the field and play a game. I liked getting to Pocatello, though, because I had girl there, Daisy Bates.

Our manager, Lou Rochelli, was one of the nicest managers I've ever had. We were all kids on that club. They didn't put any veterans in the low minors. There was no point to that. And Lou looked out for us and advised us and taught us a lot of fundamental baseball. I think the managers in the minors were not always sharpies, but they were good with young guys.

We didn't win the pennant, I don't think, though I wasn't there for the finish. I was drafted into the army late in July 1953, just when I was getting to going good. I was one of the more popular players on the team. I was a good kid in those days. Hell, I didn't even try to make it with Daisy. And when it came time for me to take a train to Ashland, they threw a night for me and passed the hat, and raised three hundred dollars so I could fly home and have a few extra days at home before reporting to Fort Knox, Kentucky.

I still have a letter written by general manager Nick Mariana of the Great Falls club to my parents, which is so complimentary it is embarrassing, but I guess it shows what kind of kid I was in those days. He said I was "one of the finest examples of American youth as can be found anywhere in this land of ours." He said I had "set an example of conduct, hustle, ability to take orders, and all-around good sportsmanship and fair play that will be remembered as long as they have baseball there."

It might be cornball, but it was kind for him to write such a complimentary letter. I know they always gave nights for guys going into the service there in those days, but they told me that was the most money ever raised. It came in nice, because while my salary had doubled to three hundred dollars a month that season, my spending had doubled too. Daisy and all. I was learning. I even found out about pawn shops. I was broke between paydays a few times and had to hock something to keep going.

I guess I was just a kid finding my way, though I still had a long way to go and I don't think I ever really got there, being as backwards as I always was about high living. In fact, the thing I remember best about Great Falls was getting there.

A couple of my teammates from Sheboygan were assigned with me from the Dodgers' minor-league training camp in Florida and we had some time to kill in Chicago en route. We went downtown to see what the big city was like and we went into a burlesque theater for the first time. The star stripper was someone famous, like maybe Sally Rand. She did a lot of stuff with veils. And on a bed on stage. She had a great-looking body for an older lady. I remember all those ladies taking off most of their clothes—not really clothes, but costumes. Still, it was something someone like me was bound to remember.

To tell the truth, I was shook by it. I was so shook I didn't enjoy it as much as I should have, not as much as my buddies did. I kept thinking it was wrong and I kept wondering when the cops were going to come crashing in and haul all of us in for doing this depraved thing. It did seem depraved to me. Not that I didn't like looking at the ladies, though they embarrassed me. I noticed older men in the front rows leering at the ladies and hollering obscenities at them, and I thought there were a lot of sexually weird people in the world and maybe now here I was one of them.

6.

I DIDN'T drink, I didn't smoke, I didn't curse, at least not much, and I didn't chase women, not as much as I might have wanted to, so soldiering in the United States Army was not exactly right up my alley. From the day I got in, I heard words I'd never heard before. It was fuckin' this and motherfuckin' that from day one. It was said by boys before they even were soldiers, and I can't for the life of me figure out how they caught on so fast. It was that way when I got to the big leagues, too, and I got used to it. It wasn't that way when I was in the minors with baseball babies, and I wasn't used to it.

Those soldiers just lived for the nights when they could go sit in saloons, smoking and drinking and trying to make out with women of all sorts. It wasn't the way I wanted to live.

It's not that I was right and they were wrong. Different strokes for different folks. It was just something I wasn't used to and something I never really got used to. The language, yes, but not the boozing and chasing.

I guess going into the service I went through things a lot of guys have gone through. Recruits came from all over Ohio and met in Cincinnati to be trucked to Kentucky. A bunch of scared kids. There was a war in Korea. They called it a conflict, but kids were getting killed.

We pulled up at Fort Knox and got the word from the sergeants:

"Out of that fuckin' truck. Hit the motherfuckin' ground."

They shaved the hair off our heads, sent our fancy civvies

home, and gave us uniforms that didn't fit. They taught us to make our bunks so a coin would bounce when it was dropped on the blanket and to store our toiletries just so.

One kid didn't wash as much as some thought he should, so a bunch of the guys hauled him into the shower room and scrubbed him down with stiff-bristled GI brushes. He was a bad dude, so we all lay awake all night wondering if he would cut our throats. He didn't.

The bugle blew at five-thirty every morning and we had to bounce out of bed to stand at attention. We had to clean up, eat, and get out to drill or work while it was still dark. There was seldom a time when they were not shouting some profanities at us.

In training, they treat recruits like dirt. As far as that goes, in the service I found that officers treated enlisted men like dirt. I didn't run into any real racial prejudice. Some, especially Southerners, didn't like living with niggers, but black and white were lumped together and I made friends. We were all treated alike, like dirt.

It's tough to have to stop being your own man. I hated it. I guess all the guys who go in hate all the chickenshit that goes with life in the service. I was always worried I'd lose my temper and slug someone and spend six months in the stockade.

That's bad time and it doesn't count against your service time. I didn't want to be in any longer than I had to be. So I took crap like everyone else.

One thing I decided was if you have a kid who has problems, who's too wild to live in society and busts the law, you'd be better off sending him into the service than putting him in jail. The worst that would happen is he'd wind up in the army jail. Otherwise, he'd learn to accept authority and be able to get along when he got back to civilian life, or else he'd stay in the service. Either way, society would be better off.

We were in because there was a war on. They were training us to fight a war we didn't want to fight.

One of the things I liked least was gas-mask training. You had to wear your mask into a building that was filled with gas, take it off, wait 'til you were ready to die and starting to panic, then get out of there. The gas burned your eyes, your nose, and your throat. Tears ran down your face, you gagged, and you couldn't breathe. It was sickening and took hours to recover. I swore I'd never do it again. Then when I went to work for the sheriff's department in Pomona for a while a few years ago, I had to go through it again.

They gave us guns and taught us to march. I didn't mind marching. I enjoyed singing and beating the drum while we marched. I got to beat the drum sometimes because I told them I'd had schooling in it. I didn't tell 'em I'd flunked. They didn't know the difference. I didn't like the all-night hikes they took us on, or running up and down hills with full packs. But it got me in the best shape I've ever been in.

I like guns, but I don't like killing and that's why we were given ours. They taught us to take our rifles apart, put them together again, and shoot them. I did well shooting at targets on the rifle range, but I don't know how well I'd have done shooting at people in battle. I guess if they're shooting at you, you shoot back. I guess if you have to, you do it. I guess if I'd gotten into battle, I'd have been grateful for the training. But I didn't have any confidence in what we were taught.

They taught us how to handle hand grenades. They have this drill where they have you hold the lever down so the grenade won't go off when you take the pin out; then you take the pin out, count to ten, and put the pin back in again. Which is all right if you don't let up on the lever or drop the damn grenade. You hold your life in your hands and it's scary. Then you get to throw three or four. You take the pin out, count to three, and throw. It's worse than pitching to Johnny Bench with the bases loaded. If your arm freezes and you don't throw, you're dead.

We worried about the time when we would have to run the infiltration course. We had to advance against real gunfire and bomb bursts. Carrying our rifles, with live ammo firing over our heads and live bombs exploding alongside us, we had to crawl under barbed wire and climb over obstacles. We had to run across a log like a telephone pole as if it were spanning a gully or something. When I got to the course, I did what I had to do until I got to the log. I was told that if I went on it slowly I'd slip off, but if I hit it hard I'd be across it before I knew it. I hauled ass and hit it hard. My foot slipped and I fell on my face, straddling the pole. I snapped my rifle in half and smashed hell out of my face. I had to be helped back to the barracks. I carried a scar on the left side of my face for a long time, which was good in that it got me out of some hard duty for a while.

It really was hard duty. I was relieved when I had a few hours off and could just take it easy. I never took a pass while I was there because I didn't want to hang around in bars. I sacked out and wrote letters home and worried about my base-ball career going down the drain. I waited for recruit training to end and hoped I wouldn't have to go into battle. I didn't like my leaders and didn't want my life in their hands.

We got the word that half our group was going to Korea, the other half to Germany. When the assignments were posted, I was listed for Germany, and relieved. Screw war.

My group was sent to Fort Dix, New Jersey, then trucked to New York, where we boarded a troop ship bound for Bremerhaven, Germany. I had seen pictures of an ocean. I was scared and excited, and I figured it would be like a lake or river, only bigger. I had no idea how much bigger. It was smooth while we went by the Statue of Liberty but it began to get rough when we got out to sea. Soon we couldn't see land and the waves were larger than I'd dreamed possible. It wasn't too bad, but we bounced about. The ship handled it, but I wasn't sure. I figured if that mother went under, there was a hell of a lot of water to drink.

They had thousands of us crammed on that ship. The bunks below decks were four high and you slept with someone's butt in your face, slung in one of those canvas hammocks right on top of you. There wasn't much air to breathe and the body odor got bad even though everyone tried to shower as much as they could. You used to pray no one would throw up be-cause the stink stayed in the compartment. But everyone was throwing up from seasickness and the stench of bodies and sweat and vomit. I don't know how they assigned the work details, but my job was to take the garbage from meals and throw it through an opening in the side of the ship. I threw up as much as I threw out.

You had to go on deck to get fresh air, but those waves worried me. It was two weeks before we saw land again. I knew there was no way I could walk home, so I promised the Lord if he let me get off the ocean safely, I'd never get on it again. I lied. I knew I had to get back on it to get home, but I didn't want to think about that. I thought maybe I'd make my home in Germany so I wouldn't have to ship home. I just wanted to get to Germany and get off that big boat and that big ocean. I guess I was lucky they took me in the army instead of the navy.

Finally, we landed at Bremerhaven. We were sent to the 28th Division headquarters in Goppingem and quartered in Lapeim, about sixty miles away. I didn't see a lot of Germany, but what I saw I liked. There was a lot of beautiful countryside and some interesting towns with buildings that went back centuries. But Lapeim wasn't one of the more interesting towns, and I didn't take any passes into town. Later, I was transferred near Nuremberg, in the north, and I took a pass to see that and it was interesting. And I got to Berlin once on pass and that was interesting, as much as I saw of it.

I didn't want to go around alone and I didn't want to go with the guys when they were going into town because all they were going after was booze and broads and all they ever saw was the inside of some saloon and some broad's bedroom. All the guys ever talked about was getting drunk in the beer halls and *gasthofs* and fucking frauleins. I'm sure there were attractive taverns and good restaurants and nice women, but the soldiers never saw them. I wanted to have a good time and I wanted a woman, but I didn't drink and I didn't see how I could sit in some beer joint without drinking, I didn't speak German, I was afraid of getting screwed up with strangers, and I was afraid of knocking up some damsel or getting disease. Lots of guys did get messed up.

In Berlin I did get up the guts to go with some guys to a whore house. It was called the Telephone Booth and I thought it was a club. There were tables and a dance floor and a band. But the tables were numbered and had telephones and you could call a woman who looked good to you and make a date

and she'd leave her table and take you upstairs to a bedroom. The guys who used to tease me about not going out
said they were going to get me laid that night, and I wanted to
get laid and I didn't want them to think I was a fag so I went
along with them.

They fixed me up with a fat fraulein and I went with her. I
wanted to and I didn't want to. I was scared, didn't know what
to do, you know, didn't know if I wanted to do it with this
chick who had a chest on her like you wouldn't believe. In the
room she took off her clothes and when she took off her bra
her bazooms fell to her waist. One had a big black, hairy mole
on it and I couldn't take my eyes off it. Finally, I realized I
had to get undressed, so I did.

I got on the bed with her and did what I could. I swear I
don't know what I did. I guess I got up and got into her, but I
swear I don't know for sure. I don't know if I got off, but I'm
sure she didn't. I don't remember her saying a word to me or
me saying a word to her. We fumbled around for a few minutes and when we were finished we got up and got dressed and
went back downstairs and went our separate ways.

The guys were giggling and smirking and hitting me on the
back and asking me about my first fuck, and I guess that's
what it was, but I didn't know what the hell to tell them because I didn't know what the hell had happened.

For me, it was easier to stay on the base and not embarrass
myself by getting into things I didn't know anything about. I
guess in the service a lot of guys learned a lot about life and
about ladies, but I guess I just wasn't ready for it and didn't
have the guts to get into it. I didn't like the way those soldiers
went at it, and I guess I had to wait awhile before I learned
how to handle those things the best way I could, which never
was and never will be the easiest way in the world.

I remember I took a course in German that was offered at
the base there, and several wives of officers and enlisted men
enrolled too, and the instructor, who was a German from the
town, put them in the front row and was more interested in
talking to them and putting the make on them than he was in
teaching the rest of us. They'd learned a little German from
maids they had, and they'd carry on these conversations with

the instructor in German, giggling and all, until a lot of us got fed up with it and dropped out.

There wasn't much to do. There was a service club where you could play pool or cards. I won some money at pool and lost some at cards. I'm a good cardplayer and I can do well in an honest game, but they had some characters there I'm convinced were crooked and cheated. Elmer from Philadelphia sat me down one day and showed me how to set a pair of dice the way I wanted them in my hand, click them without moving them, and roll them straight so whatever I wanted would come up. That's why they make you bank the dice off a wall at a lot of gambling joints. You didn't do that there so I skipped craps because I saw how easy it was to cheat and I didn't want to cheat or be cheated.

I didn't have much money anyway. I was making $110 a month and sending $80 or so home to be banked for me, so I only had $20 or $30 to spend on a bite to eat at the canteen and stuff I needed from the PX. I tried to run my money up a couple of times, but I blew everything I had in a poker game one night and was left with most of the month to go and no money. I sent a special-delivery letter home asking the folks to take some money from my savings account and send it to me as fast as possible. I didn't hear from them the whole month. I guess they wanted to teach me a lesson. I skipped poker after that.

We didn't have much work to do, either. Just staying ready in case we had to fight. I was assigned to a reconnaissance company as a mortar man on a half-track that held a .50 caliber machine gun and mortars and we spent a lot of time learning to fire the mortars at the proper trajectory to clear whatever was in between and hit the target. We went on some maneuvers, and we took turns standing watches. But my captain turned out to be a real jock lover and it turned out all he wanted from me was that I play on his baseball team. I wasn't a big leaguer yet, but I was a pro and he figured I'd help the company club. I got there in the winter and just had to wait for spring and the start of the baseball season to be transferred into a special unit for athletes who played games to entertain the other troops.

One bitter-cold winter night I was standing watch from three to six in the morning at the ammo dump, though I don't know who the hell I was guarding it from. The wind was whipping around me and my feet were freezing. It was dark and no one was around. Finally I figured I had to get warm some way, so I took some wood from some broken crates and started a little fire against a concrete wall in a bunker. I was warming myself when sirens sounded an alert like war had been declared. It was just a practice drill, but here was the captain of the guard, running on his rounds to check security at the airfield, the motor pool, the ammo dump, and here I was with a fire at the ammo dump. I couldn't figure out how to put that fire out fast except to urinate on it, which I did, just as he got there. A stream of white smoke was rising from the charred wood and any idiot could see what had happened.

He said, "Soldier, if this was wartime I'd have you shot for this."

I said, "I'm sorry."

He said, "Sorry, my ass. Consider yourself under arrest. Report to the guardhouse. I'm going to get you six months at least, if I don't get you shot."

So I went to the guardhouse. I didn't think much of going to the guardhouse or getting six months or getting shot, but no one there thought much of a guy who would start a fire in an ammo dump and might have gotten them all blown to hell. They did think it was sort of funny, since the worst hadn't happened.

My company captain got to me and he was upset but not so upset he wanted to lose me from the company baseball team. So he said he'd fix it, and he did. He got to the other officer and got it worked out so my only punishment was thirty days without a pass. Which, of course, was no punishment for me. I spent my time at the canteen, playing pool and watching three hundred soldiers try to put the make on three Red Cross women who worked there. And I was not assigned to guard the ammo dump again.

Come baseball season I was assigned to the billet for the ballplayers and joined the team and started to play games all over Germany, which gave me a chance to see some of the country. It turned out I was one of the best ballplayers over there. I was the best outfielder. They had real bad equipment, but I made do. The longest bat they had was the shortest one I ever used in my life. It was a thirty-three-incher, but with it I hit seventeen or eighteen home runs in the twenty-five or thirty games we played. I ran, threw, and caught like a pro, which I was, and I really liked getting back to baseball and finding out I hadn't lost it.

They had a contest to name the most valuable player in Army ball in Germany and the prize was a trip home to see the World Series. The finalists were me, Yankee catcher Johnny Blanchard, and a clever left-handed pitcher named George Peckatoosis or something like that, whose name I couldn't spell then and sure can't spell now. He won, although my captain had given our whole company one whole day off, herded them into the cafeteria, and had them clip thousands of ballots out of the *Stars and Stripes* newspaper to fill out in my favor and send them in. I'll never figure out how I lost, unless the other guy's captain did the same thing.

I was sorry when the season ended. I had to go back to regular duty. None of the athletes wanted to go back to duty and a lot of them went to other teams. One of my roomies was a guy named John Farrell. He wasn't a good athlete, but he never did anything but athletics. He told the football coach he had played quarterback at Oregon State, so he was put on the football team. After the coach saw he couldn't play quarterback, he let him help coach. Farrell coached the track team and the boxing team and any other team he could find that would keep him off regular duty. He was one of the great guys and one of the great con artists I've known.

A lot of guys got away with that sort of thing and they had a good life, lying around between games and eating good training-table chow. I could have done it legitimately. I had played high-school and college football and I could run. But I heard those games over there were really rough, with a lot of guys who didn't know what to do except hit hard and hurt one another, and I was scared of an injury that would hurt my baseball career. So I went back to soldiering, with a new company commander who was West Point and Army all the way and hated jocks and goof-offs. I had a hard winter doing dumb things so bad I was always being put on punishment and getting restricted to base, which is where I would have remained anyway.

Finally, we were moved to a new location in the countryside near Nuremberg and put up in one of the most beautiful buildings I have seen in my life. It was made of marble and stone and had high ceilings, long halls, and huge rooms. It was converted to our use, but we had no business being in a place like that palace. I remember at night they'd turn an armed forces radio station on the loudspeakers. They had a program of jazz music that started with a theme of a train chugging into or out of a station. I'll always remember the sound of that train echoing down those long halls and the sound of that music filling those large rooms; I've wanted to be a disc jockey ever since.

I was, of course, a baseball player. I entered my second season of service ball in the best shape of my career, thanks to daily calisthenics and fitness routines forced on us by our West Point drillmaster. I got away from him and got back on a ball field. A lot of guys had gone home, so we got together a lot of new guys. Farrell was back, and a big Greek named Dan Theodosian, who had played at Georgia Tech, and another big guy named Mel Johnson, who had played at Colorado. Football players. We became good buddies and played a lot of good baseball, but I didn't run with them when they ran after frauleins at night. I hit about .350 with power and fielded fabulously.

My hitch ended before the season did. They threw me a going-away party at a *gasthof* in town. Some sergeant who hated athletes started to chew out one of our guys whose uniform was sort of sloppy. Theodosian and Farrell took the sergeant into a back room to talk it over. When I got there to hear what was being said, I saw they were mixing with the guy. I jumped in to get my two fists' worth in, but they grabbed me and got me out of there and got me to my senses. As they pointed out, I was headed home the next day and it was no time for me to be headed for trouble. Then they went back in the other room and beat the hell out of the guy.

And I went home, on a big ship, over that big ocean, sick all the way.

7.

I GOT back home to Ohio, got in touch with the Dodgers, and was told to get to Pueblo, Colorado, to play in the Western League. I was also told to get a catcher's mitt and get back behind the plate.

I was disappointed. After tearing up Germany as an army ace, I assumed my reputation had preceded me and I would be welcomed home as a hero and moved right into the majors. I also thought I was the world's greatest outfielder.

A Dodgers' official told me confidentially that Roy Campanella was getting old and slowing down. They were looking for a catcher for the future. They had signed me as a catcher and wanted me to get back to it and learn it.

I thought I was being conned. Campy was having a great year. But he was well into his thirties, and as it turned out it was to be his last good year.

This was the midsummer of 1955 and I was twenty-two years old and on my way to the top. I thought I was being sidetracked, but I would make it to the majors in two years and become a regular in the big leagues in less than three years.

Actually, I had moved up to Class A ball and I wasn't ready for that.

I had hit in D and in C ball, but I had a hard time hitting in A ball. Army ball had softened me up. Most pitchers in Germany just threw. They didn't put much on their pitches and they couldn't put them where they wanted them. Here they threw curves, change-ups, everything with control.

I didn't do too badly. I averaged .278, but I didn't hit with any power or get many extra-base hits and didn't produce runs.

I wasn't concentrating on my hitting because I was worried about my fielding. I didn't make too many errors, but I was having a hard time handling the pitchers and keeping the ball in control. I was worried and went to my manager, Goldie Holt, and asked for help.

I never will forget it. I said, "Goldie, I'm butchering the ball behind the plate and I have to have help."

He said, "Kid, you're in A ball now. By now you should know how to play."

So that was that. I went on butchering the ball behind the plate a few games, and he put me in the outfield a few games. Without having given me any help, he must have told the Dodgers I couldn't cut it, because I was sent down to B ball, to Cedar Rapids, Iowa, in the Three-I League.

Pueblo was all right, but I hardly got to know the town. Or the league. I did get to know Salt Lake City. One night after a game we left the beat-up hotel where they roomed the blacks and Latins and we were walking through town looking for a place to eat. There were four of us, all black, so we didn't try white places. The word was that Salt Lake City didn't welcome blacks in white places. Finally we came on a Chinese restaurant and figured that would be all right. There were only a few people there, all white. We sat down at a table and waited to be served, but no one came to wait on us until this Chinese man came up and said, "I'm sorry, boys, but I can't serve you. It's not that I mind, it's my other customers." We looked around at the few white faces, who were looking away, and we left.

I had been out in the world enough that I had reached the point where I was pissed off at being treated like a second-class citizen. I thought, "What the hell is this, we can't even eat at a Chinese restaurant? And why are Chinese better than blacks? For that matter, why are whites?"

I'm sorry I didn't have the guts to do anything about it. Not that I lacked courage, but what could I have done? Raised hell? Refused to leave? Insisted on service? Called the cops? Gotten locked up for disturbing the peace? I had the guts for a fistfight, but I didn't know what to do about bigotry.

I blame the Dodgers some. They have always been a first-class organization, but at that time when they signed blacks and Latins and assigned them they should have made certain they would be welcome. We weren't even welcome in Florida where the Dodgers spent spring training. I'll get into that later.

They should have insisted that their teams do things together so the majority could protect the minority. If black Dodgers weren't welcome in a motel, hotel, restaurant, or theater, the white Dodgers should have fought for their rights or at least walked out. The Dodgers should not have gone where all players were not welcome. That's the way the Dodgers are today, but it's not the way they were.

In fairness to the Dodgers, they were the first to have a black player and they eventually fought for their rights. All teams went through the same racial transitions and most were a lot less considerate than the Dodgers. Some teams were still going through these transitions in recent years and some still aren't all the way through to the other side. When I was with the Twins in Minnesota and the Senators in Washington a few years ago, they were torn with racial tension, and, as far as I can see, a couple of clubs today are being troubled by bigotry.

Anyway, I lasted thirty-two games in the Western League and moved on to the Three-I League. I was playing in Waterloo or some such small city where the fans are right on top of the field. I was in the on-deck circle and apparently blocking the view from a box seat behind me, because a fan started to yell, "Hey, Sambo, out of the way." I turned and gave him a glare and he said, "Cool it, nigger, and move it, or I'll come out and kick it." Like a fucking fool I hung my head. I wish to hell I'd started a riot or two. It's for sure my glare never did much for me.

It didn't make much difference where you were, racial prejudice was everywhere. I didn't move, but I didn't make a move either. I thought, "Who needs this trouble?" I was a kid and my career was in trouble. I had not only been demoted, but at mid-season. The Dodgers wanted me to become a catcher, and I was no catcher. The Dodgers didn't care if I was black or white. The Dodgers didn't care if I had race troubles to go with my growing-up troubles and my playing troubles. It was harder for a black to make it than it was for a white because blacks had to contend with all kinds of extra crap. But black or white, a player either makes it or he doesn't.

I don't think I'd have made it if it hadn't been for Ray Perry. He was player-manager at Cedar Rapids. He was all the manager Goldie Holt was not. Ray Perry knew why I had been sent down and when I reported to him I told him that while I had caught in high-school and college ball, I was not a good catcher, had never had any instruction in catching, and had to have help if I was going to become the catcher the Dodgers wanted. He said he'd give me all the help I could handle and told me to report to him at the ball park at three every afternoon.

The other players reported for the night games at five, but I reported early every day and Perry was always there to help. He wasn't a catcher but he knew how to catch, and he put on catcher's gear and got down in the dirt with me to help me. He pitched to me and had me pitch to him and he laid down bunts for me and had me lay down bunts for him. He hit pop-fly fouls behind the plate for me and he had me hit pop-fly fouls for him. He taught me how to catch a pop-fly foul, field a bunt, throw to first, block pitches in the dirt, and throw to second on steals. He also took time to work on the infield with Clarence Moore, a kid the Dodgers had sent to him to learn the infield. Clarence Moore never made it, but I did, thanks to Ray Perry. He worked hard to do the job he was supposed to do.

I improved. I still had a lot to learn, but at least I was on my way. I needed experience, which I was getting.

I never will forget the first time I went back on a pop-fly foul behind the plate. I thought I was camped directly under it and it fell four feet from me. A high pop-fly foul straight overhead tends to fade and creates a sort of optical illusion. You have to take this into account to get where it's going to be. It is one of those things you can be told, but have to experience before you really see what it is.

I never will forget a tag play I had to make at the plate. The throw got to me long before the runner did. I figured it would be easy and went to bang the ball on him. But, about six feet from the plate, instead of sliding straight, the runner jumped in the air and came at me, spikes high. I thought his feet were going to cut my legs off. He missed my thighs, but one of his shoes hit my shin guard. The cleats cut right through it. He almost tore my kneecap up.

I remember another tag play at the plate that was close. The throw got to me about the time the runner did, but I was down for his slide and he didn't slide. He came in standing up and hard. I turned my head and he hit me in the mouth with his elbow, knocking out three teeth.

With plays like these I learned that you always have to protect yourself, never expect the other guy to do the expected, and hurt him before he hurts you.

I hung on to the ball and made the out on both plays. I can take punishment without getting afraid, but being brave is one thing and being dumb another. You have to play it smart and think of yourself first.

Perry was a great teacher and a good guy, which isn't to say that he was soft. I still wasn't sharp on my throws to second on steals out of the crouch and a team was stealing on me and embarrassing me. My pitcher had two balls and no strikes on a batter, but I wasn't thinking about that. I was thinking that the runner on first was going to steal, so I called for a pitchout, but the runner didn't go. So I'm standing there with the ball in my hand and no place to throw it and the pitcher is standing there with three balls and no strikes on the batter. Before I knew it, Perry was standing out there too, chewing my ass out for putting the pitcher in a hole like that.

I felt like hell, but I learned. I always carried the lesson. I think I only called for a pitchout on two-and-oh one time after that. That was with the Dodgers when I was catching Roger Craig, who could put a pitch across a postage stamp. I figured I could take a chance with a control pitcher like Craig, but he didn't like it either, so that was the last time. I think the runner went that time, and I think I got him. But if you can't get a base stealer off a strike, you can't catch in the big leagues. It can't always be easy for you.

I remember later that evening in Cedar Rapids, Perry saw I was upset and he told me, "Everyone makes mistakes. The thing is to learn from them. You can't always help making a physical error, but if you make a mental error you have to profit from it so you don't make it again. You're down here to learn and if you learn right you won't make the same mistakes again and again. You may see your mistake and you may not. I'm here to make sure you know what you did wrong. And don't ever get upset when anyone who knows points out to you something you may not know. I don't think it's the last time you'll ever get chewed out, but I hope it's the last time you have to be chewed out for this thing."

I nodded and said I knew and I thanked him. I still do thank him, even all these years later.

He helped me in many ways. My catching was so screwed up that my batting got screwed up. I caught fifty-five games and batted .235 down there, one of the lowest averages of my entire career. He showed me how to keep my body still in the batter's box and keep my weight back until I swung, and then to shift my weight forward so I swung with a lot of leverage. At least I started to hit with power. I hit ten doubles and five home runs and drove home twenty runs. I was concentrating so much on my catching I wasn't concentrating enough on my hitting, so I didn't hit consistently. But at least I became a threat at bat.

It was quite a summer, from Germany to Colorado to Iowa in a few months' time. I went from $110 a month in the Army to $400 a month in pro baseball, which was still not a lot, but at least it was a raise over my earlier salaries. It was enough for me to buy my first car, a '53 red Chevy convertible. I loved that car dearly. I polished it every week and drove it all over that little midwestern town and hated it when I had to go on the road and leave my nifty little car behind. I lived with an old couple in town. I didn't exactly tear up the town. I don't recall having any dates. But I was ready.

8.

ALL the time I was in the service I corresponded with Mary, who was still at Central State, though I didn't count on her as my girl. All the time I was in the service I saw guys who were shook up because their girls back home had broken up with them. I didn't want to get into a position where I could be hurt. Guys got "Dear John" letters all the time from girls who had fallen in love with others while the servicemen were gone, or admitted they had been unfaithful. Or the guys heard that their girls or wives were being unfaithful. Not that the guys were faithful to their ladies, but they always expect their ladies to be faithful to them.

I guess I wanted to have a girl too, someone to write to, like the other guys, so I wrote Mary, and Mary wrote me, and we wrote about wanting to see each other again, but we didn't write that we were going together or going to get married. We didn't write about being faithful because what did we have to be faithful to? We'd never slept together.

I wrote her when I was headed home and I looked forward to seeing her. But when I got home to Ohio there was a letter from her waiting for me in which she said some guy had gotten her in the woods and forced himself on her and gotten her pregnant.

She said she knew I had some of my baseball bonus money in the bank and had also saved some service money in the bank and she wanted me to give her five or six hundred dollars for an abortion.

Well, I was an inexperienced kid from the country, maybe, but I wasn't that naïve. I wrote that I was sorry for her, and I was, but she'd have to go to the guy who'd gotten her in trouble to help her out.

I don't know what happened after that because I never heard from her again. I don't know if we'd have gotten something going together, but if so it would have been because I didn't have anyone else, because I never felt like I loved her.

I got another girl at that time and we did get something going together, maybe because neither of us had anyone else. I don't know if it was love or anything like that because it's hard to look back and know, but we liked each other.

When I was home I started to visit Jim at Ohio State in Columbus and watch his football games. He was buddying up with two other players, Jim Parker, a tackle who became a great pro, and Aurelius Thomas, a good guard. I'd hang out with them there and sometimes Jim would bring them home to Ashland for a few days.

All three had girls at the school and the girls had a friend, Geraldine Fraime. They called her Jeri. She was an extra girl in the group, and Jim had told her all about me and she was sort of waiting when I got back. It was like an arranged marriage, but it was all right because when we met we took to each other and it felt natural to just start going together, like the others.

She was a lot like me, quiet and not very experienced and not too aggressive. I felt easy with her and she felt easy with me. We didn't do a lot. Nothing sexual really, just necking and stuff like that. During the season we'd go to the games, which were really exciting because those guys were really good, and then go out after games. And we kept it up after the season, too.

We'd sit around and shoot the bull or go out to eat or to a movie, the six of us. Sometimes we'd drive around in my Chevy. She met my parents and they liked her and I met her mother—her parents were divorced—and she seemed to like me. I wasn't home all winter and I was gone the next summer. We wrote and went together the next winter when I was home.

Some of the other guys and girls broke up. I remember one

time when I was with Jim at Columbus he said he had a new girl who was a nurse's aide and a singer with a local band. She turned out to be a beautiful girl, sweet, and a sensational singer. I think Woody Hayes the coach, thought a band singer was a bad influence on a player, keeping him up late at night in saloons, so he threatened to take away Jim's scholarship if he didn't split. They broke up. Her name was Nancy Wilson, and, of course, she became one of the top performers.

Jim got another girl. Other guys got girls, broke up with girls, then got other girls, but I stayed with the only girl I ever really went with up until then, Jeri. I have no idea how we got together so thick. I played baseball in Venezuela part of that winter and in Montreal the next summer, but before the summer ended we were married.

While I was away, we exchanged letters. When I was home, we went together. But I didn't feel like I was committed to her.

When I went to Montreal for the summer I moved in with a lady who rented rooms to ballplayers. She had a daughter who was good-looking and liked ballplayers. She was always talking about Chico Fernandez, who had lived there when he was playing in Montreal. He was real good-looking and always had a lot of ladies. She acted like she liked me, and her room was right next to mine, but we never got into anything except a lot of talk and she was always talking about charming Chico.

It's a swinging city, though, with a lot of nice-looking ladies and a lot of nice nightlife. The guys were always talking about banging broads, even the married guys. The ball club liked to have the married guys bring their wives with them because they couldn't control them otherwise in that town. I was ready to run a little, but I was still scared half to death. I was still going out to eat and going back to my room and to bed by myself after games.

Finally I met a nice young lady, but I still went to bed by myself. We became friends. Necking friends, but still just friends. She was half and half, black and white, and she was Jewish. She was going to McGill University, was highly educated, and was interesting to talk to. We spent time together, walking that interesting town, even walking in the rain, talking.

We used to talk about the black-white thing. She saw it from both sides. As she saw it, one thing Jews had on blacks was Jews were clannish and stuck together and tried to help one another. But when a black guy made it he was separated from the black community and wanted to get away right away and live in a white neighborhood, and the poor blacks resented him. I used to talk about making a million dollars to help my people.

She made me see both sides, and that opened up my mind and helped me, I think, but things have changed since those days. I know they don't always, but Jews are supposed to take pride in being Jewish. Since "black is beautiful" came along, blacks have begun to take pride in being black. We're brothers and sisters, and more together.

I think the thing is for everyone to get together. But until a people start to take pride in themselves they find it difficult to put themselves on a level with others and feel free to be with them.

Anyway, we spent our time together talking and philosophizing and keeping each other company, keeping each other from being lonely. We were friends, not lovers, but Jeri, my girl back home, wasn't too sure; when she found out about my friend in Montreal, she wasn't too happy about it. I forget if I wrote her or told her, but I guess that was my mistake because it got Jeri in gear.

Columbus was with Montreal in the International League at that time and whenever I was in Ohio with the team Jeri lived in town and I spent my time with her, of course. I don't remember proposing, but maybe I did. I think we just started talking about what it would be like to be married and about getting married.

I remember we were walking in downtown Columbus one day, looking in windows, and then we were looking in jewelry-shop windows at engagement rings. Next thing we were in one of the stores buying a ring and then she was wearing it.

I don't mean to say she talked me into it or anything like that. I don't remember too much talk. And I don't think she maneuvered me into it, either. It just sort of happened. Before I knew it, we had set the date.

That broke the other thing up, of course, and it's too bad because that was one of the finest friendships I ever had. It's sad, really, but ladies don't like their men having other ladies for friends, and we don't like our ladies having other men for friends.

Once I got into it I found out sex was fine, but I've found there's a lot more to life than just that. You can have good sex with a lady, but if you can't be good friends too, you can't have a good marriage.

It's really a shame that men and women can't be friends without being lovers, but most people haven't come far enough to be comfortable with that.

To this day I can't tell you why I married Jeri. It wasn't for sex, because we hadn't had any.

I can't tell you what was in her mind either, but I guess she cared for me and wanted to marry me or she wouldn't have done it. I don't know how well she knew me, but then I know I didn't know her all that well.

It was like you met a girl you liked and you got married to her. I wanted to have a girl. To keep her I thought I had to marry her sooner or later. That was the summer of 1956 and I was twenty-three and she was a year or so younger.

It just sort of happened. I liked her well enough and we got along well enough, and we got a lot out of our marriage for a long time.

We had set a date in August. We were due in Columbus for weekend games and we were supposed to get married there on Saturday. Friday night we were playing in Richmond, Virginia, and I caught a foul tip in the groin.

I don't know if you have ever been hit by a hard-hit base-ball in the groin, but it hurts like hell. I landed on my back. Doc Harvey, our trainer, ran out, grabbed me by the belt, and lifted me off the ground and dropped me back down a couple of times. I think that's supposed to get your testicles back where they belong. It's a hell of a way to handle the problem.

I got back to where I could breathe, but I had to get out of the ball game because I was walking half doubled over like some kind of cripple for a long time. My testicles were swollen and I was in pain through the night and into the next day, my wedding day.

Knowing I was about to be married, the other guys thought it was funny, of course. They couldn't stop talking about it. They just had a hell of ,a good time. And when I got to Columbus and told my dad and brother and buddies, they thought that was a real laugher too.

When Jeri found out about it, I don't think she thought it was so funny. Except for whatever it was I did with that prostitute in Germany, we were both virgins when we married, and Jeri and I had sex for the first time on our wedding night, but it was too painful for me to satisfy either of us. However, whatever else went wrong, sex turned out to be all right for us from then on.

I do remember being scared half to death of what I was doing on my wedding day. It was all formal, in a church with our families there. I wore a white tux and I recall I was soaked with sweat before the ceremony even started. I don't know how I got through it.

I remember being surprised by her during the day. She had never had much to say, until we got married and got to the reception. Then she took over and told the photographer and others what to do and directed the whole show and ordered people around. I remember how surprised I was that she was so forceful. I found out she had a lot to say from that day on.

I'm not knocking her. I guess marriage gave her the confidence to do what she thought a married lady should do. It brought her out of her shell It's just that I was surprised that she was so different than I had thought. But marriage made me a different person too. It made me a married man, not just a kid who was scared of women. And when we had kids, I had to grow up.

It wasn't just growing up overnight, of course. We were young when we got married and we both had a lot of changing ahead of us. It took time, and in time we changed so much we grew apart. Meanwhile, we went through a lot together.

We honeymooned in Montreal as I got back to baseball,

and she went on to the top with me and later back down again.

We were just kids when we got married, and we hadn't thought it through and we didn't have a lot going for us, but it wasn't so bad. Our marriage lasted a long time and we got three terrific kids out of it. We had lots of good times, and we didn't have any really bad days until my career came to a close and our marriage ended and a lot of bitterness came between us.

9.

For me, 1955 proved an adventurous year. After returning from Germany to the United States, I wound up in Venezuela.

Following my fourth season of pro baseball, I went home to Ohio to be with my brother and his buddies, to go with my new girl, and to go to work. I got a job in a New London foundry where they made pottery-type tiles.

There was a train rack of tiles fresh from the hot kiln. Without testing it, I went to strongarm it with a push of my shoulder. It was hot and burned me from my shoulder to my arm. My dad took one look and said I was finished with the foundry before I was finished with baseball.

I was out of work when a call came from the Dodgers asking me to report to a team in Venezuela for winter baseball. The team needed a catcher and I needed work on my catching. I was offered four hundred dollars a month and accepted.

I had an overnight layover in Miami and was booked into the Sir John Hotel, where blacks stayed at that time. Roy Hamilton was playing the club there. Roy was a great singer. "Ebb Tide," famous in the black community, was one of his hits. Standing on the balcony of my room, overlooking the front of the hotel, I watched the well-dressed people pour in to see his show. I wanted to see the show in the worst way, but I didn't have the guts to go.

There was a woman there trying to make out with every man who came by alone. I could hear her saying she needed rent money and would turn a trick for ten bucks or five or whatever they offered. There were no takers. As the crowd thinned out, she looked up at the balcony and said, "How about you, broad shoulders, want to buy a little bit?" I'd never seen anything like that. I was shocked but I was also tempted, and I backed into my room fast. I'll never forget it. I hope he made out—the next day I found out it was a man dressed like a woman.

We had a stop in Jamaica on the way down. I recall the water was green and clear, as beautiful as anything I had seen. Then we landed in Caracas, where the Caribbean Sea and the beach also were beautiful. From there I went on to Maracaibo, on the Gulf of Venezuela, another lovely place. I was struck by all that beauty. I was becoming a world traveler. But I was scared half to death. I didn't speak Spanish and was among strangers.

Someone from the Cabimas ball club met me and took me to the team lodgings in a large house. All the rooms were taken, so I got the basement. But it had been made into a room and I was content—until Don Demeter and I found we were making four hundred dollars a month while others were making almost twice that, and we were carrying the club.

Don never made it big in the majors, but he did last eleven or twelve years with four or five teams, and when he was on the way up he looked like he was going to be great. He was a tall, lanky centerfielder who covered a lot of territory—he could run, catch and throw, and hit with power. I was becoming a better catcher, ran well, and hit well. When we found out about the money, we bitched to Buzzie Bavasi on the phone and he raised us each to seven hundred a month.

Buzzie was the general manager of the Dodgers for many years and he was all right, smart and fair. He had a weakness for good living, I was to find out, and he had a weakness for players who lived high, which I didn't, but I always played hard for him and he always played fair with me.

I found out from him many years later that Clay Bryant, manager of the Cabimas club, didn't want an inexperienced black kid, but Buzzie said he told Bryant if I couldn't go there, he could come home. Buzzie said they were only stocking the team to provide experience for promising players. There'd be no point to it if a player like myself couldn't go down there to play.

To Bryant's credit, he never let on he didn't want me. He played me and he helped me. A former pitcher, he could help a catcher. He had gray hair and gray eyes, a feline look to him, was nicknamed Tiger, and was temperamental and tough. It was exciting to play for him. We became friends and remain so to this day.

It was exciting to play there. There was a main league, which had all its teams in Caracas. We were in a secondary league and had to play teams in towns all over. Whenever we had to leave Maracaibo for road games, we had to ferry across the inlet from the bay and drive to the different towns. The cars were old and the drivers were wild and we had to cross a lot of mountains. We had many a hairy moment careening around narrow roads on the edges of long drops. I wasn't the only one scared.

The games themselves were scary. The people came to see a good game and to see their team win. Many of them couldn't afford the money they paid to get into the game and if they weren't happy with the outcome, they let us know about it. They were very volatile. Booing was the least of it. I learned a lot of Spanish cuss words. I couldn't speak Spanish, but I got to where I could cuss Spanish. They spit at you and threw things at you. Some of them carried guns. I didn't see anyone shot, but it gave you something to think about.

I remember one game when the home team was losing badly and the home fans turned mean. When a fight broke out between two players on the field, a lot of fans came out of the seats and surged down to the metal railing. They were hooting and hollering and building up behind that railing until it gave way and they fell onto the field. The players ducked into the dugouts, but the militia, which was always there to keep control, moved in with their machetes and guns and drove the fans right back into the stands. They were flailing away with the flat sides of those machetes and cutting a couple of people with the sharp edges. It was scary to play there, but the playing helped me, and I survived.

It was a little lonely, but I made friends with Demeter, who was soft-spoken and religious, and Earl Battey, a catcher playing for a team across the water from our base. Earl became a major leaguer. We went around together and saw some of the country on our travels. We saw a lot of poverty —animals roaming free and people living like animals on hillsides and in open fields, or in cardboard shacks, their kids half dressed and dirty. A lot of it was worse than the worst ghetto life in the USA, which is still no excuse for ghettos. It made me grateful to live in the USA, which is still no excuse for the way I was sometimes treated because I'm black. You didn't have to be black to have a hard life there, you just had to be poor.

After I spent the following summer in Montreal, the Dodgers' top farm club, I was sent back to spend another winter season in Venezuela. Of course, it was summer there. I didn't mind. I liked playing ball. The experience was helping. And I was paid for it and could use the money instead of spending the winter without a salary.

This time I was assigned to the top tier, the Caracas League. All the teams were based in Caracas. I was on the Lions. I had another good season. And we didn't have to travel unless we wanted to see something. I traveled with Battey, back as my good buddy.

We lived in a downtown hotel. We ate almost all our meals at the hotel restaurant. The year before, they'd had a cook for us at the house they used for us, and the food wasn't bad, but this year, with a restaurant cook, the food was better. I was getting used to the spicy food, and I liked the seafood. Aside from playing ball, though; there wasn't a lot to do. We went to theaters that had American movies with Spanish subtitles or Spanish movies with American subtitles. We didn't chase señoritas.

Then, the next year, even after I'd started in Montreal and finished in Brooklyn, I went back to Caracas for one more winter, this time partly as a vacation trip for my new wife. It was a lot less lonely for me. We had an apartment at the hotel and we had friends among other players who had their wives and apartments there. And they had reception parties for the eam we could go to. We ate at the hotel most times, but we went to an American market to get our kind of food and fix it for ourselves. We did a lot of window-shopping and bought a few things at the open-air shopping plazas, where the prices were right.

We went on trips around the country. You played three days, then had three days off, so you had time to go places. We went to a bullfight, but I'll never go to another. It's the unfairest fight I ever saw. It's bloody and the bull doesn't have a chance. We went to every movie that came along that looked good. We went to places I hadn't gone to before because Jeri had studied Spanish and could speak it and we could communicate. We went to the beach, too, and even though I'm a good swimmer, I don't like to swim where I don't know what's underneath me. When I found out they had sharp rocks close to shore, I didn't like it. And the undertow was strong. Years later, when I was with Minnesota, one of the prospects in our system swam there. The undertow took him out to sea and he drowned.

I had a good season again, and it helped me some more, but I didn't need so much help that time. It was my third season there and I was a major leaguer by then. Jeri and I started to feel homesick and out of touch with things. They had an English-language newspaper but it just reported mostly what was happening in Venezuela. They had the *New York Times* flown in there and we used to pay the high price and spend hours going through it word by word just to catch up.

We were restless, especially after it started to get politically tense. There was turmoil, and we heard talk of a revolution. One night tanks ringed the outside of the ball park because there had been talk that there would be an uprising at the game. Nothing happened, but it was a hard game to play.

We decided to cut our season short and go home for Christmas. You couldn't just take off if you worked there. You had to take care of what they called your *serventia,* which means you had to pay taxes to the Venezuelan government. There was a lot of paperwork and red tape to cut through but we got it done and got out. After we got home, a revolution did break out there. There was war in the streets. The players had to stay in their hotel rooms and away from windows and flying bullets. It was a while before it was settled and they could get back to baseball.

A kid named Charlie Peete, out of Omaha, a prospect of the St. Louis Cardinals, played there. He was a good outfielder, a good hitter, and a good kid. He was flying in with his family when their plane crashed in the mountains outside of Caracas. It's a close landing there off the ocean and the pilot clipped a cliff. There were pictures in the paper of the wreckage strewn all over the hillside and the broken bodies and doll babies lying all around. We heard he was on that plane and then we heard he and his family had all died in the crash. I felt like I was going to cry. You know, your throat starts to get dry and your eyes start to sting and you feel like the tears are going to come. A grown man isn't supposed to cry, so I didn't cry. But I think that was the first time I felt real sorrow. I hardly knew him, but I felt for him and his family. I felt that it could have been me and mine.

I've made many trips since. And I guess I'd go back if I was offered a managerial job or something like that, but I'm not sure.

10.

I<small>N</small> <small>THE</small> spring of '56 I was reassigned to Portland of the Pacific Coast League. It was triple-A ball, but not as good as the other two triple-A leagues, the International League and the American Association. Most of the major-league teams sponsored teams in all three leagues, but the major-league teams were all in the East and the Midwest then. They kept their promising prospects close to them for quick recall. They stocked the Coast clubs with older guys on the way down.

I was on my way up, but I'd dropped down from A ball to B ball during the previous season and they didn't want to make too much of a move with me this season. But the Portland ball park had a long rightfield and a short leftfield. They wanted to pack their lineup with right-handed power-hitters. I was a left-handed hitter. The way it worked out, I never got to see the park.

Portland trained in southern California, so I went there that spring instead of to Vero Beach, Florida, the Dodgers' main base. That was my first time in the West and I really liked the good weather and life.

Our home ball park was Casey Stengel Field in Pasadena. We slept late, because if we got to the park too early the field was still wet with dew and it ruined the baseballs. After the workout some of us would pile into Artie Wilson's Merc convertible and drive down to Sunset Strip to eat at a drive-in restaurant and watch the girls. Mainly, I looked at movies. I'm still a film freak. I lived downtown at the Mayfair Hotel and I went to a different film every night.

I don't remember too much about the ball club. We were just getting into exhibition games when they got me out of there.

Before expansion, a lot of good players spent their careers in the minors, and they were good careers in big cities like Los Angeles and Minneapolis and Montreal, before they were in the big leagues. It wasn't the big time though, and it wasn't the big money, and they had little left to show for it when they finished. When there were only sixteen teams in the big leagues maybe better ballplayers than I never made it.

I learned later that Greg Mulleavy, the Montreal manager, really had to fight to get me moved to Montreal. Just before the season started, the Dodgers made final assignments of all the players who weren't going to play with the big club. Mulleavy had his choice of two or three former big-league catchers, including Dixie Howell and Johnny Bucha. He surprised everyone when he said he wanted Roseboro. Here I was, a kid out of B ball with one winter of winter ball behind me, picked over proven and experienced receivers.

Buzzie Bavasi and Fresco Thompson of the Dodgers' front office admitted they resisted the idea. They thought I needed more seasoning at a lower level. But Mulleavy said he fought for me because he wanted someone on the way up, not the way down. He thought I had a lot of potential when he saw me, and he heard I had improved a lot in Cedar Rapids and Caracas. The brass gave in on the condition that he keep me, play me, and help me. He did.

Mulleavy is a good man. A former infielder and another of those who had only a season or so in the majors, he knew the minors, ballplayers, and baseball. We had some good men and played some good ball. Our best probably was Rocky Nelson, the first baseman. He played for six or seven teams in nine or ten seasons in the majors, but he never made it the way he had in the minors. The hot hitter that year was George "Sparky" Anderson, the second baseman, now the manager of the Reds. Sparky made it to the majors for only one season, but he hit fair that season in Montreal. Clyde Parris, our third baseman, had hands as good as any I ever saw and could hit to the right as good as anyone, but he never made it to the majors. In the outfield we had Bob Wilson and Jimmy Williams and, for a while, Bobby Del Greco. I was the regular receiver. And Fred Kipp, Connie Grubb, and Billy Harris were the pitchers. Kipp won twenty that year. None became major-league pitchers of any consequence.

They call a catcher's gear "the tools of ignorance," but I was learning a lot about the art. It is a hard, difficult job. You are the only one in the game during every pitch, except the pitcher, but he doesn't play every day like you do. You squat behind the plate a half inning, then have to unlimber and swing the bat and run the bases the next half inning.

I learned from everyone. I even learned from opponents. For instance, Miami signed Satchel Paige to pitch. He must have been fifty. He was *old* old. He stood out on the mound burping and you could hear his stomach growl. He held the ball so long you were sure he wasn't going to throw it, but the minute you relaxed he laid it on you. He didn't throw hard when I faced him, but he threw where he wanted.

I was a left-handed pull-hitter. Teams played me to pull. But to stop me from pulling, they'd pitch outside to me. That's stupid. If you shift your fielders to the right, you want the batter to hit to right. Paige pitched inside to me and I hit to where the fielders were playing for me. Even today teams shift one way on batters and then pitch to them the other way. I learned from Paige that if you keep the batter off balance, and pitch and defense him properly, you can get him out most of the time without working hard or throwing hard.

Even at his age Paige was a wonder, with all his windups and deliveries and soft stuff, and it was a thrill just to bat against him.

They had some wonderful players in that league. Luke Easter, the big first baseman who was playing for Buffalo, also had a lot of age on him by the time he got to the majors, but he still hit hard. In the little ball park in Buffalo, he hit so hard he almost tore it up. He hit shots that bent the fences and some that traveled five hundred feet. I remember once when I was leading off first and had to dive back because of a pick-off attempt, Easter slapped his big glove on me and muttered,

"Get back here, you little motherfucker." It was a thrill just to be beaten black and blue by his glove.

I held my own. I had a hell of a year. We had a short right-field fence and Rocky Nelson and I leaned on it. Mulleavy suggested I pull the ball for home runs to right, and while it held my average to .273, I hit 25, which was to be my all-time high. I hit 22 doubles, I scored 76 runs, and I drove in 78 in 125 games. I played a little outfield and even first base, besides catching, and only made four errors all season.

It was an interesting league, to say the least. When we hit the road we really traveled. We went all the way from Montreal and Toronto to Miami and Havana. I lived in that room at that woman's house and walked and talked with that college girl until Jeri and I got married and moved into an apartment in the suburbs. I lived quietly and didn't dissipate.

Some of those guys could, and did, go from the end of one ball game to the beginning of the next. They thought they were major leaguers and didn't belong in the minors, and they were bitter about it. They partied to take the hurt out of it. Some of them never got out of the minors because they boozed so much or chased women so much or got such bad reputations the big teams wouldn't take a chance.

We had an outfielder who had a lot of talent. He was a black guy who dressed to the death and loved the ladies. I remember Doc Harvey calling me one night to go with him to bail the guy out of jail because it was a black area and Doc didn't want to go alone.

The guy was always so well dressed it was a shock to see him with his suit torn and dirty, his straw hat all beaten up, and a heel off one of his shoes. One of his eyes was bruised and his face was swollen. He had been with a girl and her guy caught them and threw him down the stairs.

It scared me to see the cat like that, sick and stinking, and it was embarrassing to walk out of jail with him. He swore it wouldn't happen again, but of course it did, again and again. He was one of the best ballplayers who never made the majors. Even if he blamed bad luck or dumb bosses, he really had himself to blame.

There are a lot of fellows with ability who get kicked

around, and you wonder why. Then you find out, you learn there's a reason. Maybe they chase women and booze it up or pop pills or take dope and get in fights and get into trouble. The time comes when no one wants to bother with them anymore.

I learned a lot about baseball and about ballplayers in the minor leagues. There are a lot of guys who want to be big players but don't want it enough to sacrifice for it. There are a lot of guys who get the chicks coming at them and get some money in their pockets for the first time and don't know how to handle it. They give in to temptation, and they waste themselves and their ability and their lives. It's true in every profession, but I think the temptations are stronger in sports.

I was lucky because I was sort of shy and straight and scared. I held back and didn't go over the deep end. I had ability, but not so much I could have wasted any of it and had enough left to have a good career. Maybe I was a square, but it was a blessing. I concentrated on my career and wasn't distracted by a lot of fooling around beyond the ball field.

After the season, I went back to Venezuela for the winter. I didn't stay the season, but each time I went there I learned a little more. There didn't seem to be any end of things to learn every time I took to the field.

I was even learning how to dress off the field. Mulleavy had a couple of sons who liked clothes. They got me interested and we used to shop together. One of the sons now has a clothing store. Greg Junior, the other son, is an actor—he played the husband in the "Mary Hartman" television series. Greg Senior is a scout now.

When I went back to Montreal in the spring of 1957 I was dressing like a big leaguer even though I wasn't in the big leagues yet. But I wasn't far away. The team hadn't changed much, except Rocky Nelson had moved up to the majors and Jim Gentile had taken over at first base. The Dodgers had won two straight National League titles, but they were having a hard time getting going. Gil Hodges was sick and they needed someone to take his place at first, so they called for Gentile.

I found out later from Jimmy Campanis, the son of Al

Campanis, now the Dodgers' general manager, that when they sent for Gentile they couldn't find him. Jim was a good guy and a good ballplayer, but he was out on the town and out of touch when opportunity came calling. Obviously the brass was bothered by it, because they decided to settle for another hitter and bring Roseboro up.

That's the way I got my break, which I guess I'd have gotten before long anyway. But you never know. I was having the same sort of season I'd had the year before, even to the .273 batting average. I wasn't driving in as many runs, but I'd scored thirty and hit seven home runs in forty-eight games, which was about one-third of the season, so I'd probably have finished with some fair figures. I was continuing to improve as a catcher.

I had just passed my twenty-fourth birthday and was in my sixth professional season. I don't know if I was ready, but my time had come.

11.

I GOT to the Dodgers just in time, before they left Ebbets Field and Brooklyn. That summer, 1957, was the team's last one there. I was there for only a few months, yet I feel I played a part in history.

My wife had just learned to drive. She didn't have a driver's license yet, but she had guts, and drove our car and our few belongings from Montreal to New York. We found an apartment in the Bedford-Stuyvesant section of Brooklyn.

It was a hot summer, we had no air-conditioning, and we were uncomfortable a lot of the time. It was a poor, black neighborhood, but not nearly the drug-ridden, crime-ridden place it is now. We were a little nervous on the streets at times, but mostly we enjoyed the experience.

We had never lived in a really big city. We couldn't believe how many people there were. All kinds of people. All kinds of life. It was exciting.

I remember passing a church on Fulton Street and hearing the darnedest music. I was used to quiet churches and hymns. Here, they had a band, and even the kids in the audience had tambourines. When they made that foot-stomping, hand-clapping music and everyone got to jumpin' around and whooping it up, I practically went out of my mind. Jeri couldn't understand why I suddenly started to go to church. I went for the music and the excitement.

We were in the big town and there was excitement all around. We'd go to Times Square and walk down Broadway.

You could do that then without fear. We went to shows and ate in fancy restaurants. We were black, but we were welcome anywhere. It was a good experience to be treated decently. Because I was a ballplayer, I was especially welcome and treated well wherever I was recognized. I enjoyed the attention. It was new to me, and I liked it.

We went to tourist places like the Empire State Building and the Statue of Liberty. We went to theaters in Harlem and Brooklyn where we watched great black performers. Brother Jim came from Canada, injured and out of football, and we showed him our town, the good and the bad.

I have never seen anything like Harlem. As bad as Watts is, it isn't as bad as Harlem. All those blacks and Latins living in the worst sort of poverty, congested together along filthy streets. Maybe the Bowery was just as bad. All those drunks and bums sprawled in doorways and begging for pennies. I was being paid ten grand a year and felt rich.

Every time Leo Durocher came to town he'd take a trip to the Bowery to see an old broadcaster whose life had gone bad, and he'd give the guy some money.

Bedford-Stuyvesant was soiled and congested too, so as soon as we could, we rented a house in Jamaica, which was suburban, nicer, cleaner, less crowded. But I really loved the whole town, the good and the bad. I can't explain it, except I was excited.

Ebbets Field was exciting too. It was a little old bandbox of a ball park, but it had a great history and a lot of tradition. It wasn't like the new ball parks, which are all alike. It had its own character. For instance, instead of bleachers it had double-deck stands in the outfield.

Fans could buy the cheapest seats and sit in the shade upstairs and have a hell of a view of the action.

The stands were built close to the field and you felt the fans were a part of everything. They were the greatest fans I've known.

I can't put down the fans at Chavez Ravine in LA. They set attendance records and they support the team tremendously. But they're sort of sophisticated. They don't make the noise the fans in Brooklyn did. They don't know the game the way the fans in Brooklyn did.

Fans in Brooklyn were special. They lived and died with the Dodgers. "Dem Bums" was that town's team. The Dodgers *were* that town. They were more important to the town than anything else, and the town has never been the same since the team left. I don't think any team and town have ever been so close.

I heard about it before I got there, but I didn't believe it until I got there. I wasn't there long, but long enough. Hilda Chester with her signs and her clanging cow bell. The Sym-Phony with the worst pack of pickup musicians you ever heard. The atmosphere was something else. Baseball was a religion there. The Dodgers conducted a kind of church. The fans believed.

Those fans had been around. They could accept a physical error, but if you made a mental mistake they booed your butt. And they knew when you made a mental mistake. They knew the game's fine points. If I had any doubt about maybe making a bad play, the fans let me know. You could learn from them, and I really loved them. They cheered sometimes and booed sometimes, but they were always loyal.

The park held less than thirty-five thousand, but it was packed a lot. They drew more than a million fans that year, which was what they usually drew, and that was a lot for those days. Walter O'Malley, the owner, talked a lot about the ball park being too small and not having enough parking space and all, but it wasn't that the team wasn't drawing or making money, it was that he thought he could do better elsewhere.

He talked all year about making a move to LA, but he also talked about staying if the city would build him a bigger ball park with better parking. Maybe he'd made his deal already, but he tried not to let on until the very end. He had a lot of people in town trying to save the team. He got the Giants to go to the West Coast with him in the end.

The West Coast—Los Angeles, anyway—deserved big-league baseball. The LA franchise has to be the best in baseball. But it didn't have to be the Dodgers. It could have been a team from a town that was in trouble, or an expansion

team. I don't blame O'Malley. A man goes where the mc
is. I do blame baseball. I don't believe baseball has been to
same since the Dodgers left Brooklyn.

The Dodger-Giant rivalry has to have been the best that
sports ever had. No city ever had two teams in the same
league for so long. When I got to New York, I couldn't believe the feeling when those two teams met. They played
twenty-two games a year and every game was a war. The
Giants were low in the league that year, but their games with
the Dodgers were real battles. The whole town got up for the
games and the players felt it, too.

Both had funny ball parks. The Polo Grounds, across the
Harlem River from the Bronx, was horseshoe-shaped. If you
pulled the ball to left or right you had a short home run. It
had double-deck stands and a lot of fly balls bounced off the
facade of the top tier for home runs. But if you hit to left-
center or right-center, or, God forgive you, straightaway center, you could run out and retrieve the ball and hit it again and
still not hit it out. It was 260 feet to right and 280 to left but
about 480 to center.

You could get lost out there. But Willie Mays knew the
way. It was a park meant for a great centerfielder and Mays
was great. He could run a quarter of a mile to make one of
his basket catches out there.

The clubhouses were side by side in dead center. They were
raised and you had to walk up stairs by the bleachers to get
to yours. If you were the enemy, the fans would lean over
the rail and razz you and cuss you and spit at you and drop
things on you every step of the way.

You could also look out the clubhouse window with bin-
oculars and see the opposing catcher's crotch as he gave signals to the pitcher. You'd figure out his finger signs and you'd
give the signals to your batter. Maybe wave a white towel for
a fast ball or something like that, maybe more subtle.

I didn't like the ball park, but I miss it because it was
special and different, sort of the way Fenway Park in Boston
and Wrigley Field in Chicago are today. I didn't like it because it didn't forgive you if you made a mistake and a lot of
games were won and lost on flukes.

Ებbets Field was special too, different from the others but
ot as crazy as the Polo Grounds. However, it was crooked.
The most striking part of the place was the short right-field
foul line, less than 250 feet, topped by a towering wire screen.
A lot of home runs were lifted over that fence, and when the
balls bounced on Bedford Avenue boys who waited there
would scramble for them. It was a lot like left field in Fenway.

It was less than 350 feet to left and less than 400 feet to
dead center. It was a compact park, a hitter's heaven, and in
those days the Dodgers had the heavy hitters, like Gil Hodges,
Duke Snider, and Roy Campanella, to take advantage of it.

My first Dodgers' team, the last Brooklyn club, had Hodges
on first, Jim Gilliam on second, Charlie Neal at short, Pee
Wee Reese on third, Gino Cimoli in left, Snider in center,
Carl Furillo in right, Roy Campanella catching, Don Zimmer,
Sandy Amoros, Elmer Valo, and Rube Walker on the bench,
and Don Newcombe, Don Drysdale, Johnny Podres, Sandy
Koufax, Roger Craig, Danny McDevitt, Sal Maglie, Clem
Labine, and Ed Roebuck pitching.

Hodges was a heavy hitter, but he had weaknesses, which
is why he had slumps. He didn't like the ball on the outside
part of the plate and wouldn't swing at anything he didn't
like until he had two strikes on him, so you could pitch to
him.

Snider hit with power too, but he didn't like left-handers
and used to be taken out at times when a good one was going.
Campy was powerful, but he was having a bad year. Furillo
hit line drives.

Hodges had hands on him you wouldn't believe, and he
was a magician at making pickups of balls thrown in the dirt
to him with a sort of circular move of his glove. He used to
have his teammates throw in the dirt deliberately during infield warmups so he could show off.

Neal had a lot of hot dog in him. He was better at second
than at short. He was as mean as any player I've known and
wasn't afraid to fight. He used to throw low to first so the
runner would have to duck or hit the dirt, because Charlie
would as soon hit them between the eyes with the ball as not.

Charlie had jets on his legs and covered so much ground

that when we later had Jim Lefebvre at second, barely covering the bag, I suggested to Walter Alston that we bring back
Neal from some semipro circuit in Kansas, even though he
was thirty-five or thirty-six. He could have gotten off his death
bed and got to more balls than Lefebvre. The skipper passed,
but it wasn't a bad idea.

When I got to the team, Neal was just about to take over
second from Gilliam. The sportswriters called Gilliam "Junior," but we called him "The Devil." Like Neal, he could be
mean. And he could do a lot of things with a bat and glove
to beat you. But he was slow-footed and slow-armed and had
to cheat like hell to get by in the infield. For instance, I don't
think he ever in his life touched second base as he went by
the bag in the middle of a double play.

But then, I seldom did when I was speeding past while
running the bases. There's a lot of things you're supposed to
do that you don't do in big-league baseball, I learned, because
you can get away with them. And you get away with whatever
you can. Winning is the aim—winning games, not sportsmanship trophies for fair play.

Gilliam wound up playing third after Reese retired. Reese
had shifted from shortstop to get in one more season. He
could still make magic with a bat and glove, but he had
slowed down and that was his last season.

Snider wasn't Willie Mays, but he covered centerfield well
and threw well. He was smooth in the field as well as at bat.
Furillo was slow, but he caught everything hit at him and
threw as well as any outfielder I ever saw. He had a rifle for
an arm and fired bullets home. Cimoli was a good, but not
great, all-around fielder and hitter, but he was one of those
good-looking Italian kids who got on great with the gals and
didn't take good care of himself.

Campy had slowed down but was still a strong receiver
and smart with pitchers. And we had some top pitchers,
though some were too old and some were too young.

We didn't have a 20-game winner that year. Newcombe had
won twenty-seven the year before and I was scared to death
of handling him. He didn't have very good stuff and was
struggling, though he was still throwing hard. He was on his

way out, though I didn't know that then. Maglie was washed up, but the ex-Giant was still tough to score on. The Barber could still put the ball where he wanted it and liked to give the batters close shaves to keep them loose. Erskine could dot an *i* with the ball and he had a good curve ball, but he wasn't throwing hard.

Drysdale led us in wins that year. He threw hard and he threw sidearmed and he was mean enough to knock people down, but the big guy was just a kid at that time and wasn't a smart pitcher or sure of himself. Koufax threw harder than anyone, but he wasn't mean enough to knock anyone down and he didn't know where the hell the ball was going when he threw it, and he didn't win many.

We spotted a lot of starters and used a lot of relievers. Podres led the league in low earned-run average that season but he was strictly a seven-inning pitcher. John had good stuff and he was smart, but he was never in good shape and was always shaky. When a manager goes out in the seventh or eighth inning to ask a pitcher if he can finish, the pitcher usually begs to stay in, but John always said, "Good to see you. It's about time. Get me the hell out of here before they get to me."

Craig started a lot of games and he had incredible control, but he hadn't mastered his pitches yet. McDevitt started some and he had great stuff, but he was a wild kid and inconsistent.

Labine was our star reliever. He was near the end of the line, but he could get a lot on the ball low and he could come in and get some guys to hit the ball on the ground and others to strike out. Roebuck relieved effectively. He threw low sidearm, almost underhand. He was a one-pitch pitcher. He couldn't throw hard, but he could throw a sinker low that batters beat into the ground.

It was a good team, but it had been a great team and it wasn't what it had been. Milwaukee now was the best with Warren Spahn and Lew Burdette and Bob Buhl on the mound and Henry Aaron, Red Schoendienst, and Eddie Mathews behind them. We spent most of the season fighting for second place with St. Louis, Cincinnati, and Philadelphia. The Phillies had pitchers—Robin Roberts, Curt Simmons, Jack San-

ford. The Reds had a balanced ball club. The Cards had
sluggers such as Stan Musial and Del Ennis.

The Cards were the first team I faced in the big leagues. I
packed a bag, grabbed a plane, flew to New York, and caught
a cab to Ebbets Field. I remember it had been raining and I
wondered if we'd get the game in. I was surprised to be going
up and scared to go into the clubhouse. I had to talk my way
in because the attendant didn't know who I was. I walked into
the clubhouse and the Dodgers were dressing.

It was unbelievable to me that I was there with those guys.
I knew a few of them from past training camps, but I'd never
worked out with the big club and I didn't know the big guys,
at least not well, personally. There was Newcombe. There was
Campanella. There was Reese. I was awed. An attendant came
up to me and I told him who I was and he showed me where
my locker was. A uniform had been set out for me and I got
into it. I will never forget getting into a Dodgers' uniform for
the first time, those white flannels with the blue script *Dodgers*
on it.

I don't remember anyone greeting me and making me feel
at home. A few looked at me sort of fish-eyed. A few I knew
nodded and said hello but most paid no attention to me at all.
I was as alone as a man can be. Then, the manager, Walt
Alston, who had been there three years, came up and introduced himself and handed me a first baseman's mitt. He told
me I was playing first that night. At that point, I had to go to
the bathroom.

Here I'd been converting from the outfield to catching,
and now I had to play first, which I'd played only a few times
in my life. But the reason they'd called me up in the first place
was because Gil Hodges was out of the lineup for a few days.

While it scared me to have to go right out and play, I
learned later that that was one of Walter's pet tactics—get a
new guy right into a game instead of having him sit around
getting nervous and wondering when he was going to get in.
It's good, too, because it gets you over your jitters right off.

I went out to the field and just stood there for a second,
soaking it in. The park was awesome. Not that it was so big,
but the double-deck stands were so high I felt small and closed

in. The high screen in right looked so close I couldn't believe it. I noticed right away advertising signs on the fences offering prizes for players who hit them. There was a big scoreboard at the base of the right-field fence and a long sign at the base of the scoreboard advertising Abe Stark Clothes and offering a free suit if you hit it. I figured right off for sure I'd win some suits. I never won a one. Don't know anyone who did. The fielder would have had to fall down in front of it for a ball to get to it.

The stands were filling up. The Dodgers were taking batting practice real loose, laughing a lot, and there were a lot of photographers and writers standing around the cage, talking to the players who were waiting. No one talked to me while I waited. I was a starter that night and I remembered from spring training that the regulars got two bunts and five swings in turn. I laid down my bunts and took my swings two or three times in turn. The bat weighed a ton. Then I took infield practice with the regulars. The glove felt funny. I was scared, not of doing bad but of looking bad. I got through it somehow, though, and the game got under way.

There I was in Ebbets Field, playing with Reese and Snider and Furillo and Campanella, against Musial and Del Ennis and Alvin Dark and Ken Boyer. I don't remember if we won or lost, but I remember a couple of things about that game.

I remember I felt I had to get a hit and the best way for me to make sure I'd get it was to bunt, because I could lay the ball down and run. And I did, for my first hit as a big leaguer. I also remember Boyer was on first base, fooling around with a little lead, and the pitcher was throwing to me, trying to pick him off, and I thought to myself if the pitcher made another throw to me I was going to block the base to see if I could trap the dude. The pitcher threw, and I not only blocked Boyer but bumped him a little bit. He got through me and beat the throw back, but I remember he started to complain to the coach at first. The coach said, "The next time this fucking rookie does that, you cut his goddamn leg off." That scared the hell out of me. I thought, "Here I am, my first game in the bigs, and I'm in trouble already." I didn't do anything funny after that.

I wasn't fancy at first, of course. In fact, in my fourth or fifth game a ball was hit between first and second and I went after it instead of letting Gilliam get it and I jarred the hell out of Jim, running right into him. It was the last out of the inning, and as we got back to the dugout Gilliam told Alston, "Get that goddamn rookie off first before he kills somebody out there." Well, Hodges was ready to return, and it was time anyway.

I went to the bullpen then, to catch the relievers. I worked out there under Rube Walker, who was Campy's backup catcher. Once in a while I got to catch or pinch-hit or pinch-run, but I only got into thirty-five games and didn't do much.

There was one other incident I recall from that season when I was breaking into the big leagues. I was catching Drysdale in a game against Milwaukee and Johnny Logan was at bat. I had been at it long enough to be getting into some of the psychology of catching. I knew that most batters knew their weaknesses and knew how most pitchers tried to set them up to hit the pitch they wanted them to hit. The batters try to guess what the pitcher is going to throw them. I knew that when the pitcher shook off the catcher's sign, it tended to make the batter uncertain. So the catchers have a signal asking the pitcher to pretend to shake off a sign. I did that to Drysdale to get Logan to thinking.

Drysdale liked to loosen up the batters by throwing high and inside to them, and that set them up for his "out" pitch, which was low and outside. He got two strikes on Logan, who was then looking low and outside. And I gave Drysdale the sign for it, but also the sign to shake me off. I shifted to the inside, stuck up my glove as if for a target high, gave it a good whack right by the batter's ear, and hollered "Gimme the good curve." When Drysdale let the ball go, Logan let go and backed out of the batter's box. At that moment the ball clipped the corner low and outside for strike three. Logan was as embarrassed as he could be.

Now, Johnny Logan was a hard-ass sonofagun. I didn't know him then the way I knew him later, but he could go off the field as hard as he could on it. He was not a great player but he was a peppery one and he didn't take crap from anyone. He hollered, "What are you, one of these wise-ass rookies?" And then he made a move on me. I stood right up to him and replied, "That's just what I am."

I was scared, but I wasn't going to let on. My dad had taught me you had to stand up to people and show 'em you weren't afraid. A lot of the time they'd back off, but if you backed off they'd think you were afraid and they'd be all over you from then on. I wasn't afraid to fight, but I was a rookie and I didn't want to get in trouble, and I figured if I started getting into fights right off I'd have to fight the rest of my career.

I yanked my mask off and stood face to face, nose to nose, with him. "Wise fucking rookie," he said. I didn't say anything, just glared right back at him. Then the umpire got between us and Logan just walked off and I put my mask back on and went back behind the plate, real relieved.

I never had words with Logan again. He never made a move on me again. I guess I'd made my point. It was a bluff, but I got by with it. I guess Alston and the Dodgers were impressed. At least they knew then that I had the guts to antagonize opponents and not back down when they confronted me.

Still, it was the bullpen for me most of that season, sitting around most games, watching, listening to Rube Walker talk about the pitchers and the hitters and about catching and about Jackie Robinson. It's funny, but he talked to me as much about Robinson as anything else.

Traded to the Giants the previous winter, Robinson had refused to report and had retired. I'm sorry I never got to know him and play with him, but I feel like I did because he remained so much a part of that team even after he had left. He'd had such an impact that they couldn't stop talking about him. I heard at least a hundred stories about him.

It was not just that he had broken the color barrier, but the way he'd broken it—taking all kinds of crap that apparently was thrown at him without making any bad scenes, but also without bowing his head. They said he set up fights beyond the ball park. And they talked about the way he played—all out all the time, a good glove man, a line-drive hitter, a clutch hitter, a terror on the bases, a guy who set records stealing home, an incredibly intense competitor.

He was regarded as a god by his former teammates and it seemed strange to me to sit in the bullpen with a white Southerner from North Carolina speaking so respectfully of him. They all liked Campy, who was a good-natured guy and a great player, but he was not a leader like Robinson. There was an incident where some blacks were refused service and Campy just took it and left and everyone was saying Robinson wouldn't have taken it.

Even though I missed playing with him by one lousy year, I feel like I did. He remains one of the most memorable personalities from my first team of Dodgers.

Reese was another. Apparently, when Robinson reported to the Dodgers and Dixie Walker and some other rednecks were bitching about it, Reese befriended Robinson. I can believe it, because there was something special about Pee Wee and it didn't take you long to see it. He was captain of the club when I got there and such a great gentleman and natural leader that while I played only that half season with him, I will always think of him as the captain.

Maury Wills became captain later, and he had become my buddy and roommate by then. I think they made him captain just to keep him happy. He knows the game and might make a marvelous manager, but he was a bit of a hot dog. He wasn't graceful about getting on guys who didn't put out. Wills made enemies as well as friends, he loved the ladies and bright lights, and he was not cut out to be a captain.

Reese did everything right, and he was so nice that everyone liked him and respected him. I never felt I was black and he was white. I felt like he was my captain.

But I think the most memorable of the fellows on my first Dodgers' team was Campy. If Walker taught me a lot on the field, Campy taught me a lot off the field. He was a fun-loving guy, happy-go-lucky, always snapping his fingers and doing a dance to whatever music was on. But he had his serious side. He could take the responsibility of turning a rookie into a major leaguer. He befriended me and became like a father to me. He became my roommate and guided me through the big cities—Philadelphia, Pittsburgh, St. Louis, Cincinnati, Chicago, and Milwaukee—as I traveled the big-time tour for the first time. He believed in traveling first-class and he took me with him.

He taught me how to handle fans politely, even when they became a bother. He taught me how to respond to the press properly, telling them the truth short of making a teammate look bad. He took me to the best restaurants and taught me how to order and about different foods. He taught me how to dress and took me to the finest stores and helped me shop for the right clothes. He used to tell me and the other young players on our team, "Kid, you're a big leaguer now and you better begin to dress and act like one."

He made me feel like a big leaguer, like I belonged on the Brooklyn Dodgers. Campy had a boat. Hell, it was a yacht. It must have been forty feet long. It had a living room in the middle and a front bedroom and a back bedroom and bedrooms all over the place. He had a home in Glen Cove, right on the ocean, and he'd take us sailing on his yacht. Sometimes when we had a game in the Polo Grounds on a Sunday he'd sail it right up the Harlem River, dock it, and we'd take cabs to the ball park, then return to sail home at twilight. We'd bring our wives and he and his wife always made us feel welcome.

Sometimes he'd bring a five-gallon barrel of iced crab fingers with him to the ball park. He had this special spicy sauce he made up himself, and after the game we'd dig into that barrel and dip those crab fingers in his sauce and suck it up with beer or soft drinks. We'd sit around licking our fingers, having fun. Lord, how he loved those crab fingers! Lord, how he loved to have fun! He was always taking us sailing or throwing a feast or having fun with us. He was a great guy, and he had earned the good life. He was enjoying it and was letting us enjoy it with him.

But he had a bad season that year, the second one he'd had. He'd had a couple of operations on his left hand and he couldn't grip the bat too well. He seemed to have lost the strength in his left hand, but he'd been a great ballplayer for ten years, he was thirty-six, and the talk was that he was through as a regular and would become a player-coach the next season. There was talk that I was the Dodgers' catcher of the future, but I didn't think about that. I'd been up half a season, served as a bullpen catcher, and had an experienced receiver ahead of me. I figured my future was still well ahead of me.

Before the season ended, with the Dodgers finishing third, we got the word that we were on our way to Los Angeles. I hoped to go with the team, but I hated to leave Brooklyn. I remember McDevitt shut out the Pirates, 2–0, in the last game at Ebbets Field, and the organist, Gladys Goodding, played "Auld Lang Syne." There were less than seven thousand fans in the stands that sad day, and many of them cried, before they tore the place apart in search of souvenirs. Some of the players cried too. And then we left for the last time. After we were gone, they replaced the park with an apartment house. I've never gone back.

I was at home in Ohio early the following year, in January, just before we were to go to Vero Beach to begin spring training, when my mother told me that she'd heard Campy had crashed his car and was in bad shape back in New York. It shook me and choked me up. I tried to get through to him, but, of course, I couldn't. I felt terrible; and spent difficult days trying to find out how he was. He wasn't very good, of course. He was paralyzed from the neck down and would be for the rest of his days, though it took a while for that to sink in. I never thought about it being a break for me. I wish to hell it hadn't happened, but it had.

12.

STARTING in 1953, I went to spring training at Vero Beach with the Dodgers for fifteen years. It has changed a lot now. Walter O'Malley has made it a sort of a resort for year-round use, with fancy apartments and a golf course. But it changed only a little all the seasons I was there.

It was a converted service base with barracks, set out in the middle of nowhere. There was little to do except play ball, which was the idea. It still is one of the few spring-training facilities owned by the club that trains there, which is the only reason I can think of that a California club would still train there.

For the black players while I was there it was still Florida, Dixie, the deep South, a bad place to be. The Dodgers broke the color barrier and have always had as many blacks as any team, so I can't condemn the club, but they did not always protect their black players the way they should have. The fact that Florida was a bad place for blacks did not stop them from staying there. Beyond the base there was bigotry, even if there was none on the base.

I remember my first trip. In Washington, another black ball-player got on the train bound for Vero and we buddied up. He was Maury Wills, just another hopeful at the time. He'd been there before and as we passed through Gifford, just before getting to Vero, he said it was the colored town where the niggers went out on the town after the day's work was done. We went right down the main street. There was a movie house, a drugstore, a barber shop, and a pool hall. That was downtown Gifford, a poor place.

Just past Gifford, on a curve, there was a house that looked like it would be blown down by the first strong wind. All those years I went to Vero, every time we got out of Gifford and hit that curve I'd look to see if that house had gone down, but it was always still standing there. I don't know if anyone lived in it. I know no one ever did anything to it. It was just there.

When we got to Vero Beach, the white town, it wasn't much better. It was a tiny, tourist-type town. But when you go to the beach across the causeway, a road that runs like a bridge over the water, you go past golf courses and get into an area where there are some nice hotels and motels, nice restaurants and shops. Blacks weren't welcome there.

When we got off the train we had to call the Dodgers' complex for a ride to the camp, which was about a mile out of town, because we weren't allowed in the white taxicabs. The camp was nice-looking, surrounded by orange groves, and you could pick all the oranges you wanted. They always had oranges and freshly squeezed orange juice available at the base. They had a swimming pool and tennis courts, a recreation room with Ping-Pong and pool tables, a lounge with a television set, and a telephone area.

The ballplayers lived in barracks, had eight fields to play on and a cafeteria to eat in, and there was a medical facility where you could get treatment. A path cut through the complex, dividing it into major-league and minor-league areas. You were segregated by ability, not color. The major-league area contained not only the major leaguers but the triple-A players who might make it to the majors that year. The minor-league area contained the others who might make it some year.

The minor leaguers dreamed of the day they might cross that path to the other side. The odds were against them. Fifteen to twenty-five years ago, major-league clubs supported a lot of minor-league teams and had two or three hundred players under contact. Today, teams own less than a hundred. A young player was surrounded by so many other players that the competition was cutthroat just to get noticed.

It took me five or six years to make the majors. It took

Maury eight years. In those days, that wasn't unusual. Today, kids come up in a day. If they don't make it in a year or two, they're ready to give up. And maybe they should. There are so many more teams and open positions and so few players that if a guy doesn't get to the top fast there's something missing. A great player would be great in any era. A good player would be good. But you don't have to be as good to make it to the majors today as you did yesterday.

The minor leaguers slept in army bunks, eight to a room. There were two central restrooms, where you also took showers and shaved. You didn't have to take showers, and they were usually so crowded that you sometimes didn't. Every room had face bowls and you used those. You were supposed to wash your own uniforms, but you didn't always. You hung them in the windows, sweaty or wet, to dry. It was always hot in Florida in the spring, hot and humid. Our rooms weren't air-conditioned, and they got gamey after a while. We spent as little time in them as possible.

I moved over to the other side in 1956. I felt like I'd made the big time. On the major-league side you had two rooms with a bathroom in between, and only two players to a room. After a while, Wills and I shared a room every year. When you move up to the majors and start making more money, you can afford to get your uniforms washed. We still didn't have air-conditioning, but we could take as many showers as we wanted in comfort. You didn't mind sitting around those rooms, relaxing and shooting the bull.

It was like being in the army. A guy came around and blew a whistle at seven every morning. You'd wash, have breakfast in the cafeteria, and then you'd go to your dressing room and put on your uniform and work out until noon. A lot of calisthenics and drilling on fundamentals. After lunch, more of the same, until we got into games. Then we'd either have a game at home or travel to one by bus at another team's camp. The big leaguers might go to Miami, say, and stay awhile. Usually, by late afternoon you were free. Curfew came at eleven every night, when that dude with the whistle came around to put us to bed.

There wasn't a lot to do in our free time. Some of the guys

brought radios or record players and we'd listen to a lot of music in our rooms. Later on they started to bring tape-players. No one ever brought television sets for fear they'd be stolen, so the only television we saw was on the set in the lounge or one at a saloon or someone's house in town. We didn't leave valuables in our rooms, so there wasn't much thieving. You had to pay a dollar for your room key and if you lost it you had to pay another damn dollar for another key. We used to leave the key above the door and dare any thieves to take whatever they wanted.

We'd go to the lounge and watch TV or read. There was a gift shop where you could buy paperbacks, magazines, and newspapers, as well as toilet articles and cigarettes. We played a lot of checkers and chess, and I got to be pretty good. I think I miss checkers and chess in spring training more than anything else.

We played a lot of table tennis, too, but the winner of a game always took on the next guy in turn, so you had to be pretty good to get in many games and I was never very good. I was better at pool, but Walt Alston and Jim Gilliam were the best. Alston had a hand for it and could do it all, but The Devil was sneaky-good, playing perfect position and just tapping the ball so it barely fell in. They had a kid catcher in those camps who made money hustling at the tables, but the skipper and The Devil did him in.

Over the years I made a lot of money I needed playing cards, but I never tried to con or hustle anyone, and they discouraged cardplaying for money at camp. I never got into tennis. Few did in those days. It was too much sweaty work on those hot afternoons. I got into golf a little with Ron Fairly, who was one of the great natural all-around athletes I ever saw. Ron was a great natural golfer, and he tried to teach me, but I didn't have the patience to pursue it.

We used to go to a driving range because blacks weren't welcome on the country-club courses. It was something for the whites to do the blacks couldn't do and eventually Jim Murray of the *Los Angeles Times* wrote an article about this and other injustices. People started to talk, and pressure built until O'Malley had a nine-hole course constructed for all the players, which is now a full-scale eighteen-hole course.

O'Malley and other officials tried to treat us well, but there was a lot of unfairness they never got into. The white guys could make deals to get a boat for free and spend an afternoon fishing out on the ocean, but we never got to do that. The white guys could go to a first-class theater in Vero to see first-run movies, but the blacks had to go to a dump in Gifford to see some of the first movies ever made, like Buck Jones westerns and Buck Rogers serials. We could go to a white theater in Fort Pierce, but if we did we had to go around back, climb up a fire escape to a door leading to the balcony, and sit there where it was hot and where we couldn't get to the snack stand. It was humiliating. The Dodgers tried to make up for it by showing good movies on the base.

It was years before the blacks got the right to sit anywhere they wanted in the white theater in Vero. The first time I did, some cracker behind me was crabbing, "There sure are a lot of niggers in here tonight." You had to take it or risk getting lynched or at least having your head knocked off. The whites had the numbers and they were always picking fights when blacks dared enter Vero. We always felt like we were walking on eggshells when we had to be in that town.

Blacks weren't welcome in most of the stores and restaurants in Florida. I remember one time Lou Johnson came storming into the dressing room all steamed up because he'd put some laundry in a machine in a laundromat in Vero and been told to take it out because blacks weren't supposed to clean their clothes where whites did. Lou was very volatile, and I guess he cussed out the lady who laid that on him. He raised the roof and the Dodgers later received complaints about the incident. To their credit, they ignored them; to their discredit, they didn't do anything about it.

Once when we were returning from a road game and stopped to eat as a team in some town along the way, the people in the restaurant agreed to serve us, but we had to sit behind a screen at the rear while the rest ate in the main room. We were hungry, so we stayed and ate, but some of the older guys observed that if Robinson had been with us he'd never have let the team take that kind of stuff. Campy was with us at that time, but he just took it along with the rest of us. He was sort of our leader, but he was not a man of action where race was concerned and would not fight for our rights. As good a guy as he was, he was not a real leader.

I got a haircut in town one time and the barber cut me up a bit when he was trimming my sideburns. I didn't think much of it, but the cut got infected and the side of my face swelled up and became painful. The doctor at Dodgertown felt I needed care I couldn't get there, so he sent me to a doctor in nearby Melbourne. This doctor treated me, but in a little room in the back, out of sight of the rest of his patients. I got better, but all the blacks cut each other's hair after that.

Years later, I applied for an insurance policy and had to have a physical exam by a doctor in Vero. He seemed annoyed to see me, and he took me to another room out of the way. When he asked me how much insurance I'd applied for and I told him $200,000, I could see he didn't believe any nigger was going to come up with the cash for that kind of policy. It made him mad. He treated me as if I was trash. I'm lucky he passed me.

I hate to think of the kind of medical care blacks got in the South over the years, and maybe still get if they have to use white doctors. I've heard a lot of stories about those who went blind or died because they couldn't get good care.

The Dodgers had a bus that took the players to town, dropping the whites off in Vero and the blacks in Gifford. It was a bad bus with a bad bus driver and one day he stalled it on the railroad tracks just outside Gifford. I remember Lacey Curry saying, "Hey, bussie, first thing you're supposed to learn in spring training is not to stall your bus on the train tracks." We got off before the train got there, but every time we went across those tracks we crossed ourselves. I don't remember, but I hope to hell it wasn't Steve Garrvey's old man, who I guess did drive the Dodger bus a long time.

Eventually the Dodgers started to provide cars for the players to take to town. They had to divide the cars among the whites and blacks because we went in different directions, so it was segregation, but it couldn't be helped. A Newcombe or Gilliam might drive a car to camp and keep it to use, but there weren't many private cars around. One year Wills rented a car for us by phone, but when he showed up to get it, they took one look at him and decided they were all out of cars.

Springtime was basketball-tournament time in Gifford, and Tommy Davis and Willie Davis and I used to go in to catch games played by the black high schools in the area. It was also a good place to pick up teachers. Most of the single women in Gifford were teachers or servants for the whites. The domestics and waitresses wore white uniforms a lot. We used to say the woman might be black but she always wore white. Not all the women were single, of course. Some had husbands who were having a hard time making it, and the women were living a poor life and were attracted to the big-league ballplayers who came to town throwing dough around. The husbands envied and hated the ballplayers because of this. We weren't much more welcome in their town than in the white man's town.

When I could get a car to myself, I liked to go driving out to the beach or, better yet, to the marshy areas inland where I could be by myself and walk and hunt snakes and spiders for fun. I used to carry an old army machete on my hunts. One afternoon when I was in the back country in one of the team cars, I noticed I was being followed. I got trapped at the end of an inlet and got out of the car with my machete in hand.

It turned out to be a black dude who wanted to check me out because a cat in the same kind of car had been carrying on with his girl friend. I knew of the girl, the foxiest female in that town, but I'd never met her. He didn't know these were company cars, which all looked alike. Once he realized who I was, he calmed down. I told him he was lucky I didn't take his head off with my machete because I was nervous as hell down there anyway. He just laughed. I think he was armed, and I think the really lucky cat was the Dodger who was making out with that chick until I warned him off.

The white players got into most of the trouble in that town because they had most of the opportunities. They could go wherever they wanted. They could go into the saloons and drink. Guys like Podres and Drysdale could really lap it up. And there were always some guys getting screwed up with women, especially young players. I think one of the things the Dodgers have always liked about Vero is that it's so far from bright lights, but there are always guys who are going to get there, no matter what, and always guys who are going to get screwed up.

The wives seldom went with the players in those days and some of the older guys didn't like to go to bed alone. They had to in the barracks, but they didn't have to be in the barracks. Not 'til curfew, which most of them missed a time or two. Even a straight guy like Koufax.

Sandy and Larry Sherry went out early one night and came back late. They may have gone to Miami. When they got back, they had to get by Alston's room to get to theirs. They tip-toed, but he heard them. Alston was a light sleeper. Alston came out as they ran down the dark hallway to their room. He followed them and knocked on their door, but they didn't answer. He started to pound on that door, hollering, and then all the doors were flying open up and down the hall. He pounded that door so hard he cracked his World Series ring. He fined them.

Lacey Curry, a black guy, now a minister in Chicago, was caught coming in after curfew by Fresco Thompson. He took off, ran back outside the barracks, with Thompson in pursuit, and almost cut his head off on a wire support for a palm tree.

Roseboro didn't run much. I made friends with some schoolteachers who had me to their houses for home-cooked meals. We'd watch TV or play checkers or whist or talk, but I didn't try to make out with many.

I think the schoolteachers were clean ladies, but there were chicks in that town that weren't. One of our players got dis-eased by some dame there. He contracted syphilis and didn't admit it to anyone until he was so screwed up the doctors couldn't do much for him. He gave it to his pregnant wife and they lost their baby. She left him. I ran into her at a club in Oakland some years later and asked how he was. She said he had died on the operating table when his heart stopped, but they had brought him back. She said it was a lousy life be-cause he was sort of crippled. She said she wanted to go back to him to help him. I don't know if she did.

I do know at least three ballplayers who were broken by broads with syphilis, and I know it is one of the things that always scared me off strange women.

One year shortly after the birth of one of our children, I brought my wife to Florida on a vacation. We always spent time in Miami. I had gotten to know the town and some people there and I wanted to show her a good time. The blacks usually stayed at the Sir John Hotel in the colored community, but that year they opened the McAllister Hotel to us and we stayed there. We had a good time, then drove back to Vero. It was late and we decided to stop at a motel. There were no more than four or five cars in the lot, but when we went to register, the desk clerk told us they were full. Same thing across the street. I saw then that Vero hadn't changed at all, though it was supposed to have. Because we were black, we couldn't get a bed for the night. I could bitch about it, but I'd be told "watch your mouth, boy." We had to drive back toward Miami before we found a Holiday Inn that would give us a room. And when we returned to Vero the next day I had to get the clubhouse boy to find a friend who would put Jeri up for a few nights. The humiliation is still with me. I think of it when people give me all that crap about how times have changed.

Even when you stayed at the Sir John you had problems. You changed into your uniform in your room, went to the Miami ball park, played the game, and went back to your room to change back into your civvies. You didn't use the dressing room with the whites. You did have room service at the hotel, because you couldn't use the dining room. When we got into the McAllister it was like getting out of the ghetto. You still had to watch your step.

We had a black catcher, Nate Smith, who was trying to make the team. He was married to a blue-eyed black girl who looked white. She joined him at the McAllister one spring. In the morning when Jim Gilliam and I got to the dining room, there they were, sitting at a table. Gilliam saw them, swung around, and got right out of there. I got after him to ask him his problem.

"Stupid sonofabitch has brought a white girl in here," he said.

I said, "She might look white, but she's black."

He said, "She might be black, but she looks white."

I said, "Whatever she is, she's his wife."

He said, "That's his problem." And he took off.

No one wanted to be with them because the black-white look was downright dangerous and made most black men nervous to be around them in that town.

I felt sorry for them and wanted to show them a good time. I had made a friend who played drums with the house band at the Sir John. I called to ask him for a table for the show that night and he said he'd reserve one right up front for us like he always did for the ballplayers. But when we got there the man outside demanded identification showing that she was Nate's wife and that she was black. Then the man inside took one look at them and led us to a corner table so far from the entertainment that we were out of it. And we hadn't been there more than a few minutes when a couple of white detectives turned up and made us show the identification again and stand up to be searched.

When things like this happen to you because you're black, you get so mad you want to kill. But what can you do? You can leave, which we did. Nate and his wife went through scenes like this all the time. I guess it became too much hassle for them to handle. I talked to him on the telephone not too long ago and he told me he and his wife had divorced. Now he's married to a black woman who looks black. She teaches school in Atlanta.

After a while I got to where I could get around pretty good and avoid hassles. Preston Gomez, a Cuban, has been a Dodgers' coach a long time and managed a couple of teams in between. He knew a lot of people in Miami and was nice to everyone. Through him I got to meet Muhammad Ali, who used to spend a lot of time in Miami, training and sometimes fighting.

Maury Wills and I used to watch him work out and went to a couple of his fights. Maury, an incorrigible panty-bandit, even tried to make out with Muhammad's girl friend when she wound up alongside him at ringside one night. The big guy kept sending down with withering looks at Wills, but Wills figured Ali wouldn't leave the fight just to fight him.

When I first went to see Ali they were having trouble getting sparring partners for him. They are offering good money to guys who would go even a round with him. I'm big, I'm handy with my dukes, and I figured I could stay out of trouble and could take a few hits for one round. I was ready to volunteer until I really took a look at him in action. He looked like the biggest 6′ 3″, 220-pound dude I ever saw, the fastest, and the meanest, and I forgot about a fistic career.

Half-fighter, half-huckster, I found him a fascinating fellow and thought him one of the greatest athletes I've seen. Unlike Wills, I'd be afraid to mess with one of his women.

I wasn't afraid to fly. I realized my dream of learning to fly in Florida. One spring Koufax and McDevitt were sneaking off to an airfield alongside a Piper Aircraft factory and taking lessons early in the morning. I took it up, too.

I was doing well, and one morning I brought Wills with me. That day I was given a new plane, which tended to sway. Wills sat behind me and the instructor. When I took off I didn't compensate enough for the sway and we started to drift off at an angle. Wills started to holler. The instructor straightened it out for me, and I flew it fine the rest of the way and made a good landing, but Wills wouldn't fly with me after that.

Another time, the instructor was showing me what would happen if I pointed too steep in a climb. We stalled and went into a tailspin. The world was spinning and I didn't know where I was or what to do. He showed me how to come out of it, then made me do it myself. I was scared half to death, but I stalled it, spun it, and straightened it out.

I loved flying like I thought I would, especially at night, near the stars, with the lights of the cities beneath me. On the last day of spring training, I soloed. I thought I'd be nervous but I wasn't. The man turned it over to me and watched me take off. I banked out over the ocean, brought it back, and landed.

I have my certificate framed, along with a photo of me receiving it, but I've only flown a few times since. When the Dodgers found out about it, they ruled it out. Then Kenny Hubbs of the Cubs was killed in a crash of his small plane, and that scared me off for a while. But I still like to fly.

That was my best spring. After a while spring training becomes a bore. I think the pitchers need it because their arms stiffen and tighten up over the winter and it takes them time to loosen up, but most of us need no more than a week or two instead of the seven or eight we spend at that drudgery, playing games that mean nothing but risk. For a catcher, spring training is dangerous. He catches during batting practice and pitching practice, and the risk of his fingers getting smashed up or split is three times greater than in the regular season. I got injured one year, missed spring practice, and had one of my best seasons. Spring training is overrated.

The one spring that meant a lot to me was in 1958, after it was clear that Campy couldn't come back and the catching job was wide open. I thought at best I'd be the backup to Rube Walker. I was competing with Joe Pignatano for the second-string duty. And Walker did open our first season in Los Angeles. But Alston and the brass simply didn't want to break in a rookie under that sort of pressure. They did want to give a young guy a chance, one who might take over for a long time to come. I'd had a good spring, I got into games early, I did well, and I did take over for a long time.

But I could have done that without the hassle of dear old Dixie.

13.

THERE were a lot of guys who had just about lost their legs, or their arms, when we moved from Brooklyn to Los Angeles in 1958. Sal Maglie, the Barber, didn't even make the move. Campy, of course, couldn't. The Captain, Pee Wee Reese, went with us, but he played little and left after that season. Newk's arm was used up. So was Erskine's. Newk was sent to Cincinnati early in the season. Erskine hung on a couple of seasons but didn't do much. Labine had a few seasons left. Hodges had three, Furillo three, Snider four.

Although I wasn't with them too long, some of those guys who were with us a little while in LA left a deep impression. Newk made maybe the deepest. He was a giant in both reputation and size and I was in awe of him. He came on strong and seemed a mean man.

Newk called blacks "niggers" and whites "blue-eyed bitches." I don't know why. Most of the time he called most people some nasty name. He was a loud dude.

I was scared of catching for him because if I made a mistake I thought he'd have my ass. But in my first year Campy told me, "Son, Newk is the easiest guy in the world to work with. You just get behind the plate and put down whatever you want him to throw and he'll bring it to you." He did that. All he had was his hard one. He only had a little curve. And his heat was cooling off by the time I got to him. He was the easiest pitcher I ever worked with.

Newk's bark was worse than his bite. He was *bodacious.*

That's a word we used in baseball to mean a man who comes on loud and strong. *Hellacious* means much the same thing, except maybe a man who's more outrageous in his acts. I learned these words when I got to the big leagues.

There was a whole lingo I had to learn. If I was seen with a mullion, that meant I was with a chick whose looks were the other side of bad. When Lou Johnson ordered coffee for us once, he asked me if I wanted mine Booker T. or George. I had to ask to find out he meant which Washington, black or white? Without cream or with?

Everyone had nicknames. You never used players' real names. I was afraid to open my mouth and betray my ignorance the first few years I was in the majors, so Ed Roebuck hung the nickname Gabby on me. It stuck with me the rest of my career. I used to say I'd rather listen and learn than shoot off my mouth. He used to say I had the smallest ears he'd ever seen so he didn't know how I could hear anything. Because Norm Larker had big ears, he became Dumbo, the cartoon elephant. Newcombe was Tiger. He could tear a town apart.

Newk used to carry his record player on the road with him. He called it his "sin box." We roomed together on the road the first part of the '68 season. Whatever town we were in, he stayed by himself or with friends without bothering me. Many players took extra rooms to be with ladies. They'd show off in front of their roomie or make him sit in the lobby and wait. When Wills was my roomie and started to turn up with women, I told him to take an extra room. I wasn't about to wait in the lobby wondering if he'd finished his performance.

One night Newk left for his spare room and told me that if anyone on the team ran a room check to tell them he'd ducked down to the coffee shop to get a bite. I went to sleep and woke up about one, with Bavasi on the telephone checking us out. He asked me to put Tiger on. I told him Tiger was in the coffee shop. He said "Okay."

I called Newk to tell him, but Newk wasn't ready to return. When Buzzie buzzed back, I said Newk was still in the coffee shop. Buzzie said to tell him not to spend so much money because he was fined three hundred dollars for missing curfew.

I was scared Newk would figure I'd messed him up, but when he returned and I told him the bad news, he shrugged it off.

Newk later met and married a good woman who helped him beat the booze. The little I was with him I did not see him drink at that time, but he later talked openly about boozing so much that he became an alcoholic. He didn't say it at the time, but says at times he took the mound drunk. He claims now it shortened his career, but with the help of Alcoholics Anonymous and the woman he married, he overcame it. He made a second career outside baseball. He works part time in public relations for the Dodgers, and lectures on the evils of drink. Later on, when I needed help, he befriended me.

Hodges was another impressive person. He was very strong and straight. He was a family man and never ran. As a player he was hot and cold, but he never bitched about it and never put his problems on anyone else. He seldom said much, but he didn't have to.

One time Norm Larker, a real red-ass, got so mad after striking out that he threw his helmet and it hit Hodges. Larker was always throwing his bat or his helmet, but he had never hit Hodges. Gil looked up at him, real level like, and said simply, "That's the last time." That's all he had to say. Norm got the message. He never threw anything anywhere near Gil again. Hodges commanded respect.

On the record Gil became a marvelous manager, which is what I would have expected, but I heard he had one weakness. It was hard for him to communicate well with players. I might have expected that, because he never had much to say. But he was one of those soft-spoken fellows you listen to when they do speak. I imagine that's the way it was when he was managing. Maybe a guy who wasn't playing well and wasn't getting to play might bitch about not getting through to Hodges, but I'm sure Hodges had little patience with players who bitched all the time and blamed their problems on their manager. Hodges was one of the nicest guys you'd ever want to know, but it's hard to be a nice guy when you're a manager and the players are bitching and the press and the public are putting pressure on you. Anyway, he won a World Series with the Mets before he died of a heart attack.

Alston was another one who didn't have a lot to say, but when he spoke you listened. He was the strong, silent type. He managed by the book, which made you mad sometimes because he wouldn't take a chance when maybe it was meant to be taken, but in time I came to see that it made him a very consistent type of manager. He might have a bad year with a team, but he could bring it back the next year. He was patient and relied on the law of averages. If you played hard he let you play, and if you made a mistake he didn't put a lot of pressure on you. In baseball, you play a long season and if a manager puts a lot of pressure on you it just wears you out. He wasn't a holler guy, but after you've heard a guy holler a lot it doesn't mean much to you and just unsettles the team.

It took a lot to make Alston mad, but when he got mad he showed it. When the team was going bad and bitching on a bus in Pittsburgh, Alston stopped the bus and challenged anyone who wanted a piece of him to step off to the side of the road and try him. He got off, but no one else did. He wasn't a kid by then, and even the biggest, baddest ballplayers wanted no part of him. They shut up. We had two buses that time and I was on the other one, so I didn't see it. I heard about it.

I did see the incident at Vero Beach, where he broke his ring banging on the door to get at Koufax and Sherry. And I saw an incident with Gino Cimoli. Gino was a real puss. In ballplayer lingo that means he was a little too fancy to suit us and inclined to temperament. Alston took him out for a pinch hitter and Cimoli threw his bat and helmet and stormed down the bench and into the clubhouse. He tore off his uniform and threw it on the floor as he went into the shower. Alston followed him right into the shower room and he snapped, "If you want to show some spirit, take me on. If not, don't ever try to show me up again." Gino didn't.

Furillo was a funny guy. I liked him, but I didn't understand him. He was called Skoonj. He hit clotheslines—hard drives, straight as a string. He threw frozen ropes—hard and straight. He was slow, but he hustled. He was nice but strange, and he was as chintzy as any player I've known. He borrowed newspapers rather than spend a dime. He spent only enough on clothes to keep covered. If you finish high, there's bonus money, sometimes World Series shares, to be divided by vote at the end of every season. Furillo had a Polish word he used, *oogots,* which means "nothing." When we'd vote shares for fringe players who hadn't been with us all season, or the clubhouse or dugout people, Furillo always said *oogots.* After every name, *oogots.* "Nothing."

After an argument with management over money, Skoonj left the team and never returned.

Labine was another puss, but he was a top pitcher. Clem was the kind of guy who carried a book with him wherever he went. It helped him look like an intellectual. He used to carry *Mein Kampf* on plane trips and display it to impress stews. It was heavy stuff. You had to figure if he didn't like Hitler, he liked heavy stuff. He kept his place marked and the marker never moved. One day when he wasn't looking, we tore out several pages past his place and he never noticed. We weren't even sure he could read. That's the kind of guy he was. But I got to like him later in life when I got to know him better. He had a son who lost a leg in Viet Nam and Clem handled it well. He had more to him than he had shown us.

Carl Erskine—we called him Oisk—had a lot to him. He had a son who was mentally retarded and he handled it terrifically well, without complaint. Oisk was a smart man, a smart pitcher. He had good stuff, but he made up a lot of it as he went along. He figured out a way of jamming the ball between his thumb and index finger so that when he threw it hard it came out as the best change-up you ever saw. And he was willing to teach anything he had to anyone. When Hal Jeffcoat was converting from the outfield to pitching, Carl worked with him even though Hal played for another team. Oisk had considerable class and had everyone's respect. He would have made a marvelous pitching coach and I don't know why no one got him for that, unless he didn't want it. He stayed in Indiana where he's in business and helps a high-school team.

Snider was a hell of a guy. Newk called Duke a blue-eyed bastard, meaning he looked better than he was, but he was one of the best. Duke came from Compton originally, and when we first got to southern California my wife and I rented a house in Compton from my South American buddy Earl Battey. Duke and I got to know each other fast, talking about his old home town. That was before it became a black ghetto. It was mixed then, more white than black, and all right, not too far from the Coliseum, where we played our first two seasons. Our wives became buddies. The Dooker and Cliff Dapper, a former catcher and player-manager in the minors, had an avocado ranch in Fallbrook. I didn't even know what avocados were before I got to LA. We'd be invited as a team to the ranch for cookouts and we'd have a great time.

The Duke was a Dodger through and through, and it was sad when he returned to New York to play with the Mets the last few years of his career. It was sadder still when he wound up working and broadcasting for any club but the Dodgers. No matter who they played for or worked for later, The Duke and Newk and Gil and Campy and Pee Wee and Oisk will always be remembered as Dodgers. Whatever else they were, the Dodgers always have been known as a class organization with great tradition and faithful fans. When you play for them a long time they leave a mark on you. It's the same way Ruth and Gehrig and DiMag and Mantle and Whitey and Yogi will always be Yankees, but it is not true of many teams in sports.

I hope I always will be thought of as a Dodger, though I was not as important a player as those I have been describing, and those such as Sandy and Don, Podres and Perranoski, and Maury and others, who played prominent parts on my Dodgers' teams. We were always a family, black and white alike. We did not all love one another, but no one loves everyone in his family. We had the family feeling where we would fight for one another far more than we would fight with one another. There always was a spirit of togetherness on the Dodgers. When someone retired who had been with us a long time or was traded, we felt like we were losing a member of the family.

I came to feel like an important part of the Dodgers family. Like Tommy Lasorda says, when I was cut I came to expect Dodgers blue blood. Most of the time, I wore number eight. The kind of guy John Roseboro was, he was a boy who took a long time to grow up, a sucker who had a great time on the field, but never could have a good time off the field, who made a lot of money on the field, but blew it all off the field. It's taking Rosey a long time to learn how to live without baseball. He may not make it. When he got back in the game he thought that was where he belonged. He was a boy playing a game for almost twenty years and those were the best years of his life. Others may see me differently, but that's the way I see me.

My first full year in the major leagues was the Dodgers' first year in Los Angeles. It was exciting in southern California. Some of the fringe benefits the ballplayers expected didn't materialize. I think most of the endorsements and commercials came out of New York at that time anyway. A few guys got bit parts in movies, but that didn't amount to much. I played a Detective Brown on a "Dragnet" TV show. After that, every time Roberto Clemente came to the plate, he'd ask, *"Como esta,* Sergeant Brown? You do any more "Dragnet's?"* I think he was jealous. But it didn't come to much. Actually, we had gotten more gifts from the people in Brooklyn.

We did get to meet some film stars. Some were fans, some became fans. Some knew baseball from the Pacific Coast League, but others started to go to games only when the big leagues came to town, and as a group they were not as knowledgeable as the Brooklyn fans. Milton Berle, Cary Grant, and Doris Day were among the most enthusiastic. Berle and Grant still go, though I doubt Doris does. She was burned by stories that she was having an affair with Maury Wills. She saw him a lot, as did her late husband, Marty Melcher. Wills says he never had a romance with the lady, and I never saw any.

Grant used to go to games with his wife at that time, Dyan Cannon. He kept to himself, but he met the players. I must say I have never seen a more handsome man, regardless of age. I wouldn't have expected it, but Lauren Bacall was probably the most beautiful of the lady stars I saw. She was striking in person in a way that she was not on the screen. It was interesting to meet these people in person and they were all nice to us. The way others were fans of theirs, they were fans of ours.

We used to get invited to a lot of parties. I didn't go to a lot because I'm not the party type, but my wife always wanted to go and the other players and their wives went. Jeri and Don Drysdale's wife and Steve Allen's wife and Sammy Cahn's wife and Milton Berle's wife got together and worked in the Kennedy presidential campaign in 1960. It was social, which Jeri really liked. She became a part of SHARE, which is a charitable organization run by Hollywood wives.

The Melchers, the Allens, the Berles, and Bob Cummings threw a lot of parties for the players. There was always a lot of drinking and dancing. I don't drink and don't like to be around drunks. And I don't dance well and don't like to dance. I sweat a lot and always feel like everybody's watching me. One time one of the coaches' wives pulled me out on the floor and proceeded to do the grind. I was about as embarrassed as I could be. I told my wife later, "I'm not going to any more of these goddam parties." But she always wanted to go. At the games, she was always in some star's box, socializing.

There were a whole lot of stars who went to the games. Jerry Lewis and Chuck Connors were others who come to mind. Connors, of course, played for the Dodgers for a short time before he became an actor. It became an "in" thing to go to our games. I think some of this has worn off with the Hollywood set, but Berle and Grant and others still attend. It was a big thing at one time, especially after we bounced back from a bad season in 1958 to win the World Series in 1959.

Our first home field in Los Angeles before Dodger Stadium was built in Chavez Ravine was the Coliseum. It had been built for the 1932 Olympics and became the big football stadium in town, but it was never meant for baseball. It was a sprawling place with wooden bench seats all around the oval. The closest seats were a long way from the field and the farthest ones were ridiculous.

The fans didn't seem to mind, although we did better when we got our real ball park. We played four years in the Coliseum and drew a bit short of two million the first and fourth seasons and more than two million the middle two seasons. We drew more than seventy-eight thousand for a game with the Giants our first season, more than twice what Ebbets Field held, and more than ninety-three thousand, which remains a major-league record, for a game honoring Roy Campanella our second season. It was a night game, all the lights were turned out, and all the fans held up lighted matches to show the way as Campy was wheeled in. It brought scalding-hot tears to my eyes.

They just squeezed a baseball field into that football stadium. It had to be set in at an angle so it was 300 feet to right, 440 feet to center, and 250 feet to left. They strung a steel mesh fence from right to center to form the field, then had to erect a 40-foot-high screen along the left-field stands so that the players wouldn't hit a home run every time they hit one in the air to left. It turned out to be hard to hit one over the screen but not too hard to hit the screen. Unfortunately, our opponents hit it more often than we did.

Maybe we were trying too hard to make it in our new town, but most of us had a bad time. Some of the older guys were on their way out and the younger guys weren't ready yet. Newk was sent on his way fast. Podres, Drysdale, and Koufax were our big winners, with thirteen, twelve, and eleven wins, yet none of 'em won more than they lost. Snider was our only .300 hitter. Hodges and Neal tied for the team lead in home runs with only twenty-two. No one drove in a hundred runs. Or even ninety.

We got off to a bad start and struggled the rest of the way. Milwaukee ran away with the pennant and we must have finished twenty games behind them. We lost a dozen games more than we won, and settled for seventh place in what was then an eight-team league. It was one of those seasons some teams have where everything goes right or everything goes wrong. That season, everything went wrong. We were a better ball club than we showed.

Rube Walker had started the season as our catcher, but that was in San Francisco. I started the home season as our catcher in the Coliseum in Los Angeles and then became the regular receiver. I wasn't a complete catcher yet by any means and led the league in passed balls with fourteen. I also made eight errors, mostly on throws. I wasn't too bad at bat and averaged around .270, hit fourteen home runs, and drove home or scored a total of around a hundred runs. I also stole eleven bases, the most by a major-league catcher in twenty years. Still, there were people down on me because I lacked polish. I just didn't look good.

During the off-season, when everyone was speculating about changes the Dodgers had to have if they were going to get back in contention for a pennant, a lot of people figured they'd have to get a better receiver than me to replace Campy. That worried me, naturally. After not playing much my first half season, this had been my first full season. I didn't think I'd done too badly, and I thought I deserved more of an opportunity to prove myself.

Fortunately for me, the Dodgers were a stable, patient organization. For the most part, they believe in developing their own stars, and they do not panic and start to tear things apart after a bad season. A lot of people thought Alston would be fired after the bad year, but they always were patient with Walter and it paid off with a lot of good years. And Alston always was patient with players he thought would develop, and that paid off with a lot of good players. I became one of them.

I became a better catcher in 1959. I made as many errors but cut down on passed balls and improved my throwing. I went from thirty-six assists to fifty-four, most of these throwing out opponents trying to steal second base. My hitting went to hell as I concentrated on my catching, but I had some big hits. Working in the confines of the Coliseum, I had to learn a lot about handling pitchers and how they had to pitch to batters to avoid being burned in that bandbox.

We didn't have any really outstanding players that season, but we pulled together and had an outstanding season as a team. Our top pitchers were Drysdale and Podres, who won seventeen and fourteen. Sherry really relieved well, winning or saving ten. Wills arrived to take over short from Zimmer and teamed well with Neal. Wills and Neal worked out a play where if one of them fielded a ball out of position for the throw to first, the one would flip it to the other for the throw, and it worked well. Our defense strengthened.

Hodges and Snider led with twenty-five and twenty-three homers, while Wally Moon and Neal had nineteen each, and Don Demeter had eighteen. We got Moon in one of the best deals the Dodgers ever made. He wasn't a heavy hitter, but he was able to pull and pop it to left so it cleared the screen. He also hit a lot off the screen. He batted .300, as did Duke. No one drove in a hundred runs, but we had five different players who drove in seventy or more.

They said there was no way the Braves could be beaten when they went after their third straight pennant. And they did have more talent than the other teams, with a ton of pitching and power. But the Giants led most of the season and it wasn't until the last week of the season that the Braves caught and passed them. Then on Thursday of that last week we caught the Braves, and on Friday we passed them. But on Saturday the Cubs murdered us in Chicago, 12–2, while the Braves beat the Phillies to catch us. We bounced back to win on Sunday, the last day, but so did the Braves, so we tied for the pennant and had to go into a best-of-three playoff.

It was tense stuff and I was excited, but not too badly because I tended to take things like this in stride. You want to win, of course. You've come so close to the top, you don't want to get knocked off then. And you want to do well for yourself. It's a showcase. The country is watching, including all your friends and family. I think the only thing I was ever nervous about, the one thing most players are nervous about when going into big ball games, is doing bad and looking bad. You don't want to mess up in front of everyone because you figure it'll hurt your ball club and make everyone look bad. You've heard so much about big goats from big games over the years that you don't want to be one. You pray, "Oh, Lord, don't let me mess up and do something bad I'll be remembered for the rest of my career."

I think that's why in basketball you won't find many players who want to take the shot in the clutch. And in football few players want the ball thrown to them in the last seconds. The pressure performers are rare. It's true in baseball too, but in baseball you don't have many options. If the batter is in the box, the pitcher has to pitch to him. If the pitcher pitches, the batter has to bat. If the ball is hit to you, you have to field it.

I guarantee there are a lot of guys who don't want to be the man up under pressure or who hope the ball isn't hit to them in the clutch.

I was anxious about the playoff, fearful of not doing well. The first game was on a foggy, drizzly afternoon, in Milwaukee. We'd used up our starters, so Alston turned to McDevitt, who hadn't done much that season. He was wild and had to come out in the second with the Braves leading, 2–1. Sherry came in and shut them out the rest of the way. That year it was as though God touched Sherry on the shoulder and said, "Boy, this is your year."

Hodges singled in the tying run in the third. I hit a home run for the winning run in the sixth. Carlton Willey was pitching. He threw me a fast ball, I swung hard, and hit it well into the right-field bleachers. I thought it was gone when I hit it and I thought to myself that I was a hero and I ran around the bases. I was thrilled about it and my teammates really pounded me for it. That was it, 3–2.

That night both teams flew back to Los Angeles for the second game the next afternoon. This was a wild one. It took four hours. We used twenty players, including six pitchers. They used twenty-two players, including five pitchers. But Lew Burdette took a 5–2 lead into the last of the ninth. Lew was one of the top pitchers. He threw one of the best spitters I ever saw. But he was cute and we couldn't catch him.

He was getting old and tired. Moon, Snider, and Hodges singled to load the bases. Fred Haney, the Milwaukee manager, brought in right-handed Don McMahon, his best reliever. But the batter, Norm Larker, was left-handed. Larker hit the ball off the screen, bringing in two runs and bringing the tying run to third. I was due up, a left-hander. This time Haney played the percentages. He went to his star, left-hander Warren Spahn. Alston pulled me and put in right-handed Carl Furillo. Carl hit a fly ball caught by Henry Aaron in right, but deep enough to bring in the tying run.

So we went to extra innings. In the eleventh, both sides loaded the bases without scoring. It looked like the game was going to go on forever without any more scoring. The game was settled finally in the fourteenth inning. The turning point might have happened seven innings earlier. Breaking up a double play, Larker had crashed into my old pal Johnny Logan so hard at second that Johnny went flying and had to be helped off the field and replaced at short by Felix Mantilla. In the fourteenth, Hodges walked, and Joe Pignatano, my sub, singled him to second. Furillo grounded to right. Mantilla got to it, but he hurried his throw and threw wild past first as Hodges continued on around third to home plate for the winning run.

We had champagne in the shower room. In my third season in the majors I had made it to the World Series, and that was a thrill.

I heard later that all Vince Scully said on the air as the winning run scored was, "We go to Chicago."

I think now that the biggest thrill for me may have been our arrival in Chicago. We flew in with our wives and were put up at the swank Conrad Hilton Hotel, looking out at Lake Michigan. When we went to the ball park to practice, we used two buses. Suddenly we were surrounded by motorcycle cops. We took off with a police car leading the way, its siren sounding. We were escorted screaming through that town without stopping for a light.

These were the Go-Go White Sox, who had won the American League pennant primarily on the flying feet of Luis Aparicio, Nellie Fox, Jim Landis, and Jim Rivera. They had good defense and good pitching, only fair hitting, but terrific speed, and they stole more than a hundred bases that season. The newspapers and the television and radio stations in town were full of stories that the Sox would steal the Series from the Dodgers' young catcher. They said I was the weak link that would come apart under pressure. Alston made me feel like a million by telling reporters, "They don't know how well Roseboro throws. They can go, but he'll cut them down."

I did. I threw out everyone who tried to steal on me in the first two games. Landis stole one on me in the third game and Aparicio stole one in the fourth game, but that was it. I threw out everyone who went in the last two games. They stopped running. I threw out Fox and Landis and Aparicio, and that discouraged them. Of course, I had help. The Dodgers always worked hard on details. Our pitchers learned how to hold runners on first base so they didn't dare take too big a lead and never got a big jump. I often gave the signal to the pitcher to make a pick-off attempt. Drysdale, especially, had a terrific pick-off move.

Although I only had two hits in the Series, I was considered one of the stars. Neal, who had a lot of power for a little guy, was the hitting star. But the star of stars was Sherry, who relieved in four of the six games, gave up one run, saved two games and won two games, including the deciding game. He had a fast ball that hopped, a big curve, a sneaky slider, and exceptional control, but his pitches never worked the way they did that Series. Like I said, someone touched him with magic.

We were shut out by burly old Early Wynn and blown out of the first game, 11–0, but we were a tough team and could deal with that. We came back to win the second game in Chicago, 4–3. Chuck Essegian pinch-hit the tying homer and Neal hit the winning homer. They almost tied it in the eighth, but Wills relayed Moon's throw to me at the plate and I put the ball on Sherm Lollar and held on to it as he smashed into me.

Each of the three games in the Coliseum in LA drew more than ninety thousand fans. It was something. Sherry bailed out Drysdale in the third game of the Series and Roger Craig in the fourth as we won both. Although both had relief help, Bob Shaw outpitched Koufax as the White Sox won the fifth game, 1–0, to stay alive. But we went back to Chicago and killed them off in their little old ball park in the sixth game, 9–3. Snider, Moon, and Essegian hit home runs. Chuck's was his second pinch-hit homer, a World Series record. Sherry shut them out after he picked up for Podres in the fourth, and we ran off the field the world champs.

That dressing-room scene was something. I took it in stride, but some of my teammates went ape and it was exciting to be a part of it.

It took the Dodgers sixty-five years to bring a championship to Brooklyn but only two years to bring one to Los Angeles. However, even counting our two playoff victories, we won only eighty-eight games during the regular season, a record low for a pennant winner, and we weren't the team we would be, a team that could continue on top.

We fell to fourth in 1960 as Pittsburgh, led by the pitching of Vernon Law, Bob Friend, and Elroy Face, won the pennant. We came back to finish second in 1961 as Cincinnati won, led by the hitting of Frank Robinson and Vada Pinson. We only finished four games back, but we had fallen too far back when we lost ten in a row in August.

That was the year, '61, when the American League expanded to ten teams, and one of them was the Los Angeles Angels, who played in Wrigley Field, where the Pacific Coast League team had played. That was also our last year in the Coliseum, as our own stadium now was ready in Chavez Ravine, near downtown.

The thing I remember best about those first years in southern California has to be winning that first World Series. I didn't drink, but I asked for and was given one of those big bottles of champagne they had and kept it as a treasured souvenir for years and years. I forgot to take it with me when I moved out. I wonder if my ex-wife still has it.

14.

I MADE the minimum major-league salary of $7,500 in 1958, my first full season. I got a raise to $11,500 my second season. I went to $14,000 my third and $16,000 my fourth, 1961. So, it was slow. It took a while to move up to big money. In time, I made it. I was not a spectacular player— solid, but not spectacular. I didn't bring people into the ball park. I had to work my way up in money slowly but surely.

Still, it wasn't bad dough for those days. I never needed much. I never walked around with a hundred dollars in my pocket unless I was going on the road and the club had paid us our per diem in cash in advance. That's the meal money and incidental dough that the club pays a player on the road. I think it used to be about ten dollars a day. Today it's three times that. But I was never a big spender.

I used to think that if I'd lived one year on less than eight thousand, by the time I got to sixteen thousand I should be able to save half of it. But I never got to that. The money never got to the savings account. The kids started coming and our expenses went up. We bought a house and had expenses there. Then we bought an apartment house as an investment and lost a lot there. That was the first of a series of bad investments. I was always aware I couldn't play ball forever and was always looking for that one solid investment that would set me up for the future.

We bought a house on Arbutus Street in Compton in 1958. It was a nice street in a nice neighborhood. We were among the first blacks to move in, but there was no hassle. The house was small but comfortable. There were a lot of trees out front and trees and a yard out back. There also was a kind of cottage the previous owner had built by the garage. I converted it into a den for all my trophies and junk. Charlie Neal had a cousin named Adolphus who drank pretty good but was good with his hands. We gave him a six pack of beer and a few bucks a day for a few weeks and he built us a beautiful bar out there and we had our few parties there.

That winter Jeri's mom and dad suddenly packed up and moved from Columbus to Compton, right into our den. I don't think they liked us putting them back by the garage, so they soon moved out, but they stayed nearby. I asked Jeri how they were going to get by, because I couldn't carry them. She said her dad, who had promoted dances and athletic events in Columbus, was going into promotions in California. I said there was no way anyone new was going to make it in promotions because every other person here already was in promotions. That's the way it worked out. They went to work as domestics for a family in Laguna Beach for a while, then wound up moving back to Ohio.

It was tough to make a buck here. As they say, they don't have to give you good wages, because they're giving you good weather. Rather than sit around, I went to work for a downtown clothing store my first summer in southern California. I was on a small base salary and three-percent commission on any clothing I sold. I didn't mind shooting the bull with the customers and signing autographs, but I didn't like selling. And because I was a baseball star, a lot of customers would wait around just so I could wait on them. The other salesman didn't like that.

If you couldn't sell a customer, you were supposed to turn him over to another salesman so he could try, but those guys would lose the sale rather than give up on the commission they might make. It was cutthroat and they thought I was taking the food off their tables. Finally I went to the boss and told him I'd give up my commissions and he could split them among the other guys when I sold something. So I didn't make much money. But I did work at something every winter and brought in a little money.

I learned a lot about the business. How they put markups of three or four hundred percent on most merchandise, which is true of all such stores. And how when they advertised a sale, such as after Christmas, they'd pull the good stuff off the floor and bring out all the seconds and bad stuff that hadn't sold. But I got to buy my clothes cheap and I was getting to like clothes a lot. Clothes became my weakness and I always dressed well.

In Compton we were about a half-hour drive from the Coliseum, an hour from downtown where the stadium later was built. We had only one car, an old Plymouth convertible, and Jeri needed that, so she'd drive me to where I could catch the streetcar to ride downtown. It was what they called the "old red car." Then she'd pick me up when I got off it in the evening. I used to ride that streetcar to work wearing a business suit, a derby hat, and carrying an umbrella over my arm. Very British. Derby hats were back and big for about a year. But we didn't sell many derby hats. And it never rained, so I never needed that umbrella. But I looked good.

After we won the World Series in '59, my share of the winners' money came to more than eleven grand, a record because of our big crowds. We traded in our old Plymouth for a new Thunderbird. But a family needs two cars in southern California, because the public transportation is terrible. I'm a sports-car freak and I bought an Austin-Healey.

I remember our trainer, Bill Buhler, asked me one day what kind of car I had. I said Jeri had a Thunderbird and I had an Austin-Healey. He asked how the hell I could afford those kind of cars on the money I was making. I asked what the hell business it was of his. But it made me think.

Over the years I've become aware of how people want to know how much money you make and how you spend it and they judge you by your home and your clothes and your cars and the image you make. We all have our weaknesses, but I never wanted to be considered a hot dog of any kind. I saw that everyone expected blacks to buy Cadillacs as soon as they came into cash, so for years I wouldn't even consider a Caddy.

We were content in Compton for awhile. Then we moved

to south LA in 1960. We still had an apartment house in Compton we had bought as an investment. Then there were the race riots in the summer of '65 in Watts, which borders Compton. The area had started to run down, a lot of businesses moved out and the financial institutions no longer would come in, so we were cut off economically. We saw we had to sell, but we couldn't find any buyers. We finally just had to let it go. After all the figuring was finished, I think we wound up with three thousand dollars. Years later, after I had left the Dodgers and sold the house in south LA, after we returned to southern California, we bought a house a little to the northeast, in West Covina. We also bought a couple of houses in that Covina-Pomona area as investments.

We started our family in Compton. Actually, our first child would have been born in Ashland in '58 after our half season in Brooklyn, but Jeri had a miscarriage. She started to feel sick so I took her to the hospital there and the doctor checked her out and said she was all right. When she got worse, I took her back, but she lost the baby.

Before she got pregnant again I took her to a doctor in Beverly Hills who was recommended to us, Dr. Leon Kron. He examined her and discovered that her womb was tipped in such a way that it would be difficult to keep the fertilized egg in it and difficult to deliver a baby from it. He said she would keep having miscarriages unless what they call a pessary was inserted into her vagina to tilt the womb into the proper position. That was done and she was all right, but I was left with a bad feeling about small-town doctors who don't know what they're doing.

Our first daughter, Shelley, was born in June 1959. That was my real thrill of that year. It meant much more to me than the pennant and the World Series. I used to lay her on my chest and talk to her and play with her and let her go to sleep right there and watch her sleeping. I did that with all my kids. I talked to them and played with them and watched them and loved them. Our second daughter, Stacy, was born in February 1961. I had hoped to have a son, but I was satisfied with Stacy. She was a little doll and I adored her. However, when we got a chance to adopt a son, we did. That was Jaime, who was born in May 1966. He completed our family. The kids were the best thing in my life and I hated to see them grow up.

I used to buy them all kinds of clothes and toys on road trips. You have a lot of time to kill on the road and I liked to shop and I liked to bring them things when I came home. I did that for years until one day Jeri said to me, "If you can't bring gifts for everyone, don't bring anything for anyone." I didn't even know what she meant until I saw she was offended that I hadn't been bringing her anything. I had never even thought of it.

She had never lacked anything. I signed my paychecks over and she took care of our money. I never took much and never asked her what she took. I never complained about what she bought. After that I bought presents for her too, but it wasn't the same, buying for someone because you'd been told to instead of because you wanted to. I guess it was my fault not to have thought of her more, not having wanted to give her more. But I guess I didn't like the way she wanted more. One Christmas I caught her counting the presents under the tree to see if she had gotten as many as the kids. That was the way she thought it should be. I just bought presents and never counted them, but that was her way.

Whatever else she was, she was a good mother. I have to give her that. And I hope whatever else I was, I was a good father. I can't say we got along badly. We just didn't get along well. We just got along. We didn't argue or anything, we just drifted apart. We not only didn't argue, we didn't talk. A lot of that was my fault, but I seldom had much to say. If an argument started she had to carry it on by herself, because I'd just clam up. Maybe I'd go into the other room and turn on the television so I didn't have to hear her. Sometimes I'd leave the house so she couldn't continue it. I just hate arguments, but differences do come up between couples and have to be decided. It had to be dissatisfying to her never to get anything settled. After a while we just lived together. I tend to keep things to myself. I find it hard to share me with someone. Even with my wife. So if I had a problem or felt bad about something, I kept it to myself and didn't give my wife the chance to help. I think that's wrong, but that was my nature and for the most part still is. But she didn't share her thoughts with me much, either. I never knew what she was thinking. But then, I never asked. We never talked baseball. She went to the games but she rarely watched them. She was always socializing. She liked being the wife of a big-league ballplayer. I liked being a big-league ballplayer. In a way, for a while, we gave each other what we wanted.

15.

M Y WIFE used to say I liked life on the road better than I did at home. It wasn't true. I missed the kids when I was away. But she used to say I lived a different life on the road. That was true and I did like that. I liked doing whatever I wanted to do without worrying about what someone else wanted to do. I think it's true of most ballplayers.

You have to be at the ball park a certain number of hours, but the rest of the time you're on your own. The players like that. A lot of time is spent traveling, but it wasn't too bad with the Dodgers because the club had its own plane. Before the league expanded we had longer series and spent more time in each town.

I was sort of straight, which a lot of the ballplayers weren't. I don't mean I always stayed on the straight and narrow, but I didn't go out looking for the ladies. Wills was always on my ass because I was always staying in my room and having room service.

Most games were at night. I'd get up early and call room service for breakfast. Then I'd watch a couple of game shows on TV, or read a newspaper, magazine, or book. I'd take a nap and then call room service for my pregame meal. After I got back from the ball park I'd call room service for my late meal. I'd go to bed early so I could get up early for breakfast.

Other players rated towns by their women, but I rated them by room service. Some of the places shut down room service at night before we got back from the ball park. They rated low with me because I had to order two meals with my pre-game meal so I'd have one waiting for me when I got back. I used to leave the television set on and put my late meal under a towel on top of it so it would stay warm. St. Louis was my favorite town because the hotel had a creamed chicken omelet I just loved. I'd have a creamed chicken omelet for breakfast, lunch, and dinner every day I was in that town. In Chicago we had a hotel that made a marvelous Monte Cristo sandwich. I'd have that three times a day.

It was better than wandering the streets looking for a Howard Johnson's or a White Castle or some place to grab something decent to eat at night after a game.

The only thing I liked about Houston was a clubhouse man named Norm Germann, who put out a spread of ham, chicken, knockwurst, and deviled eggs for the visiting team after games. A lot of teams had good clubhouse men who put out spreads with everything from delicatessen sandwiches to watermelon, but Norm was the best. His deviled eggs were so good the guys gobbled them up in a few minutes, win or lose, but he used to hide six for me, so I was always set.

Sometimes I didn't want to leave the clubhouse to go back to the hotel.

Wills got on me all the time about going out to eat at the good restaurants. After he became a star he wanted to shine. For a while there I went out with him some.

We always dressed up, which was all right with me. In Montreal, Mulleavy's sons had turned me on to nice clothes. For a while we all used to wear slacks and shirts and alpaca sweaters. That was the southern California look. When we started to win pennants, we started to dress like winners, in suits. I always leaned to conservative clothes, none of the jazzy stuff athletes wear today, but Wills went cool. He always wore bow ties with good coats until he didn't even look like a goddamn ballplayer and the stewardesses on airplanes would ask what we did for a living.

It was all right rooming with Wills because we set it up that we each went our own way right off. Lots of times we'd eat together but when he went after the women I went to our room. One good thing about our relationship was whatever we did, we split everything down the middle. We were roomies and we agreed it was simplest to share expenses without counting coins. You wouldn't believe most ballplayers. They're making big money but when they go out they're always arguing about expenses, even down to a dollar and change. A lot of roommates have split over that chintzy stuff.

I liked New York because of the nice stores. I liked Chicago because we played day games and that gave me a chance to go to movies at night. I used to go to the Loop for the movies. I'd see one, find a place to have a steak and salad and baked potato, catch another movie, then a third if there was still time.

I hated Houston. It was so hot and humid and full of bugs you hated to leave the hotel. You could ruin a shirt just walking around downtown. And you got bitten by bugs as big as dive-bombers playing on that rinky-dink field they used before they moved into the Astrodome.

Houston is southern, of course. One time I followed some white boys across a street against the light and a traffic cop shouted at me, "Back on the curb, boy." Waving at the whites, I asked, "What about them?" He said, "I'm not talking to them, I'm talking to you, boy." He was a pouchy old guy and I could have broken his back in about ten different places, but he was the law so I had to do what he wanted. But I hated it and I remember it. That's where the hate comes from. I don't hold on to hate, but I know where it's at.

Barnstorming during an off-season, we went to a black club in Houston to hear Dinah Washington. She and Don Newcombe were friends, so we had a ringside table and she sat with us between sets. I don't drink and I don't chitchat too well, so I'm usually a drag in these scenes. But this time I decided what the hell, and I had orange juice and vodka. It was all right. So I had another. And another. Soon I was drinking anything I could get my hands on. My hands weren't too steady. I spilled a drink on Dinah. She called me everything but John Roseboro. I had never heard a lady use such language. I was sick for two days. They'd paid us in dollar bills that night, so I pulled out a role of singles and peeled some off and told her to get her dress cleaned. Some of the guys got me back to my hotel room. I don't think I ever got drunk again. I still remember my embarrassment.

I met a lady in Houston through Maury. I didn't date her, but after Wills was traded I took her and her son to the circus one night. She was beautiful and she had hopes of getting into show business. She showed me a set of shots *Playboy* magazine had done on her and said she was going to be a Playmate of the Month. I didn't believe that because the magazine didn't make many black ladies, even light-skinned ones, their playmates, but I pocketed one of the pictures.

Back in LA, I was showing it around to the guys, hinting that I'd had some of this fine stuff, which I hadn't, when I got a call from her. She said, "John, I'm missing one of my pictures and I figured out it had to be you who took it. I have to have it because they're proofs. If I don't return the complete set to the magazine they'll be upset and I may not make it. It means a lot to me, both in money and opportunity." She hit me where it hurt. I said I was sorry and sent the picture right back. To my surprise, she not only made the centerfold as Playmate of the Month, but I think she became Playmate of the Year, and she became the first black bunny. She also got into show business and I saw her in a play in LA not long ago. I went to her afterwards and wished her well. And she wished me well. I wish I still had that picture.

I guess I bragged because all ballplayers brag. It was a lie, but a lot of it is lies. Most of the ballplayers run around, about half of the married ones, especially on the road. If you don't run you feel left out. It is almost easier to run than not to, because the females who follow ballplayers make it easy for them.

They are always around where the players are and they throw themselves at ballplayers. White ladies go for black ballplayers, too. But few white ballplayers go for black ladies. The ladies will ask for an autograph and ask for a room number, too. Or they will give their phone numbers.

I have had ladies call me up and give me all kinds of crap. One said Henry Aaron told her to call when I got to town. No way Henry would do that.

Another said she wanted to interview me for her college

newspaper. A third said she was taking a survey of men on the road. I strung her along until she got to the place where she asked what I did for excitement in a strange town and if I liked ladies and might like to have some excitement with her. That's when I turned her off because it could be a trap. Those are all common pitches and players do wind up being black-mailed.

We called them "groupies" and they were always available. If the average guy had an athlete's temptations and oppor-tunities, he probably wouldn't stay straight either. Some of the wildest I've known were among the managers and coaches and some of the reporters and broadcasters. I was with four different teams in my time, so don't assume these were all part of Dodgers' parties. Others were worse.

Some of the writers were the worst. They snickered about ballplayers' bad habits, but they had habits an athlete wouldn't touch. They'd plan their parties on the plane and they'd spend half their time on the road bragging about their conquests. Some of them got tight with star players so they could have leftovers, but a lot of them took out the mullions the players wouldn't touch. Some glamour rubbed off on them and an ugly gal would go out with them if she couldn't get a player.

It's a bad influence on a young ballplayer, but some man-agers and coaches don't crack down on it. They're looking for their own ladies. The minute the athletes hit a plane to start a trip they start up with the stews, but the managers and coaches laugh it off. The players make pitches, pinch fannies, and grab feels. You may have twenty-five players and only three stews, so the stews are outnumbered, but many of them like those odds. Many of them aren't available, but many are.

One stew sued our ball club because a pitcher pinched too hard, but all she got for it was fired by her airline. I guess they are supposed to handle it. I remember one who seemed real nice seemed to handle it real well, but when we got to town she checked into our hotel and half the playboys on the team had her the first night, the other half the next. She just laid all over the place.

One time my wife and kids made a trip East for a vacation. They were waiting for me outside the stadium in New York when Jeri saw one of our married players come out with a gal on each arm. That made her mad and she gave me the business about married ballplayers going out with girls on the road. Then we got to Philadelphia and she saw the same two girls in the lobby of our hotel. That really got her mad, and she wondered whether they were waiting for me. She used to dial direct to my rooms on the road to see if a lady answered. And one time I walked into my room on the road and found her waiting there. She said she just wanted to surprise me, but I think she had hoped to catch me. It would have been hard for her to catch me. There weren't many times I was doing anything I shouldn't have been doing.

A lot of the wives know what's going on, but they go along with it because they like the big time and big money and don't want to risk their marriages. They figure the player will straighten out when his career comes to an end. A lot of times he doesn't. Many marriages break up after a player retires from his sport but not from the "fringe benefits." But a lot of marriages break up because the wives simply can't stand the life a lot of players lead.

Some wives run around while their husbands are on the road. What's fair for one should be fair for the other, but it doesn't work out that way. It's easy for the player and hard on his wife. A lot of the players tell their wives about other players, which is stupid. Their wives tell other wives. Players' wives form a sort of sorority and talk about each other and their husbands, and it stirs up all sorts of trouble.

My wife used to tell me about what this wife said and what that wife said and what other ballplayers were supposed to be doing. I'd say, "Hey, I don't care about all that, I don't want to hear it." But she'd gossip away. I knew better than she did what was going on, and she knew it. There was no way I was going to tell her about any of my teammates and have her spread it around in her socializing. But sometimes you get caught up in it.

I got close to Lou Johnson when he joined the team. He was a wild one. And his wife would call me to check on Lou. She always knew where I was, but she never knew where he was. I'd get home from a night game about midnight and she'd be on the phone asking my wife, "Is John home? Has he seen

Lou? Does he know where Lou is?" I never saw him, I never knew, but she called regularly. She'd even call my room on the road because Lou was never in his. I got tired of it and it taught me not to get involved in other people's lives.

A lot of the ballplayers' girl friends talked a lot too, which scared me. In Cincinnati one of the hotel maids was turning tricks for a few dollars. She'd come to clean up my room and proposition me and tell me about all my teammates she'd been with. I figured you better be careful of those broads that put it all over the street. I told her to try someone else.

For fun, I turned one telephone caller on to Vada Pinson. He was straighter than I was and she really turned his head. I'd told her not to take no for an answer because he really wanted to say yes, and he was too polite to hang up on her.

My first trip into Chicago, Newcombe was still on the team and insisted on fixing me up with the Reamer. I'd heard of her, but I didn't know what set her apart. I asked Newk, but he said I had to experience it for myself. I didn't really want to, but he insisted. He called her up and she came over. Newk left me to her. At least he didn't want to watch, which a lot of ballplayers do.

She was a mullion plus, so I couldn't figure what had made her famous. After we got undressed, she went down on me. It took me about ten seconds to reach a climax. I was embarrassed, but she couldn't have cared less. Then she went into her specialty. I don't know why I let her, but she blew hot water up my rear, then sucked it out.

Yes, it's disgusting. I don't tell it because I'm proud of it or want to attract attention to it. But because that's what she really did to a lot of ballplayers over the years and it was an act that made her famous in sports.

She charged me twenty-five dollars and I was glad to get rid of her. I couldn't help thinking that twenty-five bucks was a pair of shoes or a pair of pants or a couple of shirts. For a while after that when I was window shopping I'd think of that wasted dough, which would have bought me something I could keep and use a long time.

But if you're a ballplayer traveling with other ballplayers, it's easy to get into embarrassing situations.

I did have an affair in Chicago, which lasted a few years.

Willie Davis knew someone in South Chicago who was having a party. I went with him and met a girl. She was very pretty, very intelligent, very quiet. I liked her a lot and she seemed to take to me. She was a college graduate who was going for a master's in psychology. That was a subject I always was interested in. It gave us something to talk about. Eventually, we found we were able to talk to each other about a lot of things. We were together whenever I was in Chicago for two or three seasons.

She wrote to me sometimes at the ball park, but one time I left one of her letters around by accident and my wife found it and really laid into me. Well, I had it coming, but I couldn't confess to anything. This girl wasn't the sort to have said anything much in the letter anyway. But my wife got it into her head I had to be giving the gal mink coats and such. I said, "Hey, woman, I can't afford to buy a sweatshirt, how'm I going to get a girl a mink coat?" She figured I'd have found a way.

Anyway, it had to end. It wasn't going anywhere. I couldn't leave my kids and I don't know that she wanted to marry me. And then she got married, so that was that. But it's not a bad memory. She was a good woman, and reached a high estate in life.

Baseball took me so many places and gave me so many experiences that it rubbed a lot of the rube right out of me. Before I even got to the big leagues I got to cities like Montreal and Toronto and Miami and Havana. Winter ball took me to Venezuela. Barnstorming moved me all over Mexico as well as this country. The big leagues brought me to all the big towns in this country as well as tours of Hawaii and Japan.

Havana was in the International League when I was with Montreal. That was quite a trip, Canada to Cuba. Baseball has always been big in Cuba, and a lot of good ballplayers came from Cuba before Castro came into power and decided to keep the talent at home. Batista was in power when I was there. There was a lot of unrest and friction between rich and poor, dark and light, Cubans and Americans. It also was a wide-open town.

The guys always bought a lot of fine cigars and rum cheap.

And they really liked the nightlife, which included Las Vegas-like gambling casinos and elaborate floor shows. But I think what they liked best were the prostitutes. I don't know why ballplayers who can get all the women they want love whorehouses, but they do.

The star attraction at that time was a cat called Superman, who was supposed to be the best-hung guy in the world and who put on a show with women and animals.

My curiosity got the best of me and I went to see him one night, only to find out it was his night off.

Women weren't the only ones who went after us. Once in a while a gay guy turned up. One turned up in Jacksonville on a barnstorming tour. He was tall and slender, and a silly ass. Newcombe and Wes Covington picked up on him outside our motel rooms and were really putting him on. He was swishing around and saying, "Oh, no, you bad boys aren't going to get any of this good booty." They made me sick the way they teased the guy, but he made me sick, too. Turned out he was a third-grade schoolteacher. That would have bothered me at one time, but I don't think it would now.

Some have said there are a lot of gays in sports. I suppose there are some everywhere. But I only knew one in baseball. He was a pitcher with the Dodgers in the early fifties. He was not popular with the other players and I do not know any players who went with him. He found fellows, I guess, but not guys off the team, I don't think. The players would tease the ones they found, as Newk and Covington did that time, but they wound up waving them away.

A lot of the players didn't know he was gay until he was traded away. He was kind to some young boys who were fans of his and their parents trusted him and even let the boys take a short trip or two with him. After we found out what he was, we really felt bad about that, but we didn't know that anything bad had happened.

Most ballplayers are too busy living up to a macho image with women to take up with gays. When I was barnstorming in Mexico, one of the most famous ballplayers I've known talked me into going to a house of prostitution in Monterrey. He said, "This is one of the most famous houses in the world," and that got me to go. I was flattered, and the ladies really were beautiful, but it was a bad experience.

He told me he could maintain an erection all night and come to a climax repeatedly. I believed him. I thought maybe that was the way it was with a lot of guys, and that maybe there was something wrong with me. Mine didn't last long. In fact, all it took was some woman looking at me in the right way and I might be through for the day. I thought I was letting the ladies down. I carried the thought with me for years until I read books about sex and asked around discreetly. Then I realized the star had been shooting me a bunch of bull.

One of our players met two prostitutes in Monterrey. When we moved on to Mexico City, he took them with him. When you bring a girl from one town to another she's known as an "import," but he didn't want them for himself, he wanted to pimp for them. He put them up in the same hotel with the team, advertised around for a couple of days, and made a mint as they turned tricks right and left, until management found out about it and booted them out.

Two teams made those tours. In some cases it was one league against another. In our case, it was white against black. Harmon Killebrew's club had himself, Jim Lemon, Roy Sievers, Jim Bunning, Billy Hoeft, Paul Foytack, and others. Our team had Willie Mays, Henry Aaron, Don Newcombe, Wes Covington, me, and others. It was a chance to play with and know a lot of top players from other teams.

It was also a chance to make a couple of grand in the off-season and see some of the world. I really liked Mexico, especially Mexico City. Really liking to shop like I do, I got to buy a lot of unusual things. I bought clothes for myself and toys for the kids, a lot of handmade silver things, an alligator shoulder bag my wife used for years, and a leather golf bag I gave my dad.

But there was nowhere I bought as much stuff as in Japan. I bought cameras and stuff at good prices. I couldn't compete with Willie Davis, who bought a thousand dollars' worth of equipment to photograph his golf swing in hopes of improving his game. My wife was with me and she was into pearls and bought pins, necklaces, earrings, and all other kinds of pearl jewelry. And we were given gifts wherever we went. We went to one of those electronic plants and the owner presented us each with eight-track tape-decks.

That was in 1965, after we lost the series to the Orioles. We came back groaning with goods. The only guy who returned empty-handed was Lou Johnson. Not that he hadn't bought a lot of things, but he blew his dough before he could pay for them. That was Lou. He had some suits made to order. Then, when he didn't want them, the tailor came crying to us. He was told to sell them to his regular customers. No way the little Japanese could wear big Lou Johnson's duds.

It was quite a trip. Aside from all expenses being paid, we were offered three grand each if we went alone and fifteen hundred each if we brought our wives. Most of the guys brought their women. I took Jeri and she just bowled the Japanese over. I don't think they had seen many big black ladies, and Jeri, at five-ten, was big. But we weren't with our women all the time, because while we were traveling out of Tokyo to play in towns all over the country, the girls were traveling on tours arranged for them.

Actually, our first stop was Hawaii. We stayed in a fine hotel, went sightseeing, spent time on the beautiful beaches, and were fed feasts. An earthquake was reported near there and we were warned we might have a tidal wave at any time. I was told that a tidal wave was forty feet high and hit at four hundred miles an hour. Our hotel was right on the water, and looking at it I could see it couldn't take anything like that. They evacuated the first four floors of the hotel, but we were on the fifth. All night Jeri kept asking me if I could see it coming, and I kept telling her the window was hers, I didn't want to look that wave in the eye. It never came.

When we got to Japan we went to so many places we lost track. We were treated like visiting royalty because we were the most famous baseball players in the world and were in a baseball-mad country. They have a big-league setup. I'd say it was Class A level at that time, though they say it is triple-A today. They put together teams that were tough for us to beat. They were far more fired up than we were.

They had a couple of players who could have played in our

league. One was Sadahara Oh, who has become famous for hitting about as many home runs as Aaron or Ruth. Another was a third baseman, Nagashima. He could hit too, but when he started to hit us, we started to knock him down, and he stopped hitting. Their pitchers didn't knock you down and didn't throw hard, but they threw a lot of different pitches from a lot of different motions. However, we won most of the games. We played in a lot of bad ball parks to a lot of good crowds.

Oh and others took Jeri and me out to eat several times. I didn't dig sitting cross-legged on the floor and chewing raw fish. If I went to play there, I think I'd starve to death. We shopped in the ginzas, which are the central shopping areas. We went to a couple of clubs. We saw the sights. We even saw sumo wrestling, with the fattest, strongest athletes I've ever seen.

We went to so many cities in so short a time that in the pre-game ceremonies on the field before a ball game in one city, William Eckert, the baseball commissioner at that time, said to the crowd, "I am happy to be here in . . ." and started to stammer and stutter because he obviously couldn't remember where he was.

I think the city that impressed me the most was Hiroshima. We were shown memorials to the death and destruction our atom bomb brought. We were shown shadows scorched into cement by the brilliance of the blast. It must have been awful. However, the way they rebuilt was unbelievable. We destroyed that town and in twenty years they put it together again with more beautiful buildings, better highways, and a more efficient transportation system than LA's. We were warned that Americans would be wise not to go out at night in Hiroshima. So I didn't.

One night in Tokyo when we were on our own, Wes Covington and I went to hear a singer who had been my lawyer's secretary before getting into show business. We went to the club where she was singing and the maître d' immediately brought over two young girls and introduced them to us as our hostesses for the evening. We tried to tell him we didn't want the women, but he pretended not to understand. They were great company. We didn't speak Japanese and they didn't speak English, so we spent the evening talking to each other and they spent the evening talking to each other. We sipped drinks while we listened to the singer, but they gulped theirs. Every time they finished a drink a waiter brought another. It was a real rip-off. We ran up quite a tab, and left before we were broke. They said good-bye at the door and went back to wait for the next two suckers.

However, there were some better experiences. We went to a geisha house in the belief that we'd be entertained by the best of prostitutes. We were entertained, but the ladies were not prostitutes. They were the most unique girls I've ever seen, with their faces painted white and wearing enormous wigs. Their traditional dances didn't turn me on, but being treated like a king did.

The best was the massage parlor. We were stripped and draped with a couple of little towels. They put us in hot little steambath cabinets and after two minutes I was ready to bust out before I melted. But then they put us on tables and gave us marvelous massages. Those ladies have the strongest fingers I've ever felt and they rubbed us front and back right to the hairline. I remember Tommy Davis got embarrassed because he got an erection. But it didn't bother them. They just washed and powdered us and sent us on our way.

I wanted to go back. My wife had to head home to take care of the kids, but I told her I wanted to stay to take classes in karate and judo for maybe a month or so. I said I thought it would be terrific for me to get my act together in karate and judo and be able to protect her.

I really was interested and later on did learn a lot of it. But Jeri said if I stayed, she stayed. So that kicked that in the head and we headed home.

16.

ONE of the things I learned in my travels in baseball is that
everyone is going to do his own thing, and it's hard to change
a guy doing the wrong thing.

There's the running around with the women, of course.
That's not ever going to change. The groupies are always going
to be around, and as long as they're offering it, guys are going
to be taking it. And if a guy doesn't go for groupies, he can
always find a gal he does go for. I did, and I never even
looked.

There are a lot of ballplayers who do not run around with
women. But about as many who do. On the road, away from
home, lonely, there's a lot of lying around with little to do,
and wanting to do what the others are doing.

Guys drink, and some turn to drugs. For all the glamour
and good dough, it's not an easy life. The constant travel is
terrible and wears you down. After a while, you don't know
what town you're in or what time the game is. And you may
play twenty or thirty games in a row without a day off. I liked
playing, I never even minded a lot of games in a row, but I
understood the guys who did.

You have a short time at the top and feel you have to make
the most of it. Unlike most professions, in sports you are
judged every night and day. Thousands of people watch every
move and millions can read in the statistics how you're doing.
You're expected to perform at your peak all the time. A hundred other players are waiting to take your place. The best
can go bad and head downhill at any time. An injury, or age,

or lots of other things can kill a career overnight. There is no security.

Everyone is expendable. The manager will be good to you only as long as you give him what he wants from you, because he's the most expendable of all. With the Dodgers we had a manager who was secure because the organization operated logically. With other teams, I saw managers degraded and dismissed, coming and going, so they put as much pressure on you as anyone because they had more pressure on them. Owners don't seem to see this. They draw up schedules that don't give you a chance to catch your breath and get your act together. They put on pressure until your head caves in.

There's a lot of drinking in baseball, maybe all sports. Guys get those free drinks on planes and start to argue and fight and abuse the stews and tear things apart. The managers and coaches go up and down the aisles trying to settle things down, but sometimes antagonism lingers a long time.

Some managers and coaches drink more than their players. They can't get tension out of their systems the way the younger guys can, so they go to saloons or their hotel rooms and they sip the sauce and bitch about today's ballplayers and make a mess of themselves.

One of their tricks to shake a club out of a slump is to say the curfew is off for that night and to go out and relax by raising a little hell. When we boarded the bus the next morning after one of those nights, one of our best players looked like he'd been on skid row for two or three weeks. He was in no shape to perform for two or three days. The writers were told he was sick.

Hungover, there is no way a player can properly make the plays in the field or pitch to spots or hit a pitch coming at him ninety miles an hour. But guys do waste themselves this way. Not many, but some. One used to carry a half pint of booze in his back pocket wherever he went and he'd take a belt whenever he wanted. There were a couple of players with the Giants, a pitcher in the fifties and an infielder in the sixties, who drank their way right out of the game, and there were others. A lot of guys let it go at a few beers after games, but others go beyond.

I didn't drink, but I popped a few pills in my time. A lot of players did and still do, mainly greenies. They've cracked down on it. You can't get them from the team trainers and doctors anymore. But you can get them. A player will say, "I've got greenies," and he's the guy the other guys will go to. There are two kinds. One is supposed to work all day. It takes your appetite away and is used to take weight off, but it's an "upper" and it gives you an artificial lift. The other is a four-hour deal and gives you a quick boost. I never got much out of them and never could tell the difference. Later in my career when I was fighting weight and suffering a sore arm, doctors would give me them. But if I took one too late in the day I couldn't sleep. Maybe if I'd gotten more out of them I'd have used them more.

I think a lot of players would do all kinds of things if they thought it would help them play better. There were players who didn't think they could play without a lift. There were players who didn't play a lot who would go to the ball park thinking they weren't going to play, and then they'd see their names in the lineup and they'd say, "Oh, shit, I got to go get a greenie."

I never thought it was good to depend on them like crutches. There was no way they could be good for you in the long run. They had to screw up your system. But guys get desperate. They get tired and they look for help. Hell, I loved to play, but I can remember getting into extra innings on a hot night and being worn down. I'd think to myself maybe I'll tell the hitter the pitch so he can hit one out of here and we can get the hell out of here. I never did it, but I was tempted.

We had a pitcher who was having a hard time. The manager was second-guessing him and the pitching coach was on his ass. After every pitch he made, he'd look in the dugout to see if someone was making a face or throwing a towel. He couldn't pitch right because he couldn't relax. He told me one time he was pitching a no-hitter in the minors when a teammate sitting next to him in the dugout said to him, "Hey, man, you're pitching a no-hitter and you haven't even broken a sweat yet." The player was surprised to hear he had a no-hitter. He was so relaxed he was just doing his thing. It turned out he had smoked half a joint before the game. I said to him, "Well, you're in the big leagues now, but you're going back to the minors if you don't do your thing the way you can. So if marijuana relaxes you I'd think about using it a little."

I think he did and I think it helped him, but I also think I was out of line. It's just that when you're a player you feel for other players and you know you better do what you have to do to get by or you'll be gone. You hang on hard, with both hands, as long as you can. And "Mary Jane" is not an uncommon lady around the leagues. A lot of guys go in for it because they feel it relaxes them. A lot of people know about it, but they protect the players and no one blows the whistle on them. A lot of guys carry stuff out in their equipment bags, which are shipped separately and seldom searched. The only time you hear about the stuff is when some player gets searched and something is found in his bag. That's happened a few times.

Some guys go in for worse stuff, hard stuff, which can kill you. One club I was on, the team doctor discovered during the preseason physical that a lot of the players had messed up the membranes in their nostrils, suggesting they were sniffing cocaine. He didn't know whether to blow the whistle or not. I suggested he give them a warning first and another physical a little later to see if they'd gone off the stuff. I think he just let it go rather than get into some mess over it.

I knew one guy who made his buys at the bank, going to a particular teller's window as if he was making an ordinary transaction, but passing the money in and taking the coke out right over the counter. One player today is so messed up on drugs that he gets moved from team to team once or twice a year. He has talent, so teams are willing to take a chance on him, but when they see for themselves how shot up he is, they dump him on to another team. Soon he will run out of teams and be out of baseball and maybe wind up an addict, broke, and a bum.

I am not going to blow the whistle on particular players, but I think it is time someone made noise so the people in power will know that this has gone on for a long time and is still going on. They have tried to do a job on it with rules, and they think because they have these rules they have stopped it. It just isn't true and they can't turn their heads away from it and pretend it doesn't exist. I think the players have to be protected from themselves by being watched more closely and being penalized so severely it will scare others. The older players draw younger guys in, and it's too bad.

The Dodgers are a classy, clean-cut organization and they have kept their guard up and helped their players or gotten rid of those who wouldn't be helped. They have had less of it than a lot of other teams, but there is a lot of it in both leagues. Womanizing breaks up families and hurts people. Some of the other things break up people.

17.

In my ten years in Los Angeles with the Dodgers there were some colorful characters. I've spoken of some players already, those who were with the team when I first made it, such as Campy, Hodges, Reese, and Newcombe. The later bunch I got to know better. The teammate I got to know best had to be Wills because we more or less came up together and roomed together most of our time with the team.

Maury spent a lot of time in the minors before he got to the majors. He got to the top late, and he was hungry. I don't think many thought he would make it, much less become a star, but he did it himself. He was very intense about baseball and learned how to make the most of himself. Once he made it, he wanted to enjoy it.

Although I was never any good at it, I always loved music and playing different instruments. To kill time on the road, especially in spring training, I used to fool around with a claviol, harmonica, bongo drums, and a ukelele. Wills liked the uke and when I'd put it down he'd pick it up. Pretty soon he was playing the hell out of that thing.

Anything Wills wanted to do, he was going to do. He was smart and dedicated. He just played the uke until he mastered it, then he turned to the guitar and mastered that, then he turned to the banjo and mastered that. He liked to play "Bye, Bye, Blackbird" on the banjo and if I heard it once I heard it two hundred thousand times. I used to say, "Maury, for Christ's sake, let it alone awhile," but Wills would laugh and launch into another round.

I don't mean he mastered these instruments in that he became a master, but he got to be very good. I'd introduced him to these instruments, but after a while I was asking him to teach me. There was a beer house in St. Louis where they had banjo players on stage, and Maury would jump up and join in with them. After he became famous by breaking the records for stealing bases, he was playing clubs in Las Vegas.

Wills would carry his banjo or guitar on a plane when we went on a road trip. He'd sit in the back and start to make music and before you knew it all those stews were back there listening to him and he was starting to make time with them. He was still married, but I can say this because it was a marriage in name only. It was one of those arrangements athletes have where the wife is one place, the player another. He only went back to see his kids. Eventually he and his wife divorced.

He liked the ladies a lot. We used to go window shopping and I'd look for clothes and he'd look for ladies. Like, in Cincinnati he'd see a nice-looking lady and he'd go up to her and say, "Are you Vada Pinson's wife?" And if she knew Vada Pinson was a star in that town at that time, she'd be flattered all to hell. Either way, she'd be flattered when he'd introduce himself. Before long, they'd be going off together and I'd be walking the streets alone, looking in windows.

I don't think there was anything to the story that Wills and Doris Day had a romance. I remember when the stories started. Wills had set the record and Doris, as a fan, gave him a stereo set. Larry Sherry hollered, "Hey, you fucking her?" The players took it up. They rode him hard. He laughed it off at first, but eventually he became a bit testy about it.

However, it helped make Maury a glamorous figure and it helped him get a lot of ladies. He didn't have to go in for groupies. But Wills was discreet. Whether he was seeing a star or a nobody, he kept it to himself and didn't brag about it. He was a charming guy with a gift of gab, a very appealing person and roomie.

Success did change him. We used to go around in sports clothes for a few years, but after he had his big year in 1962 and became a star, he started to dress to the teeth and change a couple of times every day. It made me uncomfortable. We used to eat in our room, but now he wanted to eat out in fancy restaurants, which I didn't like. We had made a few friends from town to town who would take us where we wanted to go and give us a good time. Suddenly he had friends he never knew he had, and I became a buffer between him and them, which I hated.

Whatever town we were in, the phone would ring. Nine times out of ten it would be for Wills. A lot of times he didn't want to talk to people, so nine times out of ten he'd make me take the calls, and if it wasn't this guy or that gal I'd have to tell them he wasn't in and I didn't know where he was. I was his secretary. It was a pain in the ass for me, but he accepted it as his due.

We were in Cincinnati one night and I was supposed to check in with my wife so she wouldn't think I was wandering the streets, but Maury was on the phone making lovey-dovey with some lady. He was sweettalking her from midnight to almost two, while I was waiting and kept getting angrier. Finally, he hung up. I went to take the telephone, when it rang. It was the same lady he'd just sweettalked for almost two hours. They went right back to it.

I packed my bags and went down to the desk and asked for another room. I preferred to be alone anyway. Ballplayers were not supposed to room alone, as they do now. Clubs pinched pennies more. But the next day I went to Walt Alston and said, "Skipper, Maury's so popular these days, he gets so many phone calls and gets into so much business I can't get my rest. I love him like a brother, but I got to get away from him." Alston understood and assigned us separate rooms. So I broke up with the best roomie I ever had, but it was best for both of us. He understood, and we have remained best buddies.

Women were his weakness, but there was more to him than that. He was very bright, alert, sensitive, and understanding. He got carried away by his success for a while, but it just took time for him to get his feet back on the ground. He was one of the first black superstars, and you'd have to go back to see how it was for him to keep things in perspective during those years.

I think he might make a marvelous manager, except that he

is emotional and has been impulsive at times. Jumping our Japanese trip in 1965 so he could do what he wanted to do, regardless of what the Dodgers wanted, caused him to be traded, the last thing he wanted to happen. He wasn't happy with other clubs and showed it. He was happy when he was brought back to the Dodgers in '69.

He has been outspoken about wanting to be a big-league manager, but when he was offered his opportunity in 1977 with the San Francisco Giants, he turned it down. The money was less than he was making in broadcasting and the security wasn't there with only a one-year contract.

I felt bad about it because he would have brought me back as one of his coaches with the club, but after a while I saw his point. After saying he wanted it so much for so long, maybe he should have grabbed the opportunity. Another might not come along, especially after he turned one down. But his chances for success in that Giants situation were not very good.

I don't know how he has done in business, but he has become one of the best of the baseball broadcasters, makes good dough, and leads a good life. I think he's happy, but I also think that because of the kind of competitor he is, he may need more of a challenge than he's getting out of life to be all he might be.

The biggest star on the Dodgers in my days with them had to be Sandy Koufax. And now he's leading the life he always wanted to lead. He's a hermit. He's in the Santa Barbara area. He was years in Maine until the weather got to him. He lives in isolation with his wife, Richard Widmark's daughter, and seldom sees anyone from baseball.

At my suggestion, when Wills was considering the Giants job, he called Koufax about becoming his pitching coach. Sandy had told me years before that he might like to do that someday, and I think he could do it. But he told Maury he just wasn't ready to return to the game and didn't know when he would be.

I think Koufax misses baseball. Although he had all kinds of natural ability, he had to learn to pitch before he became successful and he always liked to talk about the fine points of pitching. First his finger and then his elbow went bad. He had to take painkillers, and pitched in pain the last few years. But he liked to pitch and he pitched as well as a man can.

What Sandy doesn't miss about baseball is the spotlight. He was as private a person as I've ever known, and he hated attention. Even as a coach he would attract attention. He knows it and doesn't want it. However, he learned to live with it while he had to. He's happy to be away from it, but I don't think it drove him out.

I think what drove him out was his fear of becoming crippled. There was an old pitcher named Fat Freddie Fitzsimmons who became a coach for the Cubs. He had been a screwball pitcher who twisted his arm when he threw, and he wound up with a short, bent arm. He carried it kind of funny and when Sandy saw him it scared him. Sandy's arm was already a mess.

He said, "Jeez, I don't want to wind up looking like a cripple. I want to be able to brush my teeth and comb my hair."

So he got out.

He was probably the straightest guy I ever knew. And one of the nicest. He never screwed around, never had a bad word to say about anybody. He dated, but he seemed to be waiting around for the one right girl. He was such a good-looking guy, such a star, that he could have had more women than anyone, but he didn't want just anyone. The stews used to bust their asses to serve him, but he ignored them.

I remember one time Jill St. John, the movie star, called his room. Sandy's roomie, Dick Tracewski, took the call, and Sandy said, "Tell her I'm not in." Dick couldn't believe it. We couldn't either, when we heard about it. But that was Sandy. She was a real looker, but he didn't know her so he didn't want anything to do with her.

I think he only really relaxed among his teammates. He treated them all as equals and he wanted to be just one of the guys. Sometimes he was like a big kid, kidding around with them. There is a sort of fraternity among athletes. We feel like we're the only ones who know how it is for each other. But when you leave it, you no longer belong. When you come back,' you feel like an intruder. So you hate to come back.

But you miss it. We all do. I'm sure Sandy does.

Our other pitching star of that time, Don Drysdale, was a different type. He didn't mind the spotlight. He didn't look for it, but it didn't bother him. He's still in it, as one of the better broadcasters. There's also been some talk of him becoming a manager. He's very bright, he knows the game, and he can talk and deal with people. But he has a couple of restaurants in the Los Angeles area that are doing well and he likes the area. And he and his wife have a horse ranch.

Driz, as I called him, was, however, a very volatile guy. He had a hair-trigger temper. He was a good guy, but he could be as mean as Sandy was clean. Driz could drink like no man I've ever known. My wife and I used to go out to dinner with Driz and Perranoski and their wives and long after the rest of us were done drinking, Driz was still going strong. He could hold it, too. He could drink most men under the table.

I do remember him drunk one time coming home from a winning World Series. We were playing cards on the plane and he wanted into the game. We let him in figuring he was so drunk he was easy money. It turned out he took us for everything we had. His legs might have been wobbly, but his head was still on straight.

I remember he got into an argument with his wife that night. Ginger might have had one too many that night, too. They hollered at each other right out in the open. But they were always arguing. And they also always loved each other. Even though they split up once, they've been together a long time.

Ginger was a lot like my wife in that she was into that socializing with the Hollywood set, but she was a sweet kid. And for all his temper, you had to really respect Big D.

There are screened box seats behind home plate and between the dugouts at Dodger Stadium that are built at field level. The people that sit in them actually sit below field level, with the upper part of their bodies above. A lot of stars sit in these seats. One time Liz Taylor was sitting in one in an especially low-cut dress. Driz didn't miss much. He was pitching and his first pitch went way wide, wild, and right up to the screen in front of her box. I went back to pick it up and when I looked down there was Liz, both of them. It took me a long time to pick up the ball. When I did, I didn't throw it, but took it back to the mound. When I handed it to Driz, I asked him what kind of pitch that was supposed to be. He smiled and said, "I just like to take care of my catcher."

Perranoski was Mr. Cool. Which is what made him a great reliever. He could drink right along with Driz, but Perry could put it away without getting drunk, and he always treated his teammates well. He was just a happy-go-lucky guy.

Podres was one of Buzzie Bavasi's guys, along with Don Zimmer and Al Ferrara and Willie Davis and a few others. Buzzie liked guys who liked to party, who liked to hoist a drink or three, who liked to gamble, who played poker, who followed the horses. They became a sort of club within our club.

Podres and Ferrara were Damon Runyon characters. They talked their own language and they were funny fellows. They were always talking about broads and horses. They acted like they were always standing on a streetcorner.

We called Podres "Point" because he had a pointed head. He was single and a free spirit. He was willing to do anything for a good time and he did everything you can imagine. He drank a lot and didn't hold it too well.

One time in Chicago he got drunk and got rolled, raised hell, and wound up in jail. Alston got pissed off because he had to roll out of the sack at dawn to bail out his ballplayer.

I don't think a ballplayer who got into the trouble Podres got into would be kept by the Dodgers now, but Bavasi was protective of his high-spirited pals. And, to their credit, they produced. Bavasi was a very smart general manager, but he did have a weakness for certain types.

He and Alston and Mr. O'Malley and the others put up with a lot from Willie Davis before they finally let him go, and several teams have let him go since. Willie was strange. He didn't drink a lot, but he ran a lot. I think the Dodgers talked him into marrying his girl friend because they thought it would settle him down, but it didn't. He and Gina had a rocky road before they got to the end of it.

Willie was a winner at cards. I used to play with Jim Brewer and Phil "the Vulture" Regan, and we'd hate it when Willie would sit in. Not because he won, but because of the way he won. He would sit in a poker pot with nothing and always wind up with the card he needed to win. He had long, graceful fingers and we always suspected he was cheating, but we never caught him. I guess he was just good. Real good.

Hell, I won more than my share. I made a lot of money playing cards while with the Dodgers. I have no cause to complain. It's just that Willie was too lucky to be for real. We watched him like a hawk, without drawing blood. We called him Slick, and he was that.

He was a natural athlete. Tommy Davis and I took him out to a golf course one time and he got hooked on the game. He bought golf books and studied the game and played every chance he could. By the time I had all but given up the game, he had conquered it and was shooting in the seventies. There wasn't anything he couldn't do if he put his mind to it. The trouble was, his mind was mixed up.

Nothing was ever enough for Willie and he was never satisfied. He was always screwing around with his batting stance. He was always screwing around with some new fad or religion. Later on, I heard he'd sit at his locker and chant. It didn't help him hit .300. Oh, he was a good player a lot of the time, but he was always on the verge of being the best, and he never became that.

No one knew Willie. Not really. He was always into his own thing, doing something different.

Until Lou Johnson came along, the Dodgers didn't put up with a player's problems the way they did with Willie's and Podres's. I think Willie got into debt, too, but Johnson set all the records in this respect. Lou was a good ballplayer for a while, but not that good. He wasn't a bad guy but he was unreliable.

Lou ran real hard. He spent a lot of money he never had. He got into his teammates for some we never got back, and he got into the business community pretty well.

One afternoon I was in Bavasi's office when he got a call from Sy Devore. Bavasi asked me who the hell Sy Devore was. I said, "Buzzie, you got to be kidding. He's got the top clothing store in Hollywood." So Buzzie got on the phone and said. "Hi, Sy." Then he listened a long time. Finally he said, "I'll take care of it."

It turned out that Buzzie had taken all of Johnson's credit cards from him and had him on an allowance while his back bills were being paid off, but Lou was still charging stuff all over town and he'd run up a big bill at Devore's that the Dodgers had to make good on. Before long, it became bad business for the Dodgers to keep him on the club. He only lasted three or four years.

Lou put out on the playing field, but he let it get away from him off the field. He was one of those like Willie Davis who wasted a lot of ability. And a lot of money. You can get used to fat paychecks fast and it's easy to spend dough as if it will always be rolling in. Sooner or later, you've spent more than you had to spend, the money stops, your lifestyle is shot all to hell, and, in some cases, your life too.

I don't mean to say they were all like that. Most weren't. Some were as straight as they could be, like Koufax, who got out with a lot of dough. And Drysdale has made a lot of money. I don't think Don Demeter ever made a lot of money, but he was straight. The big guy was very religious and used to get on me a lot about the bad language I used. I learned a lot of bad language in the service. It fit in the big leagues. But Don used to ask, "John, are those words necessary?" He became my buddy and I cleaned up my act for a while when he was around, but then he went on his way and I went back to my old way.

Don Sutton was, and is, another straight guy who is very religious, never goes in for bad language, and probably sets about as good an example for a youngster as an athlete can. In 1977 when an umpire complained that Don had cursed him and had been fined for it, I couldn't believe it. Don denied it, and I believe him. He might have hassled the ump, but I never heard him curse.

Frank Howard was another who never cursed or ran around. He did drink, but he didn't get drunk. It's just that he was the biggest guy I've ever known and he could put away a can of beer in one gulp and a case in one hour. He also would pick up a head of lettuce and down it in a couple of big bites. He had an appetite on him that didn't stop. If a waitress tried to take his plate away from him, he'd eat her arm. Frank was a nice guy but a real rube. He wore clothes that didn't match and he wore the same clothes all the time. I think he slept in them. I don't think he ever took them off. He looked like an unmade bed. King-size. He's still in baseball, as a coach, and I guess he's smoothed out some. I'd be afraid he'd break my back for speaking disrespectfully of him, except he was such a nice guy he'd never hurt anyone.

Jim Gilliam was a quiet guy, but he had a mean streak that the players saw, even if others didn't. Once we went out to a fine restaurant to eat with our wives and the owner himself came over. Polite as could be, he said, "Good evening, ladies and gentlemen. Happy to have you here. I hope you enjoy yourselves. Perhaps I could suggest something from the menu."

Loud and clear, The Devil snapped, "We know what we want and we don't need any help from anyone."

I was embarrassed. The other diners all looked at us in surprise and the owner walked away in shock. I was happy just to have that meal over with. That was the way Jim was.

He was suspicious of people, often curt with them, hard, direct. He said what he thought and he didn't always think things through. He had a chip on his shoulder, waiting for someone to knock it off. But I believe he has mellowed with the years. He was always a smart baseball man and he has been a good coach for the Dodgers.

A guy like Tommy Davis, he'd make a good coach, but there doesn't seem to be a place for him anymore. He was a straight, clean fellow, who loved just playing more than anything else. He bounced around to a lot of teams late in his career just so he could continue to play. Now he would make a marvelous batting coach, but he's out of baseball.

I don't want to make too much of the race thing. There's always room in baseball for a black who can play. But there doesn't seem to be much room for him after he no longer can play. There are only a few in administration and most were big stars. There has been only one black manager. Is there a team with more than one black coach? There are some with none.

TD was promised a lot of jobs that haven't happened. When I called him to ask if he was going to an old-timers' game, he said, "I don't think so, John, I'm just not ready for that yet." I know how he feels, because I couldn't bring myself to go to one of those for years after my playing career ended.

For one thing, you don't feel like an old-timer for a while. For another, you feel like maybe they haven't done much for you, so why should you do something for them? But then you see that this old-time thing they do is partly for you. So I go to them now because it's great to get together again with the Dodgers of my day.

18.

THERE were a lot of good ballplayers and some great ones during the years I was in the National League. Heading the list had to be Henry Aaron, Willie Mays, Stan Musial, and Roberto Clemente. And there were a lot of good pitchers and some great ones. Tops were Juan Marichal, Bob Gibson, and Warren Spahn.

Marichal and Gibson were about even in my mind. Maybe I'd give an edge to Marichal because he had more variety. You might think I wouldn't put him up here because of our rhubarb, but he was one of the best and no one can take that from him.

Marichal was an unusual pitcher in that he had a lot of motion and a lot of pitches. He had a great big kick up front. He gave you a lot of leg to look at. Then he came at you with a lot of different pitches.

Many pitchers have had a lot of different pitches, but few have had more than a couple that were really good. Everything Marichal threw he threw well. He had a heck of a high, hard one he wasn't afraid to throw under your chin. He had a good, straight change-up. A right-hander, he had a good slider, almost a screwball, he could throw on the outside part of the plate to left-handers. And he had an exceptional curve, especially effective against right-handed hitters.

You could never guess what or where he was going to throw because he wasn't afraid to use any of his pitches in any situation. Usually, you know a pitcher is going to go to his strength in a tough situation and you just try to match your strength to his, but you never knew what Juan was going to. And he could throw everything anywhere he wanted. For a hard thrower he had exceptional control.

Gibson threw harder. He also had a great slider. He was a powerful pitcher. He wasn't as cute as Marichal, but he didn't have to be because he could overpower you. Jim Bunning and Jim Maloney were others who could overpower you. Bunning was a little cuter, but at his best Maloney was one of the best. On his good days he was like Koufax and Ryan. You couldn't touch him.

On the other side of the coin were guys like Ferguson Jenkins and Gaylord Perry. Actually, Perry threw almost as hard as anyone and always struck out a lot of batters, but his strength also may have been that he threw hard and had a hell of a spitter. He could put his pitches wherever he wanted them. Jenkins had even control and seldom made a bad pitch. He was always in complete control.

Spahn was probably the best left-hander I opposed. He threw a good fast ball, a great curve ball, and a good change-up, and he had great control. He never gave you a good pitch to hit. He was smart. And he was remarkably consistent. Every fourth day he went out there and pitched a great game. He won twenty-one or twenty-two games a season for seven or eight straight seasons. Others had off years, but never Spahn.

Spahn and Lew Burdette were the best one-two pitching punch we had to face. Burdette had the best spitball I ever batted against. He was accused of it all the time and he denied it all the time, but if you were batting against him you knew he threw it even if you couldn't prove it. And he drove us crazy.

I don't know what he used. Maybe saliva or Vaseline or slippery elm or some kind of jelly. Different pitchers who threw spitters over the years used different lubricants. They put them on the ball different ways. But when they threw them, their fingers slipped over the moist part of the ball and it came up to the plate without any rotation at all.

Thrown hard, it dips suddenly. You can see it coming, but it's almost impossible to get your bat on the damn thing. And if you do, you're going to hit on top of it and hit it down to the ground. Burdette was a capable pitcher without it. He had different pitches that he threw well. But the spitter was his "out" pitch. And anytime he was in trouble and needed a ground ball for a force play or double play, he threw it.

A fork ball will do the same sort of thing, but not many can master the fork ball. You spread your index and middle fingers so you can jam the ball between them and when you throw the ball hard it comes up without spinning and suddenly dips. Elroy Face had mastered it and it made him the best of the relief pitchers I opposed. He'd follow a fast-ball pitcher in the late innings and throw you right off balance.

Bruce Sutter, the Cubs' relief-pitching sensation of 1977, is said to throw a fork ball like Face's.

Musial had slowed down by the time I arrived, but he hung on for quite a few years and still was able to show me some things. He was in the outfield when I came up but later finished on first base. He wasn't outstanding defensively, but he did the job and hustled hard. He was outstanding offensively. He had a strange stance, a screwed-down crouch. But he'd uncoil and kill the pitch.

Musial used a bat with a very thin handle and not much of a barrel. It was like a twig compared to the tree trunks guys like Dick Allen swung. You'd think you could kill his hands by pitching him in on his fists and stinging the thinnest part of the stick. But it didn't bother him. He had great control of the bat and a terrifically fast swing. He had sharp eyes and didn't swing at bad pitches. You'd make a great pitch to him and he'd hit it. It didn't matter where you pitched to him, he could get his bat on it and hit line drives. He hit to all fields equally well, and he hit with power.

The difference between the high-average hitters of today and the high-average hitters of yesterday is that today's don't hit with the power of a Musial or a Ted Williams. They not only got hits, but they hit home runs. And only a Rod Carew, without power, hits for anything like the average of a Musial or a Williams.

Like Carew, Pete Rose gets his hits, though he doesn't hit home runs. He gets two hundred hits or close to it every year.

He has good eyes, fast hands, and quick reflexes. He has good concentration and is intense at the plate. Some guys get a hit or two and they're relaxed and through for the day, but if Pete gets two, he wants three, and if he gets three, he wants four. He was just developing when I played against him, and he had a weakness. He couldn't hit the inside pitch too well and we got him out by jamming him. But he worked to overcome it. He'll hit anything thrown to him now, and to all fields.

The story we got out of Cincinnati was that when Pete first came up he got close to Frank Robinson and Vada Pinson. The Reds' brass thought he got too close and got rid of Robinson and Pinson to break it up. It was a black-white thing, the story goes, and also a matter of Frank being hard to handle and outspoken and maybe being a bad influence on Pete.

Robinson was a tremendous hitter, of course. He hit for high average and also with power. He had a quick bat and could hit a pitch out of any park. One of the things that bothered everyone about Robby was that he stood right on top of the plate with his elbows cocked out over the plate, just daring you to hit him with a pitch. The result was he got hit with a lot of pitches. He hollered, but he asked for it.

Actually, he had a bit of a weakness. He was hit so much that he'd pull away from the inside pitch sometimes and you could get him out on it. You had to set him up for it. If he knew it was coming, he'd dig in and hit it. But if he didn't expect it, and got it, he'd pull away. So we'd brush him back maybe twice in an at-bat. After the first one, he'd think that was that. Then he'd get a second one. We used to spin him like a top. But he was a hard out.

But the thing that bothered me most about Robby was his habit of spitting between pitches. He'd step in and spit, and if the wind wasn't right it would come right back through my mask. You hate to tell a guy to stop spitting and I didn't know if it was deliberate so I didn't want to start a fight for nothing. I have a hunch he always knew what he was doing and took any edge he could get.

Robby was respected as a smart competitor. He was a good guy but as mean as he had to be. Like Musial, Pinson was as good as a guy could be, a gentleman, without any meanness to him. He was as effortless an athlete as I ever saw. He did everything gracefully.

The showiest player was Roberto Clemente. He did everything gracefully and effectively. He was a great all-around player in all respects except that he didn't have a lot of power. But he could pull the ball a long way at times. He had good eyes, good hands, good reflexes. He stood way back in the batter's box so you thought you should be able to get him out outside, but he had it covered. He had the body and bat control to get good wood on the outside pitch and he hit to all fields.

He didn't make the marvelous catches of a Willie Mays, but he caught everything hit anywhere near him, and he had an amazing arm. When I first came up and played in Pittsburgh's old Forbes Field they had a high right-field wall a little like the one in Ebbets Field, except this one was concrete all the way and angled out sharply. A left-handed hitter, who could run, I figured if I ricocheted a hit off that wall I had to have a stand-up double or triple. They told me I couldn't do that with Clemente out there, but I didn't believe them. I figured it took two perfect plays to catch me— perfect play on the ball off the wall and a perfect peg to second. Three, really, because the second baseman had to handle the throw well, hang in there, and put the tag on me if I slid hard. I know how hard it is to hang in there when a runner is sliding into you hard, so I always slid late and hard in hopes of moving a baseman or catcher back.

The first time I banked the ball off the wall I raced for second, only to find the ball waiting for me. The second time, the same thing happened. I watched when others did it and saw how he played the carom perfectly, whirled, and fired a perfect strike to second. I've never seen any player play a particular tricky situation so well. I became cautious because I saw it was suicide to go for second every time in that situation. But I also became frustrated and there were still times when I went for it. I figured Clemente had to make a mistake sometime. I must have tried it twenty times and he never made a mistake. I never made it.

Clemente was a classy ballplayer and his premature death

in a plane crash was a real loss to baseball. He was something of a hot dog. He did things with a flourish and he was always complaining of injury or illness. But, moaning or groaning, he always went out and played perfectly.

There are guys who get to you because they have some puss in them. Pete Rose might be one. Charlie Hustle. Running all the damn time. Not afraid to get his uniform dirty. Frankly, I think he likes to get it dirty. It's his image. And I don't think anyone feels like running like crazy every time you change sides between innings. But Rose always has played hard and you have to respect him.

Ernie Banks was just too good to be believed. Maybe it's sacrilege, but I believe Banks was a con artist. He was always smiling and always telling you what a great day it was for baseball and what a great game baseball was and how lucky we all were that we were getting to play two today. No one smiles all the time naturally unless they're putting it on and putting you on. Every day of our lives isn't a good one, and there are even times when we don't want to play baseball, especially doubleheaders.

I used to say to Ernie, "Jesus, look at the dark sky. It's cloudy. It's not a great day." And he'd say, "There's a sun behind those clouds, my man." Ernie was a fair shortstop who wound up as a fair first baseman. I used to say, "C'mon, Ernie, maybe it's a great day to play two if you're fucking off at first base, but if you've got to get down in a crouch to catch eighteen innings it's nothing to look forward to." And he'd say, "You're lucky you can catch, my friend."

Ernie was a skinny guy who had hands like lightning. He used a thin, light bat and he whipped it with tremendous speed. He had more power than any player his size I ever saw. Hit a lot of home runs off us, off everyone. A great hitter. But also a great big pain in the ass. I can't believe he believed all that shit he spread around, but that was his image and it made him a kind of folk hero in the game. It made me sick.

Willie Mays was a good-natured guy, but he didn't run off at the mouth about it. He had a good disposition but he didn't rub it in. Oh, I guess he wasn't always agreeable to the press and public, but among ballplayers he acted like a big, grown-up kid. He really liked to play and I think he was the most talented. He could do it all about as well as anyone. Mays made miraculous catches and throws, and he hit for average and with power. He took advantage of any mistakes made against him. If you hesitated going to second, he threw there. If you hesitated fielding a single, he went to second. If you caught him in a rundown, he was a rundown and a half. He was sensational on the bases. It wasn't that he was so fast, it was that he had such amazing reflexes.

Willie had one weakness. He hated to be hit by pitches. He especially hated to bat against Drysdale because Don would drill him. Willie used to come to the plate sweettalking me, thinking that I wouldn't give Don the signal to drill him. Then Don would come inside and Willie would hit the dirt and he'd get up saying, in that real high, squeaky voice of his, "What's wrong with that motherfucker? What does that crazy motherfucker want to hurt me for?" And I'd just laugh and say, "Willie, he don't want to hurt you, he just wants your respect." And Willie would shake his head and step back in real carefully.

It was well known that Willie would bail out on the high, hard one inside. But what was not well known was that you couldn't hit him. He hit the dirt as fast as any player I ever saw. And when he didn't hit the dirt, he bailed out only with his front foot. Like he had stepped in a bucket and was pulling it out. It's called a bucket swing. You'd think that would make him a soft touch for an outside pitch. But he had such a powerful upper body and arms, such quick hands and hips, he could still pivot and reach out with the rest of his body and hit the outside pitch hard. His teammates told me that his philosophy of hitting was that if he was facing a tough pitcher he'd swing at anything close to get it over with, figuring he could pick on the patsies the rest of the time. Yet, he was tough on tough pitchers because, even swinging at anything, he was always dangerous.

Willie was a little on the wild side, but I believe Leo Durocher had a great influence on him and kept him in control. Even when Leo wasn't managing him, Willie always went to Leo for advice. There was never a time when Leo wasn't building Willie up. They had the ultimate manager-player relationship. Leo brought out the best in Willie. Leo brought out the best in a lot of ballplayers. Leo was special and Willie wound up with an incredible career.

I remember being introduced at an old-timers' game recently and standing on the field and listening to the announcer read off a list of acomplishments of the next player to be introduced and wondering who in the world did all those things, only to find out it was Willie. Even admiring him as I did, it was easy to have forgotten just how much he did.

Even so, I had a terrific argument with a friend when I observed that Henry Aaron was the best ballplayer I ever saw. Willie did everything with a flair, but Henry did everything Willie did. Willie had a little hot dog in him, while Henry went about his work quietly. Willie overshadowed Henry, but Henry just kept going on his own way until his accomplishments were even more than Mays had. I am not saying this because Henry broke Babe Ruth's lifetime home-run record. That just brought attention to Aaron at last. But there was never a time the ballplayers didn't see Henry for the great player he was. He maybe wasn't as fantastic a fielder as Willie was, but Henry could go get them and throw with the best of them. He didn't steal as many bases, but he wasn't thrown out as often. Willie made few mistakes, but Henry made less. Willie had a weakness, but Henry didn't. There was no way you could pitch to Henry without him being able to hit it hard. Willie would run hot and cold, but Henry was always the same, always on his game, game in and game out, year in and year out.

Which is not to put Willie down. Mays was a marvel, as was Aaron. They, an aging Musial, and the late Clemente were the best ballplayers I ever saw.

You may not have noticed, but I didn't include any catchers in my list. There were not any great catchers in the National League in my time. I thought John Bateman would become a great catcher. He had the size, the strength, and the all-around ability, but he never developed into anything but an average performer. It's hard to say why some players don't develop. Different reasons for different players, I suppose. But many of the players with the best ability did not become the best players.

Sometimes a team will take a player down with it. Houston

is one team that has held back players. I don't know why, unless playing indoors is hard on players. But Bateman never came through there. Neither did Joe Morgan until he was traded away from there. Although he was small, Joe was sturdy. You could see he had all-around ability and the quick swing to be a strong hitter, but he didn't become a star until he was sent to Cincinnati. Today, there is no player around with more ability than Cesar Cedeno, but in Houston he has deteriorated instead of developing.

I think the most complete catcher during my time in the league was Del Crandall. He was sound defensively. He could catch the bad pitch and block the plate. He didn't have a strong arm, but he made up for it with a quick release and with accuracy. At bat, he had holes you could pitch to, but he hung in there and gave you problems and hit with power at times. He was just a good basic catcher. Joe Torre was just breaking in behind him at that time, a good hitter, but never a great catcher.

Smokey Burgess attracted attention with his bat, but he couldn't catch worth a damn. He was sloppy giving signals and you could steal his signs all the time. He had trouble with the hard pitch and didn't throw well. But he could get out of bed at midnight and get a base hit, as they say. He became a super pinch hitter, toughest I ever saw. A little, dumpy guy, he could get his bat on a ball and hit the hell out of it.

Frankly, I think I became the best catcher in the league in the 1960s. No Johnny Bench by any means, but Bench didn't come along until later. Bench was by far the best all-around catcher to come along in years. You can't compare me to him. But I was at least one of the best in my years. I made a lot of all-star teams and deserved it.

19.

As a kid I learned to catch by listening to those who knew how it was done. I made the majors with a lot still to learn.

One time, I was squared around behind the plate trying to catch Sal Maglie's outside pitches. Sal said, "Kid, when I'm going to throw outside, you move outside. If the outside corner of the plate runs right down your middle, I can cut the corner of the plate by pitching right down the middle." Maglie lived on the outside part of the plate. He didn't want them to hit anything from the middle of the plate in.

Sal's arm was shot by then, but he still knew how to pitch. He couldn't throw hard, but he could throw three different kind of curves and he could cut the corner of the plate with each one. He said, "Baby, if I throw my fast ball, you can bet I'm gonna knock them on their asses with it. I will never let them hit my fast ball because it isn't fast enough. I'm gonna make them hit the pitch I want them to hit. I'm gonna throw inside to drive them back, then outside to get them out. I'm gonna show them the fast ball, then hook them on the curve."

From Maglie and others I learned that there was much more to catching than the technical, physical part. The pitcher runs the show. He can shake off any sign you give him. But you don't want him to shake off any more signs than necessary. You want to give him the signs he wants to get. You have to get together with him before every game and decide how you want to work on every batter. You have to get together with him over so many games that you know how he wants to work.

You have to build a rapport, become buddies. You have to know your pitcher, what he can and can't do.

The Dodgers always worked on these things. They worked with their pitchers and they worked on the batters they had to pitch to. The Dodgers always had pitchers who could control their pitches well enough to work on the batters. Until he could, even Koufax couldn't win consistently. No one can. Not even Nolan Ryan. Ryan wins a lot, but he also loses a lot. You have to have the physical ability, but you also have to put the mental to it, too. When I went to other clubs I was surprised how many didn't.

A lot of managers just let their pitchers pitch. What the pitcher throws best, that's what he throws. But if that's what the batter hits best, the pitcher is in trouble. You have to balance it out. You can only go strength on strength when you're stronger. Or when the other guy is least expecting it. You have to mix up your pitches and move the ball around and try to get the batter off balance. Make him hit the pitch you want him to hit.

The thinking part of the game I found really fun. I got to feeling we could outguess the other guys. Not all of the time, but most of the time. And enough to win most of the time. Of course, I was working with pitchers who could do it. I was working with Sandy Koufax and Don Drysdale and Claude Osteen and Don Sutton and Ron Perranoski and Phil Regan, and they had the ability to do what had to be done. Without that ability, you're beat.

I was also working with the manager on behalf of the team. When a pitcher gets in trouble and a manager or pitching coach goes out to the mound to talk to him and to talk to the catcher, most pitchers will lie if they have to. They'll say they're all right, because they want to stay in. The catcher, if he wants to keep the confidence of the pitcher, can't cut the mound out from under him. Alston understood this, so we had an understanding that when I thought the pitcher didn't have it or was losing it, I'd signal to him with a wave of my glove so he knew what he had to do without asking me in front of the pitcher or asking the pitcher.

Physically, I mastered the fundamentals of catching fairly

fast. I was thrown in and it was sink or swim. I caught 100 or more games about eleven or twelve seasons in a row in the majors, usually 130 to 140 games. I didn't miss many games from injuries and I learned my trade on the job. I led the league in passed balls my first full season, but I learned to block the low, wild pitch. I learned to handle the high, twisting foul flies behind the plate. I learned to catch throws at the plate, make a tag, and take a hard hit or slide without letting the ball go. I led the league in errors early in my career, but most of those came on throws, and I was a throwing catcher. A lot of catchers won't make many errors because they won't make many throws.

When I broke in in Brooklyn I was trying to throw overhand from my crouch behind the plate. Campy told me, "Boy, you get moving with that throw, you get moving across the plate, and throw from in front of the plate, and throw overhand or sidearm or underarm or any way you can get rid of the ball fast. You get it to second as quick as you can, any way you can. You don't have to be fancy. If you throw fast, the runner can't outrun the ball. The 'speed cop' will get 'em every time." To Campy, the "speed cop" was the thrown ball, which would beat the runner every time.

I listened and I learned. I found a comfortable throwing motion, about three-quarters overarm, and I threw moving toward the base as fast as I could. I had a good arm to begin with and developed speed and accuracy. I paid attention. I got to know the base runners and the third-base coaches and the managers and the situations in which teams or runners would run so I could anticipate developments. I got to know them so I could see what they were doing and sometimes I could see them doing something different and steal a sign from a third-base coach or get a tipoff from a runner when he was going.

The pitchers helped because the Dodgers always worked on the fine points like pickoff plays and holding runners on. They taught their pitchers good pickoff motions and they had them throw to first base enough to keep the runners close to the base and to keep them from getting a good jump on the catcher. The stealer steals on both the pitcher and the catcher, as much one as the other, and if one doesn't do his job he's giving the runner the steal. Runners didn't steal much on us. We also picked off a lot of base runners. I was never afraid to throw to a base to try to pick off a runner. If I threw bad, I picked up an error. But my percentage was good.

The only pitcher we had who wouldn't try to pick off runners very often and didn't even want to throw a pitchout when I thought a runner was going to go was Koufax. He was always afraid of throwing the ball away and told me he had more confidence in his ability to get the batter out than in our chances of getting the runner with what he considered a trick play. I had to go along with him because he was Koufax. But generally I was willing to take chances because I believe aggressive baseball pays off.

I never led the league in fielding percentage, but most times it is catchers who are afraid to take chances who lead the league in fielding percentage. I still hold several big-league records for chances and putouts, yet I made less than ten errors a season most of my seasons in the majors. And I played in twenty-one World Series games and three all-star games and one playoff game without one error. Twice I was voted Golden Glove awards as the best fielding catcher in the league by the other players. I'm proud of that. I was no Roy Campanella or Johnny Bench, but Roseboro wasn't too bad a catcher.

One of the funny things that happened to me behind the plate didn't seem funny to me at the time. It was a hot night in Dodger Stadium. With all the gear we wear, a hot night can get to you. If you've eaten the wrong thing, you might start to feel sick. Umpires wear a lot, too. The umpire that night, Paul Pryor, had drunk the wrong thing. Leaning over, he threw up all over me. He'd been drinking green beer and it came out green. We wiped up, but smelled bad the rest of the night.

Poor Pryor got the nickname the Puker from that. Leo Durocher, coaching for us, liked to ride him, "Hey, Puker, that green beer will get you every time!"

I shuddered whenever it was Paul "the Puker" Pryor's turn to work behind the plate behind me after that.

It's tough back there, believe me. Even with the big glove, both hands take a beating. You catch a pitcher like Drysdale and your hands are going to be bruised. Koufax threw the fastest pitch I ever caught, but he threw what we call a light ball. It has something to do with the spin. Driz threw hard and he threw the heaviest ball I ever had to catch. It felt like a big rock bruising through your mitt. Stan Williams threw a hard, heavy ball and it hurt, too.

If you don't catch a ball right or it's fouled back into your hands, the fingers of both hands will take a beating. Some of mine are bent from the beating they took. All old catchers have bent fingers. I used to split my right index finger all the time. It seemed like every time I took a foul tip it was on the same finger. Bill Buhler, the Dodgers' trainer, used to bind the finger with gauze and soak it in an antiseptic cement that would harden like a cast so I could still catch with a split finger. He had to develop devices to protect me.

I caught so many foul tips on my feet that even with the heavy shoes I wore my toenails would split and my toes would bruise and swell up. I've got toenails growing on top of toenails to this day from all the foul tips on my poor feet. Sometimes blood clots would form beneath the nail. Buhler would take a special little drill and go right through the nail to the clot. When he hit it it hurt like hell. Blood would spurt from it like we'd struck oil. But it would relieve the pressure and the pain so I could continue to catch.

Some pitchers have pitches that sink or rise so sharply they cause more foul tips than others. Joe Moeller had a live fast ball that was always being fouled off my fingers or my toes. One day when he was pitching, Dick Stuart fouled one right back so hard it wedged right through the opening in my face mask and hit my right eye a hell of a lick. I reeled back, ripping off my mask, and went to my knees in pain, I thought I'd lost my eye. Buhler rushed me to a hospital. It turned out the ball had scratched the cornea and I saw spots for weeks.

It was about as bad as when Marichal hit me with the bat and almost knocked my eye out of its socket.

I was warming up a pitcher named Gene Snyder one time in the Coliseum bullpen when he threw the ball into the dirt at the front of the plate and it bounced up and hit me in the mouth. I had to be helped to the clubhouse, bleeding like a stuck bull. I remember walking those fifty feet or so to the dugout and seeing the horrified faces of the spectators. When I looked in the mirror, my lips were split, teeth were dangling, and blood was dripping all over me.

I had to have a dentist clean out my mouth. Eight teeth had been broken off and he had to dig out the splinters. And a bone beneath my nose had been broken and had to be set. I missed some games, but I got some good out of it. I'd always had buck teeth, but the Dodgers provided me with Hollywood teeth, about a thousand dollars' worth of the best bridgework you ever saw, making me a handsome dude.

From then on, I always smoothed dirt around the edges of the plate so the ground was even with the plate and there were no sharp edges to kick a pitch in the dirt into my face.

I lifted weights to build up my body so I could take contact at the plate without being bruised too badly. I'm stocky and built solid and have that football background. I always could take a hard blow well, but you'll be hurt if you're hit.

I had learned from football how to go out to meet a runner coming into you and how to get low to lift him. But you have to have the ball. If the runner comes in at the same time with the throw or beats the throw, you have to hold your ground and accept the hit. Your job is to block the plate, keep him from getting to it too easily.

Bob Skinner bowled me over one day and I dropped the ball. I started using a mitt smaller than the usual catcher's mitt, almost like a first baseman's glove, so I could glove it fast and keep it tight in the claw. It helped me make a quick, swiping tag on a runner without losing the ball.

Frank Robinson sliced my arm so badly sliding spikes-high one time I still have the scar. After that, I tended to tag guys so hard they'd feel it, remember it, and maybe be intimidated by it. If I knocked them head over heels they'd think twice before barreling into me next time. I got a reputation as a guy who would hurt other guys and they'd come into me cautiously, which was the ideal situation for me.

The first guy who tried to take me out was Daryl Spencer. I raised up under him and sent him somersaulting through the air. He lit on his butt and bounced a couple of times. He never tried to take me after that. Orlando Cepeda tried to run right over me. He wasn't too fast, but he was big. He was trying to hurt me, so I hurt him. I hit him with a cross-body block, caught his leg, and almost broke it. As a matter of fact, I screwed up his knee for life. I'm not proud of it, but it was him or me.

Tim McCarver hurt me. Alston was trying Tommy Davis at third. Tommy was tried a lot of places because he threw almost like a girl. A ball was hit to him and he threw a lob home. McCarver, fast for a catcher, was coming home. The ball and McCarver arrived at the same time. I braced myself, caught the ball, and made the tag as Tim hit me. He hit me so hard my glasses flew off and were broken. I was wearing glasses at that time to correct astigmatism in one eye. He hit my right knee and it has been screwed up ever since. I'll have aches and pains there the rest of my days.

I always backed up first base whenever I could. One time Julian Javier singled, saw that the first baseman was far from the bag, and rounded the base a long way to see if he could continue to second. Then he saw me moving to first base to take a throw behind him. He barged back in, burying his head in my shoulder. He almost broke his neck and was out two weeks. But he almost broke my shoulder and it's never been the same.

At times I have lost my temper and done dumb things. One time late in my career Campy Campaneris was stealing bases on me, which bothered me. We caught Campy in a rundown between third and home. I ran him back to third, which was the proper play up to the point where I didn't throw to the third baseman. Campy expected the throw, started to turn back toward home, saw me with the ball, turned back to third, and was a dead duck. I hit him in the back with the ball and both hands and both elbows.

I drove him down into the dirt and toppled onto him. He cut my pants legs in a couple of places as he kicked to get free and to get at me. I let him up and let him mouth off at me but I didn't take up his challenge to fight because I knew he was right. I had tried to humiliate him with the tag the way he had humiliated me stealing bases, and I knew I was wrong. I wanted to play hard, not dirty.

Jim Brosnan, who was a pitcher, tried to run right over me

one time. He wore glasses, read books, and actually he wrote a couple. He considered himself an intellectual. I considered him a puss. He hurled himself at me and I hit him in the middle and raised him into a full flip and he landed flat on his back with a hell of a jolt.

Brosnan later said it was a dirty play and he called me a dirty player in one of his books, but I just did to him what he was ready to do to me. You see how a guy is coming in at you and you make a judgment if he is friend or foe. Brosnan was a pitcher and he should not have come in trying to knock me over unless he was prepared to pay the price. If he had slid he wouldn't have been hurt.

There are two kinds of slides. There is the spikes-up slide, in which the slider is trying to cut or at least intimidate the baseman or the catcher. And there is the get-safe slide, in which the slider is trying to score with the skill of his slide. The good base runners like Frank Robinson or Willie Mays always slid late so they could take a split second longer to see if you had the ball, where you had it, and what you were going to do with it, so that they could come in hard at the toughest place for you to put a tag on them.

I always left the outside part of the plate unprotected so the runner would see it and go for it, and I'd know where to go for him. Nine times out of ten it worked. If I knew where they were going, I could get them. That way they weren't going to get me, I was going to get them.

The really skillful slider uses both legs. He hooks with one, scissors with the other, and makes it tough to get a piece of him. You have to get down in the dirt with him, get right into his flying feet and sharp spikes, and take your chances.

I was hurt a lot. By the end of my career my right shoulder was shot, which was my throwing shoulder, and I had to take cortisone shots to keep playing. They take the longest, thickest needle you ever saw, stick it deep into your shoulder, wriggle it around, and keep sticking it in and wriggling it around until they find the sore spot. It hurts like hell until they find it. When they do, it takes the pain away for a while, so you can play.

Although there are some arrogant guys who treat trainers

and clubhouse men like servants and a few who treat them like dirt, most major leaguers respect the jobs these men do for the players. Guys like Bill Buhler, the trainer, and big John Griffin and Nobe Kawano, the clubhouse men when I was with the Dodgers, and the others when I was with other teams, not only did what they were supposed to do for me, they did a lot of extra things that prolonged my career.

These guys take care of you when you're hurt or recovering from an injury. They tape and bandage your wounds and give you the ice baths and heat packs and whirlpool treatments and massages that keep you going when you're aching and bruised and can hardly walk, much less play. Without them, I never would have lasted as long as I did.

I was a better outfielder than anyone knows, and there was a time I hoped to play there, but I came to like catching. I think if I had not concentrated on catching and taken punishment as a catcher I could have been a pretty good hitter. I always hit well in the minors, when I wasn't always catching, but I was fair at best in the majors. I averaged as little as .213 and as much as .287, wound up with the Dodgers at .251, and lost a couple of points to .249 my last two or three years with other clubs.

I usually hit less than ten homers, but I hit some big ones, and eighteen one year. I had speed and hit twenty or more doubles a couple of seasons. I drove in forty or fifty runs and scored forty or fifty most years. I stole eleven bases my first full season, the most by a catcher in the major leagues in twenty years and in the National League in thirty years. Then I stole seventeen a few years later.

Aside from concentrating on catching, the beating a catcher's body and especially his hands take make it hard for him to be a good hitter. There were times my hands hurt so bad it hurt terribly just to hold a bat, and times they were so numb I couldn't even feel the bat. You check the records and see how many times the Hall of Fame catchers caught 140 games and hit .300 or drove in 100 runs. John Bench and Thurman Munson are exceptions and belong in the Hall of Fame because of it.

I was at best a fairly good, dangerous hitter with more

speed then most catchers, basically a defensive player who was maybe a little more useful all around than most catchers. Not a great player by any means, but a good one. When I'd have a bad year at bat or the team would have a bad year there would be talk that the team might trade me. After a while I stopped worrying. I knew I was as good as any around. I threw righty but hit lefty. Because all catchers are right-handed, teams are always looking for a left-handed-hitting catcher. I wanted to stay with the Dodgers, but I knew there were plenty of other teams who wanted me. No catcher the Dodgers brought up for ten years beat me out.

In fact, from my first full season with the Dodgers in 1958 when we landed in Los Angeles to my last season with the team in 1967 when I'd slowed down, I was the only player to play regularly every year. Maury Wills didn't break into the starting lineup until 1960 and he was gone after 1966. Willie Davis lasted until 1967, but hadn't started until '61. Others came and went at other positions. Drysdale was the only pitcher who pitched regularly all the time I was with the team. Koufax was a spot starter at first and retired after '66.

I wasn't much publicized, but there were stories about my being rough and rugged, an iron man of sorts, and I think I deserved these. I didn't get a lot of credit for it, but I knew I made a major contribution to the club, and I knew my teammates and manager and general manager knew it.

I once heard Buzzie Bavasi say about Drysdale, "I don't care what the big sonofabitch does, he goes out and pitches hard for me every fourth day." I wanted to be that kind of catcher you can count on every game. And the time came when we were talking contract and Bavasi said to me, "If I paid you for your hitting, you'd starve. But I pay you to catch and you go out and catch for me, night after night, so I'm gonna pay you what you want, which you deserve."

Which was nice, except, dammit, I wasn't that bad a hitter.

20.

I N MY glory days with the Dodgers, we won four pennants
and three World Series and finished second twice, including
one time when we tied for first place and lost a playoff, all
over a span of ten and a half seasons. If there were a lot of
good players and pitchers and a few great ones in the league at
that time, the Dodgers had more of them than any other team.

From the time we moved into Dodger Stadium in 1962 until
I moved out in 1967, I was the regular catcher and Willie
Davis was the centerfielder. The first three seasons Ron Fairly
played first base. The last three he replaced Frank Howard in
right field, while Wes Parker took over at first. Tommy Davis
played left the first three seasons, Lou Johnson the last three.

Wills played short until he was traded and Gene Michael
took over my last year there, '66. The only really unstable
positions over these six seasons were at second and third base.
Jim Gilliam played second, then third. Nate Oliver, Jim
Lefebvre, and Ron Hunt followed at second. Daryl Spencer,
Ken McMullen, Johnny Kennedy, and Jim Lefebre also played
third, along with others. Along the way, Bill Skowron, Larry
Burright, and Dick Tracewski were infield reserves, Wally
Moon and Al Ferrara were outfield reserves, and Doug
Camilli, Jimmy Campanis, Joe Pignatano, and Jeff Torborg
backed me up.

We didn't hit too hard. Tommy Davis was an outstanding
hitter for a couple of years until he was hurt, but he didn't hit
with power. Willie Davis, Fairly and Parker were pretty fair

hitters, but they didn't win any hitting titles. Howard was our only power-hitter, but he couldn't hit consistently. Wills got on base one way or another and then he stole bases. He was the sparkplug of our offense and drove rival teams crazy. We scratched for runs.

One time when Drysdale wasn't with the team and was told that Koufax had pitched a no-hitter, he asked, "Did he win?" That was the way it was. If we shut out the other team, all we were sure of was a tie. But we shut out a lot of teams. And we won a lot of one-run games. If we got a run or two, we had a good chance to win. We had a good defense and great pitching. We were managed well, we had a lot of togetherness, and we played as a team.

We had good defense down the middle. I was good defensively behind the plate. Wills was better with the glove at short than people realized. He cheated a lot, played the batters smart, and made the hard play. For a while, with Neal at second and Wills at short they were an incredible combination, but Neal screwed up with management and got traded. We just made do at second after that.

Neal and Wills sometimes threw at runners coming into second in double-play situations. It is the runner's job to try to break up the double play by intimidating the man taking the throw at second and making it to first. It is the job of the man taking the throw to keep the runner honest. Hit a runner in the head and the next time he'll go down in the dirt so fast to start his slide so far from the base that he's no problem to you anymore.

One time Don Dillard came in high and Maury hit him right between the eyes with the ball and flattened him. Everyone was worried he'd been killed and went to him except Gilliam, who was playing second. Gilliam was only worried about the out, and he went to the ball and tagged the unconscious player to make sure he was out. "That's the first time I tagged out a dead man," chuckled The Devil.

Willie Davis could fly in centerfield and he caught up to turn a lot of hits into outs.

Willie should have been a better ballplayer. He thought he was. He was egotistical. I remember the first time he was interviewed in the clubhouse, a writer asked him if he thought he could hit .300 in the big leagues and Willie said, "I think I'll hit .330." Some of us almost fell off our chairs. He has never hit .330 in his career. But he should have. Most of the time he hasn't even hit .300. He could fly. He should have been able to bunt his way to .300. But one time I was asked to help him with his bunting and he told me he didn't need any help. "How many fucking bunts you beat out this year?" he asked me. I never tried to help him after that. Willie wasn't willing to work. He had extraordinary ability but he became an ordinary player.

By contrast, Ron Fairly had ordinary ability and became an extraordinary player. As a hitter he knew the strike zone, developed a good swing, and became a difficult out. As a fielder, he always played in the right place for the hitter and always threw to the right base. He was willing to do whatever he had to to become the best player he could. And at forty or so, he's still playing in the big leagues.

Hodges used to put on a show picking up low throws at first. He taught Ron Fairly, who became even better at it. Ron taught Wes Parker, who became one of the best, but I think Ron was better. Parker was a flashier fielder and won more fielding awards than Fairly, but I believe Ron went after and made more difficult plays. Wes was a good guy, but he came from a rich family, he wasn't hungry, he wasn't fiery, and he'd pass on the hard play.

With fellows like Fairly, Wills, and The Devil on the field, however, we had a fiery team with a lot of leadership.

The real strength of our teams, though, was in the pitching. When you know you are going to get a good game from the guy on the mound every time you go out there, you have a lot of confidence. And when you know that if the starter falters you're going to get a good game from the reliever you bring in, you're just that much more confident.

Confidence is the key to winning, I think. You have to have the ability, but without confidence it won't come out. You can't pretend. It has to come naturally. We had confidence that our pitchers would keep us close in the games so we always had a chance to win. We knew we needed only a few runs to win. We won more than our share.

We had confidence in Koufax, of course. For a few years he was the best I ever saw. He spent the first six seasons of his career gaining control and confidence, and the last six setting the league on its ear. Twice he lost only five games and only once he lost as many as ten. Three years he won twenty-five, twenty-six, and twenty-seven. He set all sorts of strike-out records and pitched four no-hitters. I caught two, and Torborg, a real good receiver, caught two.

Only Nolan Ryan has surpassed Sandy's strikeout records and pitched as many no-hitters, but Nolan has not surpassed Sandy in other ways. Nolan is the only other pitcher I've known that I thought might strike out every batter or pitch a no-hitter anytime he took the mound, but Nolan isn't as consistent as Koufax. Nolan has never mastered control and he loses a lot of games, especially in the early innings. He'll never pitch a perfect game, which Sandy did.

Only Ryan may have had a faster pitch, but Sandy had a better curve and better control and could set up batters. I think what set Sandy apart from all the other pitchers was his ability in his prime to throw his stuff so hard and with such accuracy. He was so afraid of hurting a hitter he wouldn't brush a batter back or knock anyone down, which used to make me mad. But he embarrassed so many and his reputation got to be so good that most batters were beaten before they stepped in to face him.

Facing other pitchers, batters would step to the plate and ask, "Is Sandy pitching tomorrow?" If I said he was, they'd curse. If not, they'd smile.

Ryan takes advantage of his wildness to intimidate hitters. He may look like the kid next door, but he's coming in the side window to steal the bread from your table. He's a baby-faced killer. He'll brush you back, knock you down, or even hit you without thinking twice about it. He's hurt a couple of players and it's helped him.

The only time I ever saw Koufax throw at anyone was when Lou Brock was being bodacious, stealing on Sandy so much that Sandy lost his temper. He threw waist tight to Lou, who turned away and got it in the back. Usually, a ball will bounce off a batter. Sandy's pitch struck so far in to Lou I thought it would stay there. It hit with a sickening thud, then fell to his feet. He dropped to his hands and knees and was out for a few days. I don't think Sandy meant to hit him, but I think he meant to scare him. It scared Sandy. I think if Sandy had scared more hitters, he'd have gone 30–0 instead of 25–5. The hitters hated to have to face him, but they weren't scared because they knew he wouldn't throw at them.

When Sandy was strongest he was wildest, and sometimes he had a hard time. When he was weak warming up and would say, "Shit, I don't have it tonight," we'd laugh because we knew he was going to have a good game. But he got to the point where he always had good games. Some were just better than others. At his best, he seemed unbeatable. Even though he was suffering from finger and elbow injuries, hurting bad, and taking shots, we always knew we could count on Koufax. It's tragic that at thirty, at his peak, he felt he didn't dare go on. He could have won for five more years.

You could always count on Drysdale too. He was a strong-arm, healthy as a horse, and always ready. He bothered batters even more than Sandy did because Driz terrified them. He didn't have Sandy's natural ability, and he couldn't throw as hard as Koufax, but Big D threw hard. He threw the meanest spitter I ever saw, he threw from a sidearm motion that terrified right-handed hitters, and he liked to teach hitters respect, right-handed or left-handed, by knocking them down. He was the meanest, most intense competitor I ever saw. Hitters came to the plate talking nice to me in hopes I wouldn't call for a close pitch, but I didn't have to flip my forefinger to get Driz to flip 'em. I could have asked hitters for twenty-dollars when they came to the plate and they'd have pulled the money out of their pocket or sent home for it to stay on my good side.

Driz never threw a no-hitter, but he threw six straight shutouts in 1965, setting a major-league mark for consecutive scoreless innings at fifty-eight. You could get hits off him, but it was hard to get games from him. He won twenty-five one year and is the only Dodger to have won more than two hundred in his career.

Driz came up a year after Sandy and lasted three years longer. He also matured faster, reached his peak earlier, and held it longer. Only it wasn't as high a peak as Sandy's. Sandy was the best left-handed pitcher of my time in the league, better even than Spahn, though Spahn sustained his success a lot longer. Drysdale ranked with Marichal and Gibson as the best right-hander, but I don't know who was best.

I don't think any team ever had a better one-two pitching punch than we had with those two. They would have won without me, but I'm proud of the part I played in catching them at the peak of their careers.

We had depth, too. Podres was a cutie for a year when we first got to Dodger Stadium. And Stan Williams gave us a good year before going on his way. He had a lot of ability, including the ability to throw a good spitter. He didn't use saliva. Few spitball pitchers do. He chewed gum or slippery elm and used that. He'd lick his fingers, then pretend to rub them dry. Never did, though. Unless the umpire went out to look at his hands. If the ump asked to see the ball, Williams rubbed it dry and waved it dry before he threw it in.

Guys have all kinds of tricks. Their teammates or catchers help them. too. Infielders or catchers nick the ball with a big belt buckle or even a knife before turning it over to a pitcher. "The rough spot is on the underside," they'll say with a smile. Service with a smile.

Williams wasn't as good as Drysdale, but he threw as hard and was as mean. We called him "the big hurt." When you played around with him, sparring, you found out he didn't know how to spar, didn't know how to play. He'd put his fist into your chest and you'd feel it to your backbone. He was big and strong and could throw a ball through a brick wall or a catcher's glove, and if he got mad at a batter he'd tell him he was going to drill him. When he drilled him the guy was drilled. He was wild and undependable, raw ability gone to waste.

A couple of years later Claude Osteen came in on a trade and he had a lot of good years. He was a lot like Podres, not overpowering but cute. He had a sinking fast ball and a sharp curve and a good change-up, but he lived off his slider. A slider breaks a little quicker than a curve and a little less, and Osteen's slider broke less than most, which really got the batter off balance. A left-hander, he could really jam right-handers. They'd swing the bat thinking they were going to get good wood on the ball, only to have it duck in and hit the handle. His only problem was that his slider sometimes wouldn't break, and when he was beaten it was usually because of this. He made mistakes with it, but he was an easy pitcher to catch.

Then Don Sutton developed into a top pitcher, and he's sustained it a long time. Sutton was a straight, religious kid, but a killer on the mound who would do what he had to do to win. I guess he still will. He was another of those pitchers who couldn't overpower you, but he was clever and could outsmart you and he had good breaking stuff. He used to try to throw a spitter, but I don't think he ever got it to where he could get outs with it.

Instead, he came up with a way of doctoring the ball so he threw with his fingers off a rough spot that would cause the pitch to dip and be a guaranteed ground ball. Sometimes I'd catch his pitch and rub the ball in the dirt to give him a rough spot to use. But he has his own ways and he's been doing it a long time without them being able to catch him at it no matter how much they try.

There are a lot of ways to do it. You can rub it rough with sandpaper or an emery board you hide on you or even nick it with a sharp object.

My last year with the team Bill Singer came along and he came up with a good spitter along with a good fast ball. He was a super pitcher until he came down with a series of sore arms. I don't know what he used, but Singer used to put slippery elm in his mouth and soap down his pants leg. One way or another he'd get some stuff on the ball. He never used spit, but it's called a spitball, and he lived off it the last few years of his baseball life. Phil Regan used to use greasy stuff in his hair and get it on his fingers when he'd wipe the sweat from his brow. He threw a super spitter.

You use it on the other guys and they use it on you. Like it or not, it's part of the game. It's cheating, but it's also competitive pitching.

You don't like to have it used to beat you, of course. That's human nature. Lew Burdette used to drive me crazy with it. And Gaylord Perry and Bob Shaw too. There was a little guy named Dennis Ribant who used to make me mad because he couldn't pitch without it, it was all he had. One night he was going to his mouth to wet the ball, and every time he'd do it, I'd step out on him and wait until the ball dried. The umpire wasn't doing anything about it either way, so Ribant finally shouted, "Get the hell in there." He was so small I wasn't afraid to fight him. I hollored back, "Go fuck yourself," The usual clever Roseboro retort. But it made him mad and the dummy threw me a plain old-fashioned fast ball. I jumped on it and hit it for a home run. Made him mad as hell. All the way around the bases I was hollering, "There you go, you stupid sonofabitch." He didn't last long.

Regan was one of the best relief pitchers we ever had and we always had a loaded bullpen. He had a good slider and spitter. He had control and he could throw low. "The Vulture" would come in in the late innings and pick them clean. But with all the warming relievers do and all the games they work in, their arms sometimes go bad quickly. He didn't last too long.

Bob Miller had good stuff and good control and lasted a while. Ron Perranoski had a good fast ball and good control and he lasted the longest. Jim Brewer lasted a long time but he wasn't as outstanding. We backed up our great starters with great relievers. Alston never hesitated to go to the bullpen and we always knew we'd get a good piece of work from our relievers. They were all able and competitive and confident, all cool in the clutch.

We lived off our pitchers. We made the plays that had to be made in the field behind them. We scratched for runs but came up with enough to win consistently. We had some good hitters but few with power. Big Don Drysdale may have been our most consistent power-hitter but he didn't get to hit much. Two different seasons he hit seven home runs, which tied a record for pitchers set by big Don Newcombe. But one way or another, we won our share and more.

Our new home, Dodger Stadium, was perfect for us, a

pitcher's park. About 330 feet down the lines and almost 400 feet to center, a pitcher could make a mistake and still get away with it. The outfielders had a lot of room to reach fly balls. It's a good park for line-drive hitters but hard on fly-ball hitters. Not many home runs hit there, unlike Ebbets Field or the Coliseum. I always liked it. They take care of it.

Dodger Stadium is set in Chavez Ravine, which used to be a garbage dump. It's a beautiful ball park in every respect and has held up through the years. It's not as colorful as the old parks, but it's cleaner, nicer-looking, and it has four decks, a lot of seats, and you can see from every seat. There's room for more than fifty-two thousand fans and we filled it many times. The year we moved in, 1962, we set a major-league record with more than 2.7 million fans, and they had close to that every other year I played there. In fact, they only fell off for a few years, starting the year I left. I don't think my leaving was responsible. In any event, the years I played there we gave those fans their money's worth.

21.

CONTROVERSY surrounded Dodger Stadium before it was built, so it was appropriate that our first season there was controversial. Walter O'Malley and Los Angeles both got what they wanted, but a lot of land was taken over and given to us over the protests of a lot of people, including some little old ladies.

We had a great team and a great season until the end of the season. Then we blew it all in a very bad scene and were considered a club that choked. We gave them a lot of excitement until we disappointed them. No one, of course, was more disappointed than we were.

Some of us had our greatest season ever. I didn't, but I drove in 55 runs, close to my best, and I had become a very good receiver. Tommy Davis drove in 150 and Frank Howard 120. Tommy hit close to 30 home runs, which was a lot for him, and Frank more than 30. Tommy was a very timely hitter and led the league with an average of close to .350. Howard hit close to .300.

The sparkplug of the club was Wills, who hit close to .300 and stole 104 bases to top Ty Cobb's single-season record. Wills's legs were bruised raw and he was exhausted as the season wore on, but he just kept going until he had topped Cobb. Along the way he drove the other teams to distraction and inspired us. He scored 130 runs. A gutsy guy, he was voted Most Valuable Player in the league that year, and he deserved it.

The pitching was exceptional until Koufax was sidelined.

Drysdale was the workhorse. Don led the league in innings pitched, strikeouts, and victories. I'm sure Sandy would have led in those but his left index finger went numb at mid-season. He had a 14–7 record. Among his early wins was his first no-hitter. Don carried on to a 25–9 record and won the Cy Young Award as the top pitcher.

Podres and Williams helped, but they were really only .500 pitchers. The help we needed we got from the bullpen. Perranoski pitched in seventy games and saved twenty. Roebuck, Sherry, and Moeller also were effective.

We swung along in first place most of the season. I hit a home run in the all-star game at Wrigley Field, Chicago, off Milt Pappas, but we lost the game. That was when the National League occasionally lost the all-star games.

We lost the pennant to the Giants. After Koufax went out, our pitching was thin. After hitting hard most of the way, we slumped. We lost a lot of close games down the stretch. The Giants had a good team and they tied for first at the finish.

They had hitters like Mays, Cepeda, and Willie McCovey, and pitchers like Marichal, Billy Pierce, Billy O'Dell, and Jack Sanford. Three of them won close to twenty each and Sanford won twenty-four. I remember because it was one less than Drysdale won. Sanford was mean and miserable but that was his season. McCovey had just come up that season, but he hurt us.

He became the only batter who could consistently destroy Drysdale. Willie wasn't intimidated by Don's inside pitches, and he had the size and strength to reach out and rap Don's outside pitches. From then on it got to be psychological, where Willie looked forward to hitting Don, and Drysdale dreaded having to pitch to Mac.

We won thirteen in a row, which is as many as any Dodgers' team ever won, and built a big lead. We still were ahead by about five games with five weeks to go. We weren't winning regularly, but the Giants had stopped winning too.

We were ahead by four games with eight games to go. We lost four out of five, but still led by two with three to go. We lost all three, the Giants won two, and we were tied.

It is said we choked, but I don't think so. Some players perform better and some worse under pressure, but with the same players we went on to perform well under pressure and win several pennants in other seasons.

Without Koufax, our pitching was thinned out and our relievers were worn out through the final weeks. Some of our hitters had been hitting better than they ever had or ever would again. They fell back to and we went into a scoring slump, putting more pressure on the pitching than it could stand.

Also, Leo Durocher and Alston were feuding. Durocher had been coaching third and taking over, as is his way, and taking chances. Alston called him down for it, took command, and became conservative. We had been an aggressive club, but we went into a shell and started trying to hang on. We spent so much time looking at the scoreboard to see how the Giants were doing, we stopped doing for ourselves. If they won, we were depressed. If they lost, we were elated, but it was as though we didn't have to win then.

I became aware of this and started to get on guys about it, but they had gotten into the habit and couldn't break it. We expected to back in, but before we knew it we were in a best-of-three playoff for the pennant.

The first game was in San Francisco and Alston turned to Sandy in desperation, but Koufax couldn't pitch with that sore finger and got knocked out. Mays hit two home runs and Pierce stopped us on three hits. We were embarrassed, 8–0.

If we had been the kind of club that choked, we would have given up. But we went back to Dodger Stadium determined to pull ourselves together and pull out the series by winning the last two. We won the second one, a wild one, 8–7, to tie the series. Wills walked and wound up with the winning run when he came home from third ahead of a throw by Mays in the last of the ninth.

The deciding game was on a weekday afternoon in Chavez Ravine and our ball park was jammed. We were all set to celebrate when we went into the ninth needing only three outs to win, 4–2. However, Roebuck had come on early and was wearing out. He admitted he was tired, but Alston thought he would get by one more inning. Durocher tried to talk Alston into taking him out, but Alston didn't want to listen. Walt even let Roebuck hit into the last out in the last of the eighth when we loaded the bases. The situation really called for a pinch hitter.

Giants' manager Alvin Dark sent Matty Alou up to pinch-hit to start the ninth and Matty bounced a single through the infield to right. That started the rally. What is not known about it generally is that Lee Walls, sitting on the bench, signaled to second baseman Larry Burright to move closer to first just before Alou bounced the ball by where Burright had been.

I like Lee, but some of us blamed him for the loss. Maybe we shouldn't have, but we did.

Some players who aren't playing feel they have to become cheerleaders on the bench. A lot of managers like it, but most players don't. We get enough hollering from the fans, and jockeying from the other bench, without being distracted by our own bench. We're pros and we know what we have to do without being told. I have stepped away from the plate and glared at my own teammates. Walls was always providing pep talks. He didn't know what to do with himself. Burright was young and needed help from the manager and coaches on where to play. It wasn't Walls's job to give it.

He did, and Alou was on first. Harvey Kuenn hit to Wills for a force-out at second. But Roebuck then walked McCovey and Felipe Alou to load the bases.

We were in trouble, with one out. Alston talked to Roebuck but decided to leave him in. Mays hit a line drive right back to Roebuck, and the ball bounced right out of his glove and rolled away. A run scored and the bases were still full. Had Roebuck caught it, he could have had an easy double play in several directions. Had he gotten to it in time, he could have had a force at home. He didn't, and Stan Williams was brought in.

Drysdale was raring to go. He told Walt he wanted to pitch and would get the last outs. I think he could have. But Alston wanted to save him to open the World Series against the Yankees, which was coming right up. Drysdale said, "We've got to get there first." Alston said, "We'll get there." He was sure we would. We all were. But he left Roebuck in too long and we didn't make it.

We all worried about Williams. He was wild and inconsistent. On Alston's orders, Durocher came to the mound to
make the change, and while we waited for Williams, Leo said
to me, "He'll walk the ball park." I said, "He'll be okay." I
wanted him to be.

He got one too good to Cepeda and the big guy hit the hell
out of it, but right at Fairly in right. That was the second out,
but it brought in the tying run from third and put the lead run
on third. Trying to throw one by Ed Bailey, Williams threw
into the dirt. I made one of the better blocks of my career and
kept the runner on third, but the runner on first went to second. That was critical because it opened up first base, and
Alston decided to give Bailey an intentional walk to load the
bases and set up a force play at any base. This was quite a
burden to load on the wild Williams, and he got too careful
pitching to Jimmy Davenport and walked him, forcing in the
lead run. That was it.

Alston finally got Williams out of there, bringing in Perranoski, who should have been pitching in the first place, if
not Drysdale. Perranoski got José Pagan to ground to second,
but Burright fumbled it to bring in an extra run. Perranoski
then struck out Bob Nieman to end it. But it was all over for
us anyway.

Their four-run rally came on four walks, a wild pitch, an
error, and only two little hits. Dark brought in his starter,
Pierce, to relieve the last of the ninth, and he nailed us one-
two-three.

The cheers had become boos in our ball park. The Giants
ran off, hollering their happiness, while we walked off, our
heads hanging. It wasn't just that we'd lost but the way we'd
lost. We were second-guessing ourselves right and left. Everyone was blaming someone else for what had happened. Some
of the players locked the clubhouse door to keep out the press.
It was the only time that happened when I was with the team.
The players just didn't want any part of the press.

There was not only champagne on ice, but bottles of whiskey that had been brought in for a victory celebration. The
booze was passed around and the players started to drink. The
more they drank, the worse they felt. It was the worst scene

I ever saw with the Dodgers. It was the one time we did not conduct ourselves with class.

The players started to get drunk. When their bottles and glasses were empty they'd throw them away and get new ones. The floor was littered with broken glass. It's a miracle no one was hurt. Some tore their uniforms to shreds. The players were bitching and cursing and moaning.

Alston had locked himself in his little office and some of the players started to yell at him, "Come out of there, you gutless sonofagun. . . . Tell us about your strategy, skipper. . . . How we gonna play the World Series, you bastard. . . ." He never came out while I was there. I felt as bad and was as bitter as anyone, but I wasn't drinking, I don't like to be around drunks, and I got dressed and got out. I walked through the reporters without saying anything, got in my car, and drove home.

I don't think the reporters ever got into the clubhouse. I heard Wally Moon went outside to apologize for the players and pleaded with the press to understand how bad they felt. I heard he said, "It cost the guys twelve grand each, so you can imagine how we feel." And I heard Alston later talked to them too, and was the only one who went into the Giants' dressing room to congratulate them. I heard the Dodgers' dressing room was a disgrace. Among other things, big John Griffin, our colorful clubhouse man, who wore a derby hat and smoked enormous cigars, got so drunk he fell into a locker and got wedged in so tight they had a tough time getting him out.

They'd had a victory party scheduled that night at the Grenadier Restaurant, run by the fellow who catered Dodger Stadium. It turned into a wake. Few showed up. O'Malley, Bavasi, and Alston didn't show up. But some of the brass did, and Durocher did. I guess they got to drinking too much, too, and there apparently was a lot of talk that if Durocher had been managing instead of Alston, we'd have won. Durocher didn't disagree, apparently. Nor did he deny it when it was spread all over the newspapers and Bavasi asked him about it. Alston wasn't fired, but Leo was.

It was a very long winter, having to explain what had happened to us. It made me mad because I don't go around asking anyone else why his work hasn't been so good lately. But the ballplayer is out in the open and the paying customers consider it their right to let him know what they think. I don't think we choked. I think we went bad, made mistakes, and got beaten. But we bounced back to win the next year.

Maybe the disappointment of '62 made us more determined in '63. But the fact is we didn't play nearly as well in '63 as we had in '62. Tommy Davis won his second straight batting title, but he didn't drive in nearly as many runs. Howard didn't drive in as many runs. No one drove in even ninety runs. Wills, shot from the previous season, stole only forty bases.

The pitching carried us. The Koufax finger had healed and he led the league in strikeouts, shutouts, and victories. He won twenty-five and lost only five and allowed less than two earned runs a game. He pitched another no-hitter, against the Giants, ironically. He had become the best and he won both the MVP and Cy Young awards. Drysdale fell off just short of twenty. Podres struggled. We let Williams go, but Bob Miller got by in his place. Perranoski had another big year. He worked almost every other game in relief, and won or saved about forty for us.

Koufax and Perranoski were the only ones to do as well as, or better than, the year before. We won ninety-nine games, which was a couple less than the year before. But we won by six games instead of losing by one. In a way, we did a lot better in '62, but we are remembered as a club that choked and blew the pennant and the playoff that year. The '63 team did not play as well but wound up winning the pennant and is remembered as a great team. Circumstances make the difference.

In '63, the Cardinals, with Stan Musial, Bill White, Dick Groat, and Ken Boyer, won nineteen out of twenty just before a three-game series in St. Louis with us. It put them within one game of us. This was the middle of the last month of the season and people were saying we were choking again. We felt the pressure, but we felt last year had nothing to do with this year and we could do what we should have done before.

Alston called on Podres in the opener and old "Point" came through for a 3–1 victory. That was the big one because it meant they could do no better than a tie by the time we left town, and because it got us to Koufax. Sandy stopped them on four hits for a 4–0 win. They weren't through. They had Bob Gibson for the last game and built a 5–1 lead. But we battled back, and a home run by rookie Dick Nen tied it in the ninth, and we won it in the thirteenth. Nen never did much in the majors except make that one big hit. But sometimes one big hit makes a big difference. Sometimes it takes luck. With a little luck, we swept that series and the Cardinals were through.

That did a lot to repair our image. Winning the World Series helped our image a lot too, of course. Winning the way we did helped. Four straight. And over the New York Yankees, who were at that time still the dominant team in baseball. They had won two straight World Series, six of seven in their long history with the Dodgers when they were in Brooklyn. Now the Yankees faced the Dodgers for the first time from Los Angeles.

Renewal of that old rivalry had everyone excited. It got so much publicity that even the players who knew nothing about the old rivalry got worked up.

For guys like Koufax and Drysdale and me, going back to New York to play in a World Series was special. Walking into towering Yankee Stadium with its tremendous tradition awed all of us. I was more nervous than I had been in my first World Series. I was nervous for maybe the only time in my career. I can't ever recall feeling as tense as I did during our off-day workout in that big ball park. You don't want to fuck up, of course. There's always that. But there was more than that this time.

Wills was nervous too. We brought a bottle of brandy into the clubhouse with us before the opening game. After pregame practice and before going back on the field for the pregame ceremonies he took the bottle, looked around to see if anyone was watching, then took a swallow. He put it in my locker and left. He knew I didn't drink, but he also knew I was nervous. I looked at the bottle, looked around, saw no one, and took a sip. I jumped when I felt a tap on the shoulder and turned around to see the skipper. Here I was sipping brandy before the big game, but all he did was smile and say,

"Have a good game, Rosey."

I had a good game. It was Alston's way to go with his regulars in big games. Players he platooned during the season weren't platooned in a World Series. The top player played. The only times he took me out during the season were when one of the better left-handed pitchers was pitching, but I played every game of the World Series, even the opening game when Whitey Ford, one of the best lefties, pitched.

In the second inning, with two on, he hung a curve inside. I got the bat around and hit a fly ball that fell into the lower right-field seats, fair by a few feet. It was the only home run I hit off a lefty all year, but it was enough to beat the Yankees in the first game. With Koufax setting a World Series record with fifteen strikeouts, my three-run homer helped us to a 5–2 victory and we were on our way.

I don't know if the brandy did it. I didn't drink any more, and got only one more hit, but we won three more in a row. It was the first time the mighty Yankees ever were swept four staight in a World Series.

Our pitching stopped Mickey Mantle and Roger Maris and the rest of the Yankees almost cold. Podres, with help from Perranoski, stopped them, 4–1, in the second game. Wills's running got the winning rally going. Tommy Davis tripled twice. And Moose Skowron, an ex-Yankee filling in at first for us, hit a home run.

The Series shifted to Los Angeles. A walk by Jim Bouton, a wild pitch, and a ground ball by Tommy Davis, which bounced off Bobby Richardson's shin, gave Drysdale the only run he needed in a 1–0 victory. Big D allowed only three hits and one walk and was in complete control in maybe the best game he ever pitched.

Finally, Koufax got by Ford in the fourth and final. Ford gave up only two hits, but one was the first ball ever hit into the second deck of Dodger Stadium. Howard hit it in the fifth inning to give us the lead, 1–0. Koufax gave up only six hits, but one was a home run by Mantle in the seventh to tie it. It was Mantle's only big hit of the series.

Typically, we scratched out the winning run. Gilliam got the job done, opportunistically. He bounced the ball to Clete

Boyer, but when Boyer's throw got through Joe Pepitone at first, The Devil went all the way to third. Willie Davis followed with a fly ball for the running run.

The Yankees threatened in the ninth. Richardson led off with a single. Sandy struck out Tom Tresh and Mantle. He got Elston Howard to hit to Wills for what should have been the third out, but Dick Tracewski dropped the throw at second. Koufax calmly got Hector Lopez to hit to Wills, who threw to first for the final out.

We had brought the first World Series victory to Dodger Stadium and its faithful fans.

It was a thrill, of course, but I did not go as wild as you might expect. Few of us did. Some drank champagne, but the celebration was subdued. I think the memory of the bad scene in the clubhouse following the playoff loss the year before was still with us. I think we were proud we had proved something, but there was no way we were going to forget the bad memories. I think we were a bit bitter about the way we had been treated. It turned us hard, cold. We were professionals. We took pride in our performance, but baseball had become a business for us.

The series had been played in big ball parks and been well attended. There were crowds of more than sixty-five thousand for each of the first two games in New York and more than fifty-five thousand for each of the last two in LA. The players' pool was a record of more than a million dollars and I don't think the cheering of our fans meant as much to us as having won the championship and each of us having earned more than twelve thousand dollars extra.

We did not win in 1964. It's hard to sustain success. It takes away some of your desire. I think we wanted to win but weren't quite as intense as we had been. Maybe more important, a lot of little things went wrong. Howard held out, reported late, and had a bad year. Tommy Davis had a bad year. We had no one who drove in a hundred runs or hit .300. I was the second highest hitter on the team at .287, highest of my career.

We couldn't score runs and put too much pressure on our pitchers. Koufax pitched another no-hitter and was sailing along at 19–5 in August when he hurt his left elbow sliding and was sidelined for the season. What the hell was a pitcher like Koufax doing sliding into a base? That's the way the game is played, but it's stupid. Drysdale didn't give up many runs, but he lost a lot of close games and settled for 18–16. None of the others did much, except Perranoski, and even he fell off a little.

Maybe I shouldn't have had my best year personally, but I did. I had developed a bad knee, sat out the preseason, and didn't take batting practice all season. So I hit the highest I have ever hit. Water would collect in my knee and the doctor would have to drain it with a large needle that hurt. I played in pain all season and wound up with the award as the best fielding catcher in the league.

I think players sometimes play better when they are feeling bad or are hurt. To compensate, they concentrate more, bear down harder. I used Don Drysdale bats, which were enormous, a lot thicker and heavier than mine. I tried to meet the ball instead of swinging for the seats, didn't hit with a lot of power, and did get a lot of hits.

The funny thing is that I was under contract to Adirondack Bats and they supplied me my own style bats with my signature on them, but I used Don Drysdale-style Louisville Sluggers with his signature. I didn't think the wood in the Adirondacks was as good, and hits stung my hands, but I couldn't get good-wood Louisville Sluggers without using someone else's. I couldn't get a contract with the Louisville Sluggers because I wasn't a big enough name, so I used their bats but promoted Adirondacks.

In the end it was a disappointing year, of course. Not only didn't we win the pennant, but we didn't win as many games as we lost. We won eighty and lost eighty-two and finished fifth in what was at that time a ten-team league.

No one won too many games that season. The Cardinals won the pennant with only ninety-three, beating out the Reds and Phillies by only one game each, the Giants by three, the Braves by five. They were all about even and they all could be beaten. We didn't have too far to come back the following season, and we did come back.

The Dodgers have been a consistent contender over their years in LA because there has been consistency in the organization. They have had few changes of general managers or managers and they've moved men up from within the organization. They have maintained a consistent style of play that suits their big ball park. Always strong on pitching, they have made a few trades to beef up their batting, but if a Dick Allen or Frank Robinson did not fit the Dodger blue, they moved him on. They have not made many trades. They do not give up on a good ballplayer who has a bad year. They give him a chance. They have patience and do not panic with a bad year. Players feel they will be treated fairly with the Dodgers and this gives them a lot of loyalty to the team and desire to do well.

We did make a few changes for the 1965 season. We put Wes Parker at first and Ron Fairly in right, which tightened our over-all defense. The heavy-hitting but slow-footed Howard was traded for Claude Osteen, giving us another steady starter. We had some trouble with our infield defense. Jim Lefebvre was used at second and he was slow, though a good ballplayer. Gilliam had retired to coach, but he was brought back for a couple of seasons at third, slowed, but still good.

After Tommy Davis broke his ankle in a slide in May, he was out for the season and never was the same again. Lou Johnson took over in left and gave us a lift. Lou was thirty or so and had done little with other teams, but he could play and the Dodgers' spirit seemed to inspire him. You never knew where he was going when he left the ball park and what he would do through the night and next day, but he was always there ready to play another game the next night. He was as dependable on the field as he was undependable off. He was well for us several seasons. He hit hard and hustled hard. He started the habit of slapping both sides of both hands to congratulate a man for doing well and he gave us a lot of life. He was popular with the players and the fans.

Wills was still our sparkplug. He had struggled with injuries for a few years, but he came back with a year in which he stole 90-some bases and for a while looked like he was going to break his record of 104. He was an amazing guy, gutsy and determined. His slides tore his skin and beat him up. Opposing pitchers threw at his legs, trying to hurt him, scare him, slow him down. When he was on first, they'd throw there a thousand times to keep him close. He'd defy them and go when they least expected. They couldn't catch him. They'd soak their infields, but they couldn't stop him. He loved it and lived for it.

Except for Wills, we were more than ever dependent on pitching. Wills was our high hitter at .285 and drove the other teams crazy with his base running. Anytime he got on, he was in scoring position. A ground ball, an error, a fly ball, or a wild throw moved him home more times than not. Again, we didn't have a .300 hitter or 100 RBI man. I think Fairly led the team with 70 or so RBIs. I fell off in average but drove in 55 or so and was helpful with the bat. Mainly, I was helpful with the glove and with our pitchers.

All those years, Wills was our offense, Koufax our defense. In 1965, for the fourth straight season Sandy pitched a no-hitter, this one a perfect game against the Cubs. He set a major-league record with 382 strikeouts. He won twenty-six games and lost only eight. He allowed only a little more than two earned runs a game. He dominated the opposition.

Drysdale won twenty-three, lost twelve. Osteen won sixteen, lost fifteen. Perranoski and Miller were marvelous in relief. Drysdale tied his team record with forty-two starts. Over-shadowed by Koufax, Driz just kept plugging. The big guy had to hurt his arm eventually, but he was a bread-and-butter man for us for many years. You have to rank him right up with Wills and Koufax for contributions to our club over the years.

Like all good Dodgers' teams, we were opportunistic in 1965 and won the close contests. There were a lot of teams on the same level that year and we had a hard time with the Reds, Braves, Pirates, and Giants. We had a hard time with the Giants almost to the end. They won fourteen in a row and led us by four or five games with two to three weeks to go. But we won fifteen of our last sixteen games, including thirteen in a row, tying the team record, as the others sagged down the stretch.

We won ninety-seven games and we won the pennant by

two games over the Giants. That was the year Marichal hurt me. His suspension hurt them. We were not as powerful as our ill-fated team of 1962, but we were much better through the stretch in 1965. I think we had learned a lesson in 1962, never to take anything for granted. Pressed harder, we played harder. And we had Koufax all the way. We had confidence in him. He gave us confidence.

We needed that to win the World Series because we were not as strong as in 1962 or 1963. We didn't have the good defense in the field or power at the plate. The Twins took us to seven games before we beat them back. They were good, but not that good. They had good hitters like Harmon Killebrew, Tony Oliva, and Bob Allison. They had a good defense and good base running, led by shortstop Zoilo Versalles. They had good pitchers like Mudcat Grant, Jim Kaat, Jim Perry, and Alan Worthington. They extended us to the limit.

Because the first game fell on the Jewish high holy day, Yom Kippur, Koufax didn't pitch, so Drysdale started the Series in Minnesota. The Twins knocked Don out with six runs in an early inning, three of them on a home run by Versalles, and they went on to win, 8–2, behind Grant. They knocked out Koufax with a couple of runs in the middle of the second game and won, 5–1, behind Kaat. With our two top pitchers having been beaten, we went home to Los Angeles looking like losers for sure.

However, we've always tried to take 'em one at a time.

Osteen gave us a lift when he stopped them cold as we won the third game, 4–0. I singled in two runs and stole a base. Drysdale returned to form, we got ten hits, including home runs by Parker and Johnson, and we breezed, 7–2, in the fourth game to square the Series. Then Koufax came back on the beam to blank them on four hits, we got fourteen hits, four by Wills and three by Fairly, and won, 7–0, in the fifth game.

So we went back to Minnesota with the lead in the Series. However, if we thought we had it won, we were wrong. The Twins were far from finished. Grant pitched a six-hitter, Grant hit a three-run homer, and Allison a two-run job, as Osteen and the Dodgers went down, 5–1. So we had to go to a seventh and final game to decide the championship.

It was Drysdale's turn to pitch. He'd had three days of rest. But Alston decided to go with Koufax with only two days of rest. It was considered a controversial decision and it is still talked about. But we didn't consider it controversial. If you had any kind of choice at all between Koufax and another pitcher, you had to pick Sandy. Some say Drysdale was embarrassed, but I think even he understood. He never bitched about it.

I think Don would have won. I was sure Sandy would. He did, with his second straight shutout, 2–0. He gave up only three hits. He was in only one jam. With two on in the fifth, Versalles hit a hot grounder over third. The Devil dove, backhanded the ball, got up, and tagged the base for a force play. After that, Koufax was in complete command.

Sandy wasn't any tougher than Don, but he did things easier. Sandy could be beaten. He was in the first game of this Series. But he lost a lot less than Don did. Sandy seldom grooved the ball, gave up a home run or other big hit, but Don did, and a home run or big hit often beats you in a big game. Johnson's home run was enough to beat Kaat in this big game, and Parker later tripled in an extra run.

When you came down to it, it had to be Koufax. Don was great but Sandy was the greatest. Still, it took guts. It would have been easy to start Drysdale in turn. If he'd lost, there couldn't have been any complaint. But taking Koufax out of turn was tough. Had he been beaten, Alston would have been crucified.

I had another hit in the deciding game, giving me six for the Series and a .286 average. I remember it because it was by far my best of any World Series.

Although others had big hits from game to game, Fairly and Wills were our hitting stars for the Series. We actually outhit the Twins. But our pitchers were our stars. The Twins had been shut out only three times all season. We shut them out three times in the Series. Koufax shut them out his last two starts. He was our star of stars.

Because of our comeback it was an especially satisfying series.

The next season, 1966, was something else.

We won our second straight pennant, third in four years, and fourth in my time with the team. It came hard. Most of the season we were involved in a three-way battle with the Giants and the Pirates for the pennant. The Pirates had a lot of punch, led by Roberto Clemente, who was voted MVP in the league. They didn't fall out of it until the final week. The Giants had the punch in Willie Mays and Willie McCovey and the pitching in Juan Marichal and Gaylord Perry. They didn't fall out of it until the final weekend.

I don't know why the Giants didn't win more pennants than they did. They had the ability but we pulled together as a team better and we were more stable. We didn't change managers the way they did. We played with more confidence. We usually won, so we expected to win. They usually lost, so they expected to lose. If we lost, we expected to bounce back.

Marichal won twenty-five games that year, but Koufax won twenty-seven. As usual, Marichal finished second to Koufax in the voting for the Cy Young Award as top pitcher. Marichal always was overshadowed by Koufax and it must have been frustrating. just as the Giants were overshadowed by the Dodgers.

Koufax showed a lot of courage that season. He and Drysdale held out together for more money and missed most of the preseason period. Eventually, Sandy signed for $125,000, Don for $105,000. The late start did not seem to hurt Sandy, but it hurt Drysdale. Sandy led the league in strikeouts, complete games, victories, and earned-run average. He gave up a lot less than two earned runs a game. He won his third Cy Young Award. Yet he pitched in pain. He had developed arthritis in his left elbow and had to ice it after every game. It stiffened up between games. The arthritis was agony during games but he threw hard. He remained better than anybody else. I used to ask, "You all right, big guy?" And he'd say, "I'll get by, Rosey." He got by, but it hurt too much to go on much longer. Because of his record, no one would have believed it, but those of us who watched him closely could see he was thinking of giving it up. He was afraid of crippling himself.

As usual, we had little on offense and didn't score many runs. We didn't have anything close to a .300 hitter, except for Tommy Davis, who did not play regularly. Fairly, Lefebvre, Wills, and Willie Davis hit for fair averages. But Wills had slowed down on the bases quite a bit and we no longer were a running team. Lefebvre, a fair switch-hitter, led us in home runs, but I don't think he hit twenty-five. I know we didn't have any one drive in a hundred runs. Or even ninety, or eighty. I drove in fifty, about average for me. I averaged .276, high for me.

Koufax had to carry us because Drysdale had a bad year. He had worked hard for many years and he was wearing down a little. He lost more games than he won. Osteen worked well and Don Sutton came in to help. Our salvation was Phil Regan, "the Vulture." He worked in sixty to seventy games. He saved twenty and had an amazing 14–1 won-lost mark. He just kept coming out of the bullpen and saving close games. Perranoski was wearing out, but Regan had replaced him as our relief ace.

We went into the last day of the season, a Sunday in Philadelphia, needing to win one of two games in a doubleheader to clinch the pennant. Alston wanted to save Koufax for the World Series, so he tried Drysdale in the opener, but Big D was knocked out early. Fairly hit a homer that put us ahead, but Bob Miller blew the lead in relief and we lost. It took a long time to play. By the time the between-games break was over, the nightcap was really that. I remember it was after 7:00 P.M. when the second game got going. And Alston had to turn to Koufax. It was always Sandy when we needed one.

He was hurting, exhausted, but he went out, bent his back, and brought us home. He shut them out for eight innings while we knocked out Jim Bunning and built a 5–0 lead. He got into trouble in the ninth, but the skipper stayed with him. There was an error, three or four hits, three runs in and a runner on with nobody out, and we worried we might blow it. Alston didn't even have anyone warming up. We lived or died with Sandy. He struck out Bob Uecker, got Bobby Wine to ground out, and struck out Jackie Brandt.

It was over and we went wild.

In the dressing room, Sandy was so sore and weary he just sat there with a funny sort of smile on his face while we poured champagne on him. Our flight home to Los Angeles to start the World Series had been delayed by the length of the doubleheader, but we didn't care. All we cared about was that we were in it. Sandy more than anyone else had gotten us into it. We were a team and every player played a part in our victories, but he was our top gun and we all knew it. The guts of that guy really got to us. We not only loved him, we really respected him.

We did not know that he had just won his last game.

We had won ninety-five games to win the pennant by two games from the Giants and three from the Pirates, but we didn't know we wouldn't win another one that year.

Alston went back to Drysdale to start the Series against a well-balanced Baltimore Orioles' team. But Big D again was knocked out early. We knocked out Dave McNally early too, but Moe Drabowsky stopped us on one hit over the last seven innings. Frank Robinson and Brooks Robinson hit home runs and they won, 5–2.

We figured we'd get back into it the next game. We never guessed we wouldn't even score another run in the entire Series. Koufax had nothing left, he left early, and we lost the second game, 6–0. Jim Palmer blanked us on four hits. So we went to Baltimore.

Wally Bunker blanked us on six hits. Osteen allowed only three hits, but one was a home run by Paul Blair and it was enough to win, 1–0. Then McNally blanked us on four hits. Drysdale gave up only four, but one was a home run by Frank Robinson and it beat us, 1–0.

Suddenly it was all over. We sat in the dressing room thinking about how the Yankees must have felt when we won the World Series four straight from them. Again, I can't say we choked. The team hadn't choked in the tough fight for the pennant. Our lack of attack caught up to us. Our pitching could have gotten us back into it, but you can't win when you are shut out over three straight games.

We didn't feel we would lose until the last. We were a team that was used to bouncing back. We lost the first one, we thought we'd get the second one. We lost the second one, we thought we'd get back in the third. We lost that and then we were looking at defeat. We still thought we could get back. Then we ran out of games. Before we knew what was happening to us we were out of it.

It took a lot out of us. But others took more or we would have bounced back.

Koufax announced his retirement. Nobody believed it except the ballplayers who knew he always meant what he said. Without him, we were just another team. Our strength, pitching, had become ordinary.

We were scheduled for another tour of Japan and we were committed, but what was supposed to be a tour of triumph had turned into a wake. No one wanted to go, though we had a good time. Wills left the tour to do his own things, management got mad, and Maury was traded. He'd held the middle of our infield together and he left a big hole. He'd sparked our offense and we couldn't afford to lose anything from that.

We entered the 1967 season a weakened team. There was no way we could repeat our success of the past. Parker, Fairly, Willie Davis, Johnson, and Roseboro were still around, but we had Ron Hunt at second, Gene Michael at short, and Jim Lefebvre at third. Instead of Koufax, we had young Bill Singer as a starter. Drysdale was struggling. Sutton was still learning. Osteen was our ace and he was ordinary. Perranoski came back to have a good year out of the bullpen, but Regan came apart suddenly. He'd had his year. He was one of those guys God touches, I guess. He'd been given a great season as a gift, but he was never given greatness.

We weren't the Dodgers we had been. We were never in the race. We finished fifteen or sixteen games below .500, twenty-five or thirty games behind the Cardinals. It was just losing, and a long, long season.

It wasn't a bad season for me personally. I hit .272, though I didn't produce the runs I usually did. I could still catch, but I was fighting weight a little and having trouble with my knee and shoulder.

I went in to talk contract with Bavasi after the season ended. All the Dodgers, even Alston, always were on one-year contracts and had to negotiate for the next year every winter. I didn't want to wait.

I think that inside I had a feeling they were going to make changes and I didn't want to take any chances. I had been boosted to sixty grand the year before and I asked for a little raise to sixty-five grand.

Buzzie said, "With the year we had, John, I can't give raises."

I said, "You didn't have to trade Wills. With Wills traded and Koufax retired, we had to have the year we had."

He said, "Maybe, but I didn't have any choice. Maury said he had to go home to have his sore leg treated when he left us in Japan, then he turned up in Hawaii, playing in a night-club. Mr. O'Malley said we couldn't tolerate that type of defiance and I had to deal him."

I remember going to Maury's apartment after he heard of the trade and seeing him sitting there in shock. There is something about leaving the Dodgers' blue that is hard on anyone who has worn it a while. "I just can't believe it," Wills said, over and over. He was past thirty and far from his peak. He was a big name, but I think they feel that when they trade a top player they are keeping the others in line, showing them no one is superior to the system.

I said to Bavasi, "Well, I had a good year. I hit my .270 or so."

He said, "You had a good year. Maybe you deserve a raise. But how many .270 hitters do you know that are making sixty grand a year?"

I said, "Well, I'm mainly a defensive catcher. You know that. I do a job for you behind the plate."

And he said, "You've been one of the best behind the plate. You've done a job for us. We appreciate it. But you're one of the highest-paid catchers in the game now. At this point, we can't pay you more."

I think there were things he thought about saying that he didn't want to say. He hesitated, then said, "John, I'm going to give you some advice. I'll give you another contract for next season for sixty grand and I'd advise you to sign it.

"They're putting an expansion franchise in San Diego. I'm

going to buy into it and operate it. It will give me something of my own and something for my son. I won't be here much longer. I think Fresco Thompson will take over for me here. And I think he'll be a lot harder to deal with.

"Think it over," he said.

It didn't take me long to think it over. I think there was a threat there that Thompson might not want to sign me. I think Buzzie was saying that he was my friend and I should deal with him and make the best of a bad situation before it was too late. I said, "All right, I'll sign." He said, "You'll never regret it." I never did.

I hadn't thought much about being traded. There was always talk, but I never paid much attention to talk. I was young and an important part of a winning team. I knew a lot of people didn't realize how important a part of the team I was, but I knew my teammates, manager, and general manager knew.

And then suddenly I wasn't young anymore and I was on a losing team that had to rebuild for the future. I had physical problems and a limited future and I realized no one was going to rebuild around Rosey. I started to think about being traded.

That winter I went to Puerto Rico for the Prudential Insurance Company as part of an all-star team selected to make an instructional film. Among the others there was Jim Perry of the Minnesota team. We were talking and I told him I was afraid I might be traded. He said the Twins needed a catcher and might take me. They were trying to trade their shortstop, Versalles, who had slowed down suddenly. I knew the Dodgers needed a shortstop to take Wills's place. I put two and two together and it came out a trade of me for Versalles.

It's funny, but that's exactly the way it worked out. I'm sure both talked to other teams, but the end of November I was told I had been traded with Ron Perranoski and Bob Miller to the Twins for Versalles and Mudcat Grant. I was glad I was going with a couple of my good buddies, but I was sorry to be going.

I think I was friends with all the players I played with on the Dodgers. I don't think I made an enemy, at least not among those that lasted any time. All teams, good and bad, become a sort of family. Some have more frictions than others. The Dodgers didn't put up with players who caused friction.

Most players leave in the off-season. When you report to the team for the next season, some guys are simply gone. Most players who are traded in the middle of the season leave in the middle of the night. There is little of this keeping a stiff upper lip and going from guy to guy and saying good-bye. Not often.

I remember when John Podres was traded in the middle of the 1966 season. He was a woman-chaser, a gambler, and a drinker, but he never hurt anyone but himself. He helped us, and we all liked him. We were in Philadelphia and it was early in the morning. I hurried down to his hotel room to say good-bye to him. I opened the door and a cloud of smoke hit me. He was sitting in a chair with a big cigar in his mouth and tears in his eyes. He was surrounded by empty whiskey bottles and beer bottles. He hadn't slept since getting the word the night before. He'd been by himself, drinking himself drunk, crying. He said, "John, they've traded me. I can't believe they'd trade me, but they have. What the hell can I do?"

I felt terrible because I couldn't help him. The only thing I could do was to tell him to go and make the best of it. Hang on a season or two more. Maybe make a comeback. As long as you're in the game, you have hope. You could do it before, you can do it again. You just can't believe you had it and then no longer have it. It takes time to see it. Suddenly, you're out of time. Most men can do what they do all their lives. Athletes have a limited time to do what they like to do, and do best. Then suddenly you're out of time.

So Podres had gone, a grown man with tears in his eyes, a happy-go-lucky, devil-may-care kind of guy who ran into the one thing he couldn't take too well. It hurt me and I cried for him. And now it was my turn to cry. After sixteen years in pro ball, all with the Dodgers' organization, eleven with the Dodgers themselves, ten in Los Angeles, they were through with me. I was on my way to Minnesota.

I was almost thirty-five years old. Was I finished? Trades are the toughest part of sports. Unless you want one, it's tough to be told you've been traded to another team. Maybe your new team wanted you, but you always think that your old team no longer did. You've been rejected. You have no choice but to go or retire. When you're thirty-four or thirty-five you think of quitting, but I went, hoping to hang on another few years.

22.

My BEST baseball years were with the Dodgers. The few that followed couldn't be compared. The best general manager I ever played for was Buzzie Bavasi and the best manager I ever played for was Walter Alston, both of the Dodgers. The others weren't even in the same class.

Walter was the only manager I had with the Dodgers. He had his faults. We all do. He knew baseball as well as anyone, but he was slow-witted. He missed some opportunities because he didn't see them soon enough and seize them fast enough. There were certain choices that the manager was supposed to make for us, but sometimes we'd look over at Walter and he'd shrug as if to say, "I dunno, what do you think best?"

Alston was stoical. He just sat there on the bench, thinking. His strategy was almost always conservative and safety first. He played the game by the book. He didn't want to be second-guessed by the press and the public and didn't want to be criticized by the front office. He thought if he always did what he was supposed to do, who could criticize him? He wasn't wrong, because he wasn't fired the way others were.

But there are times you have to do something different. Like those seasons when Wills was leading off and getting on base and stealing ninety or a hundred bases. Gilliam always batted second. If Wills got on, Alston always signaled Gilliam to bunt him to second. Why give up an out when Wills was going to steal second anyway? And when Wills got to second,

Walter sometimes bunted him to third. Why bunt him to third when he might steal it and when he was in scoring position already?

It used to make all of us mad. We knew we were an easy team to manage against. I felt I could outsmart the man at every turn. But you think like that when you're a player, try to think the game through and think about the things the manager does. I never knew a player who wasn't critical of his manager, even the best. We still won more than our share because we executed well. The smartest baseball in the world can't beat you if you've got a Sandy Koufax pitching a shut-out.

The only time Alston took a chance was when he started a tired Koufax instead of a rested Drysdale in the final game of the 1965 World Series, but with Sandy you weren't taking much of a chance. There isn't any doubt Alston blew the third playoff game against the Giants in 1962. He shouldn't have let a substitute move his second baseman out of position. He should have gotten his tired reliever out of there sooner, he shouldn't have brought in a wild Williams; he should have turned to the dependable Perranoski, and he should have grabbed Drysdale's offer to pitch before we even got into trouble. He had no business saving a starter for a World Series before we even got into it.

I don't think there is any doubt that we would have won with Durocher managing. Durocher thought that we were too tight, conservative, cautious all down the stretch, and he was right, and I'm sure he would have driven us harder than Alston did.

Durocher would not have made the mistakes Alston made in the third game. Yet, how many mistakes did Alston make in his career? He may have lost a few close races, but he never lost one while I played for him. He lost that playoff, but had tied for first. He won seven pennants in his career, four while I was with him. How many did Leo ever win? Three, that's how many. And he blew a big lead with Chicago after he left LA. It's not fair to say he'd never have let one get away.

If you manage, you make mistakes. Because he was con-servative, Walter made fewer mistakes than any other manager

I ever saw. Because he was so aggressive and took so many chances, Leo probably made many more mistakes. I saw certain mistakes while Walter was making them in '62, and maybe I wouldn't have made them myself, but maybe I'd have made others. I wasn't in his class. He was slow, but sure.

I didn't see him get mad much. He chased Koufax and Sherry through the hall in spring training and challenged Cimoli in the shower. He stopped a team bus in Pittsburgh and challenged the players to stop bitching or take him on. But he didn't get mad much and maybe he should have chewed guys out more. He was an even-tempered guy and he'd wait a day to get on a guy about a mistake. I think he hurt guys like Howard and Willie Davis and Tommy Davis by not getting on them for their mistakes. They needed a push and he never gave it to them, so they never became the players they might have been. When he tried to tell us off in a team meeting, his tongue would get tangled and he couldn't get the words out. He was not articulate.

We felt we weren't getting as much out of our manager as we should have and it used to frustrate us. In retrospect, a lot of us look back and see that he gave us a lot more than we realized. He may have played by the book, but he taught it to us. We were always way ahead of the next team on fundamentals.

We always knew how our games were going to be played and where we stood. He didn't overmanage. He let us play our game. He didn't keep us if he didn't have confidence in us. He always showed confidence and that gave us confidence. He was patient and didn't pressure us into mistakes.

Alston was a man of integrity. He didn't have much to say, but he meant what he did say. He didn't lie or try to con us. He was a clean, decent man, on and off the field. He knew ballplayers aren't saints and knew we were doing some things off the field we shouldn't, but the line he drew was where the team morale would be disrupted. He treated the team as if it were his family. He was the sort of father who didn't interfere in everything his boys did but would disown anyone who was disrespectful.

Most important, he kept things on an even keel. He took

the games one at a time and added the wins and losses up at the end. He didn't start talking pennant after a few wins and he didn't give up after a few losses. No matter what our record was or where we were in the standings, he wanted us to do our best. If we stayed in a race, he figured we could win it in the end. If we lost it, he figured we could come back next season. Our management was that way all down the line and it helped.

He had to be the easiest man you could play for.

He surrounded himself with good coaches and let them do the job. One of his coaches, Preston Gomez, managed bad ball clubs later and is back with the Dodgers now. Everyone respects Gomez as a man and as a manager. Danny Ozark wasn't as prominent, but he has had some success managing Philadelphia, though he has been controversial.

One of the organization's scouts and batting coaches, Ken Meyer, was sensational. He had revolutionary ideas about batting and how to teach it. He was chastized by the front office for it, but he taught each player to use his own natural style the best way he could. Another batting coach. Andy High, always taught everyone the same way, and it hurt them. You can overcoach.

Tom Lasorda was managing in the minors and was not a coach with the club when I was with it. When he came up as a coach, he attracted a lot of attention. He's a colorful character who always has a lot to say. Dodgers' blue runs in his blood, is one thing he always says. From what I know of him he's smart and dedicated and very enthusiastic. He's a player's manager who gives the players a lot of enthusiasm and treats them really well. The only thing that worries me is he's a rah-rah guy and I'm afraid it'll wear thin after a while. It's a long season and you can't play every night as if the world will end if you don't win. I always wanted to be a professional who went out and did a job without a lot of cheerleading.

Lasorda was regarded as the next manager all the time he was with Alston, as if Tom was looking over Walter's shoulder, but Alston is the kind of guy who could live with that. I think the only coach Alston couldn't live with was Leo. It wasn't so much that Leo was looking to take Walter's job, which he was, but that Leo took a lot of authority away from Walter.

Alston announced Leo would coach third and relay the signs from the dugout to the batter. Leo got up and warned the guys they had to look fast: "I'm two pitches ahead of what's going to happen so I'm going to give the signs fast." Then he looked at Alston and added, "I hope you give the signs to me fast enough, Walter." And everyone laughed because we all knew Alston was slow and waited until the last second to make up his mind and sometimes waited too long and missed the play. Leo didn't wait. He gave his own signs. He often ignored Alston's signs. Alston would signal bunt; Leo would signal hit-away.

Leo knew the book, too, backwards and forwards. Better than any man I've ever known. He could play the percentages. And he could go against the grain, too. He could play a hunch. Take the other team by surprise.

You never knew what to expect when you were working against Durocher. He kept you off balance. The players liked that. It encouraged them to take chances and made them aggressive. Leo loved daring, aggressive baseball, and it was fun to play. He was fun to be with. Not a great looker, but loaded with charm, a ladies' man, close to stars like Sinatra, much as Lasorda is.

Leo was a man of many moods. He didn't handle defeat as well as Walter. Leo brooded over defeats, but maybe it was because he wasn't manager and hated having to stand by while another man managed defeats. With his ego, Leo never thought he'd lose when he was managing. Leo lost a lot, of course, but blamed the fates. He couldn't stand it when a player made mistakes. He always wanted to tell him about it right then and there. Alston always said to wait awhile and it drove Durocher crazy. He didn't want to wait. He wanted to win and he was impatient. Leo was the sort of guy who could kick you in the butt one minute and pat you on the butt the next. The players knew he never carried a grudge and was always willing to help.

One season this woman started calling me at my hotel every time the team got to New York. I kept turning her off, but she kept calling me back. She said she was from upstate and was coming to town and wanted to see me. I told her to hold up, I didn't even know who she was and I didn't make dates on the telephone. She said she was 36–24–36, a black girl with long black hair and a good figure, her folks had a greeting-card company, and she was wealthy. She had a beautiful voice and I thought maybe I was turning down the Queen of Sheba. She said she had seen me play and just got turned on by me and would dearly love to meet me. I had turned down women on the telephone before, but this one got to me. I said I'd meet her in the lobby when she got to town. She set a time and told me she'd be wearing a blue dress. I couldn't wait to see her.

When the time came, I put on my suit and went to scout the lobby. When I located a lady in a blue dress she was the darkest, fattest, sloppiest-looking woman I'd seen. But before I could beat it out of there she spotted me.

I was too chicken to call her on her lies. The last thing I wanted to do was go out with her, but I got her away from that hotel fast and got through a few hours with her. She said she had an apartment in town, so I took her there. It turned out to be a fancy building in a fancy neighborhood. I said I had to get back to the hotel and said goodnight. She went in as if she owned the place. I figured maybe she did have money, but she was a mullion of the worst kind and I didn't want anything from her.

After that, she kept calling and I kept putting her off. She started to call me in every town we went to. I have no idea how she knew which were our hotels. Then she started to call me at home in LA, where I had an unlisted number. I told Devil about her and he said she'd gone after every player on the team until she got to me and I was the first to fall for her. He said she used to be a telephone operator, which gave her an "in" to get numbers, and worked for some wealthy couple at that apartment house. I told him she was starting to get to my wife and I was worried she'd do me some harm. He told me to take it to Durocher. Not Alston, Durocher. So I did.

Leo always said if any of his players had a problem, he wanted to help him. So I took to Leo a problem I never would have taken to Walter. And Leo took care of it. He asked me for her name and number and told me not to worry. "I'll call my man, Toots Shor, and he'll handle it," Leo said. I guess he did. I don't know what he did, but I never heard from her again.

That's the kind of guy Leo was. If you needed help, he gave it. If you made a mistake, he chewed you out. But if you made a great play, he slapped you on the back. Alston never did either. Leo was involved with his players. Black or white, it never made any difference to him. There were some we suspected it made a difference to and some we knew it did. Some simply were not as comfortable around blacks as around their own kind. They treated blacks as though they were really different. But Leo had the knack of treating everyone naturally. He and Charlie Dressen were the only ones I ever knew who got involved in business deals and brought the blacks into them as fast as they did the whites. Leo didn't play favorites, except he preferred guys who put out to those who didn't. Leo put out.

Alston was the best manager I ever played for, but I would love to have played for Durocher. Leo was the smartest man I ever knew in baseball, even if his record doesn't show it.

Management sets the tone for a team and after I left the Dodgers I landed on all sorts of troubled teams that were out of control. I think it was only after I left the Dodgers that I got a realistic look at life on big-league baseball teams.

With the Dodgers, Walter O'Malley ran the organization with a strong hand but stayed in the background. Buzzie Bavasi had a lot of authority as general manager and Buzzie directed the day-to-day operations. He was a man a player could talk to. He treated people well and he was honest.

When I got to the Twins I found the Minnesota owner, Cal Griffith, the least likable person I met in baseball. He did not have the money to operate a big-league team properly and he was always cutting corners. That was all right except he acted as his own general manager, and he acted arrogantly. He never said honestly he didn't have the money for this or that; he always said you didn't deserve it.

He acted as though he was a plantation owner and the rest of us were slaves. He'd pass us without speaking or even nodding half the time. If he did talk to us, he often told us things that weren't true. He'd say someone was only making so much money and we'd find out he was making much more. He'd make side deals with some players to pay them more than their contracts called for to keep them happy. He'd make promises he wouldn't keep.

He was always out front, bragging and blustering, ranting and raving, blaming others for his own faults.

The manager when I got there, Cal Ermer, was a weak man. He was quiet like Alston, but he didn't have Walt's firmness and he didn't have the respect Walter had. It was said Ermer's wife ran him. He didn't run the team. It sort of ran itself. He made up the lineup card and he made the substitutions, but he didn't tell anyone how to play. He didn't seem to know the game too well and was slow in making decisions. He was the weakest manager I ever watched operate.

The first day I was with the Twins in spring training in Florida, Ermer got me alone and started to tell me that we didn't have a bad club and that some of the guys on it weren't as bad as they were supposed to be. He spoke about Dave Boswell and Ted Uhlaender, who'd had an argument on a plane the year before, with Boswell pulling a gun. It got a lot of publicity.

"Boswell and Uhlaender aren't bad guys, they're just hell-raisers, you know," he told me.

I cut him short. I said, "Hey, Skip, I don't want to know about it. I'll make up my own mind about them."

That made him mad. He made a face, shrugged, and walked away.

I don't believe everything I hear. I've heard too much that turns out to be nothing. I make up my own mind.

Minnesota had some interesting people. Harmon Killebrew was one of the classiest I've ever met. He was a big-name veteran but a down-to-earth guy, very straight, in a class with Reese and Erskine and Koufax. Bobby Allison was another in that league. A little more of a happy-go-lucky cat, but very straight, and he loved to talk baseball. Jim Kaat was another classy character, very decent. Tony Oliva was a little flaky but a lovely guy. Leo Cardenas was a lively, likable cat. Cesar

Tovar was a pepperpot, full of fun. Frank Quilici was a straight sort who later became manager.

Rod Carew was a young guy and wild at that time. He hadn't married and settled down and he was after all the ladies and they were all after him. Dean Chance's marriage was broken up or breaking up because he was always running around. Deano was as wild as a man can be. He'd learned from Bo Belinsky when both were with the Angels that life was one big party and that's the way he lived. He had as much ability as any pitcher I ever saw, even Koufax, but screwing the ladies eventually screwed him up.

Uhlaender and Boswell were trigger-tempered guys, but okay.

Uhlaender turned out to be a college kid, sharp mentally, a marvel at math, an artist. I got to talking to him about having learned to fly in Florida and before I knew it he was taking lessons. Within one year he had earned his license and bought his own plane. We talked about flying a lot and became buddies.

Boswell was something else. Boswell was brought up in gangs, a big guy, rough. He liked guns, but so did I. We both had gun collections, which was something we had in common and could talk about. I had a Luger I couldn't get ammunition for. I traded it to Bos for two .25 automatics. He spent all the next season cussing me out because he couldn't get ammunition for the Luger, either.

Jim Perry came on as a very religious guy. He and his wife made a big thing about being churchgoing, community-active type people and I'm always suspicious of that sort. He had a holier-than-thou attitude. There was a lot of that there. And a lot of wisecracks about blacks and Latins and Jews.

There were cliques on the club. The blacks hung out together, the Latins had their own group, and the whites stayed to themselves. It was a divided team and management did nothing to pull it together. In fact, the Latins, like Tovar, were badly underpaid and understandably bitter. Ermer had no control of the club.

All the years I was with the Dodgers there was only one racial flare-up I can recall. When Marv Breeding, a Southerner, was with the ball club, he became buddies with Tommy Davis. And they were always telling each other racial jokes. I warned Davis it could lead to trouble, but he didn't believe me. With the Dodgers, a white man could call me a nigger and I didn't mind, the way one black man can call another black man a nigger because we know where it's coming from. But you can go too far. One day one of Breeding's jokes went too far and Davis went at him and I had to break up the battle. It could have cost Breeding his place on the team, because Tommy was more important to the team. You have to keep this stuff under control, but the Twins were a troubled team, full of bickering and bitterness.

There weren't a lot of blacks in Minnesota and some of the black ballplayers were dating white girls. The good ones could get away with it, but the fringe players couldn't. A Carew could get away with it because he was important to the Twins and they didn't dare antagonize him. Even so, he took a lot of heat from management and from the public when he went with a white girl who was Jewish, who he eventually married. But they threatened to send a lesser player down to Denver when he went with a white girl. The guy gave her up so he could keep his place on the team.

The team had a lot of offense, mediocre defense, and fair pitching. Killebrew and Oliva were at their peaks, power-houses, with heavy hitters behind them. Carew was coming on, not the hitter he was to become, but a young guy with the strongest arms and fastest hands I've seen. He was playing second at the time, couldn't field worth a damn, but didn't want to be moved, so he wasn't. Cardenas was a skillful short-stop and Tovar was a good all-around player who could play a lot of positions. But most of the team was slow and clumsy.

I had a so-so season in 1968. I'm a line-drive hitter and Metropolitan Stadium was tougher for me than Dodger Stadium. Dodger Stadium was bigger, so the outfielders had to spread out and a lot of my hits found the holes. The Met was smaller, the outfielders bunched up, and a lot of my drives went right at people. I hit hard, but had a terrible .216 and didn't produce many runs. I did do a job defensively and did help the pitchers produce.

At the first meeting when the managers and coaches got together with the pitchers and catchers to go over the pitching plans they told me their signs were one finger for a fast ball, two for a curve, three for a slider, and four for an off-pitch. I waited. That was it.

I asked, "Is that all there is?" It was sandlot stuff. They said, "What more do you need?" I said, "What about where you're going to throw?" They said, "You move your glove." I said, "With the Dodgers we used a much more complicated series of signs. You moved your fingers to say exactly how and where you wanted the pitch to be thrown. It worked because we had top pitching year after year." They said, "Well, you're not with the Dodgers now." Which was the first of many hints that they were not too happy about me talking up the Dodgers and making comparisons.

I suppose I was wrong, but the lack of sophistication in their methods really made me mad. They weren't even aware of the weaknesses of the batters and didn't work on them or set them up.

We wasted a lot of our strengths, lacked leadership, and never got going. It was a long season. We lost ten games more than we won and finished seventh in the ten-team league, about thirty games behind Detroit. Strangely enough, the Dodgers also finished seventh in the other league. As it turned out, it would take time for them to build back up.

I didn't think the American League was nearly as aggressive as the National League or had the all-around strength. You can shrug it off as a black man's opinion but it is also a ballplayer's opinion that the difference is that ever since Jackie Robinson broke the color barrier in the National League, that League has welcomed more black players and has had more talent to pick from. Aaron, Mays, Banks, Clemente, Wills, Stargell, Brock, Allen, Morgan, and others have given the National an advantage. The American has had only a few stars of this type at this time. When Frank Robinson went from the National to the American he sparked his team to a series of titles.

Calvin Griffith wanted to pay slave wages. Thanks to Bavasi, I brought a sixty-thousand-dollar contract with me to Minnesota so I was set for my first season. But before I could even get to Griffith to talk contract for '69, a newspaper story said he wanted to cut me twenty grand. He was always bragging about cutting costs and salaries, which didn't endear him to the players or the public either. He was his own worst public relations man. He couldn't have cut me twenty grand if he wanted to. The maximum allowable cut was twenty percent, which for me meant twelve grand. He had the gall to send me a contract with a twenty-grand cut in it. I just sent it back.

When I went in to talk to him about it, he pointed to my batting average. I said I hit the ball hard, but in bad luck, but he wouldn't buy that. He said, "You didn't contribute to the team offensively."

I said, "You didn't get me for my offensive contributions. You knew what my offensive stats were when you traded for me. You had all the offense you needed on this team. You needed defense. You traded for a defensive catcher and you got a good one."

He said, "You hit fifty points less than the year before." Which I had. He continued, "I have to pay you a lot less than you were paid the year before for the kind of year you had here."

I said, "You want to cut me more than you can legally. Legally, the most you can cut me is twelve thousand."

He said, "Well then, that's what I'll cut you."

I said, "I won't take it."

He said, "Then you won't play."

I went home. Not to LA, but to a house we'd bought on a lake in Minnesota. It wasn't LA weather for sure. Wet summers and snowy winters. Coldest winter I ever spent, but I had a good job for the off-season with a computer company and I needed the money.

Griffith and I sent letters back and forth all winter arguing salary. I kept saying, "You got a good ballplayer, but if you expected to get a Roy Campanella or Yogi Berra you were wrong." He kept saying, "You're the kind of ballplayer who doesn't realize how lucky you are to be in baseball, much less the major leagues, and if you think I'm going to pay you one cent more than forty-eight grand, you're crazy."

At one point I suggested, "Let's sit down and talk about it. Maybe I'll take the cut, but if I have a good year, hit say .270, you can give me the twelve thousand back."

He said, "There's nothing to talk about. You'll take the cut and you'll give me a good year for the good money I'm paying you. I don't make deals like you suggested."

But he did. The next year, Harmon Killebrew and Rich Reese showed me checks they had gotten from Griffith above and beyond their contracts by agreement to compensate them for good years.

Maybe you think I was asking for too much. Maybe I was. The average man doesn't make forty-eight grand, much less sixty, but I wasn't an average man. I was a ballplayer with a limited future. Players on my level were making sixty grand.

I had to make what I could before my career ran out. But, in the end, I had to take forty-eight thousand because it was all I could get from that guy, I couldn't just go to another team, and I didn't dare quit and try to make that kind of money in civilian life.

This was before the agreements granting athletes the same rights as other citizens, the right to play out your contract and then seek a contract from any team of your choice. At that time I had no options, so I signed at the man's price.

Griffith fired Ermer and brought in Billy Martin to manage in 1969. Martin turned out to be a lot like Leo, and just about as sharp. He knew the game inside out and he was quick to seize on every opportunity. I learned a lot from Leo and Billy about baseball. If you couldn't do something, they could live with it, but both hated mental mistakes. Both chewed ass when anyone made one. Both brooded about being beaten. They had the same intensity. But both were good guys off the field. Both could be charming to the players and helpful to them.

They had their weaknesses. Both had to run their own show and both hated front-office interference. They were working stiffs, but couldn't stand to take advice from their bosses. Leo had a little diplomacy, but Billy had none. Billy would tell a boss to go fuck himself. But you don't tell a Griffith that. Billy could be one of the guys, playing cards with the players, drinking with them, telling the greatest stories of his escapades with Mantle and Ford, Yogi and Casey. But if he got mad at a player, he wanted to fight him. Billy was brought up settling disputes with his fists; using them robs a manager of his dignity. Alston threatened, but Billy did it.

When he puts on a uniform, Billy becomes a red ass. He really drives. He doesn't let up for a moment. He's a brutal bench jockey, always riding the other players, but he's almost as bad driving his own. I don't know how long you can live with that intensity, but players are willing to pay a price if it pays off. You had the feeling you would win with Billy, or else.

I went along with him on everything but one thing. Billy believed in knocking batters down. So do I, but not to the extent Billy does. You set certain batters up but you don't knock a hitter down just because the previous hitter hit a home run. That's a cheap shot by an angry pitcher. And the catcher has to call a knockdown pitch, or at least know it's coming. Billy was calling them from the dugout directly to the pitcher in all sorts of situations. It got his pitcher and catcher into all sorts of trouble.

I can remember Reggie Jackson at bat with a man on base. I called for a low, outside fast ball and Dick Woodson came in with a high, inside hard one that knocked the batter down. There was no way I could catch the pitch. As I chased it I realized Reggie was charging the mound. I turned to him and tackled him to protect my pitcher. I found myself on the ground surrounded by those funny yellow socks the A's wore, with no Twins in sight. I realized some teams didn't back up their teammates the way the Dodgers and A's did, and a guy could get killed taking on a team on his own. Luckily, the umps broke it up.

I confronted Martin, not Woodson. I knew Woodson hadn't wanted to throw the knockdown, but Billy had ordered it. I said, "Billy, if you want to call the fucking pitches, call them, but tell me about it." He said, "I'll call the ones I want." I said, "Well, you warn me or you can get yourself another catcher." Billy said, "Maybe I will."

But he didn't. He didn't mind an argument. He didn't carry grudges. But he was hard on pitchers. Every time we gave up a hit, we'd hear him rattling the bat rack. Finally, I had another confrontation with him. I said, "Dammit, Billy, you never pitched and you never caught, but if you think you can call the pitches better, be my guest, only stop rattling the bat rack and rattling your own pitchers."

When Billy would go out to take out a pitcher who had gone bad, he'd be cussing, call the guy a "choke-up," and would threaten to demote him to Denver. After a while we saw that this was just his way, that he lost his temper in tight spots, and wanted to win so badly that he lost control of himself. He'd be all right later.

The older pitchers could handle it. They ignored him or cussed him back, but they didn't let him get to them. The younger guys found it hard to handle. They kept looking for him in the dugout, so choked up they were afraid to throw the ball. I talked to Billy about it and he agreed it was a weakness, but said he was working to overcome it. I knew he was new at managing and I figured he could do it, and if he did control his temper he could be the best.

He did give me a freer hand with the pitchers than Ermer had. And I helped them. We worked up a more sophisticated system of signals and bore down better. Perry and Boswell both won twenty games, which they never had before. I can't say I pitched for them, but I can say I helped. Perranoski didn't need any help. He was sensational in relief, which made up for a lack of starters.

With Carew, Reese, and Tovar getting on base and Killebrew and Oliva driving them home, we scored a ton of runs. Killebrew was MVP that season, but the versatile Tovar could have been, as far as I was concerned. Martin was kind of crazy in that he seemed to like to create turmoil, but he drove the guys so hard they forgot about bickering and started to win. They didn't dare lose.

We won eight or nine in a row a couple of times. We won ninety-seven games in all and won our division by nine or ten games over Oakland. The league had expanded to twelve teams and split into two divisions. This was when the A's were just putting together their tremendous team and were a year or two away from developing a dynasty. It was great to be with a winner again, an exciting season. But life with Billy Martin was bound to be exciting.

In August he got into something of a mess. On Martin's orders, Twins' pitchers had to run a certain number of laps in the outfield on off days to stay in shape. When Boswell left the field after running only a couple of laps, pitching coach Art Fowler argued with him. That night, Fowler reported the incident to Martin in a Detroit tavern. Boswell was in the bar too, and when Billy went to him to ask him about it, Boswell called Fowler a squealer and went after him. Bob Allison got between them and got Boswell outside.

Bob was standing in the parking lot, with his hands in his pockets, trying to calm Boswell down, when Dave suddenly slugged him. Instinctively trying to pull his hands out of his pockets as he went down, Allison tore the seams in his pants. Before he could get up, Boswell started to kick him. But Billy came flying out of the club and landed on Dave. I don't know how he did it, but he beat the hell out of the much bigger guy.

Boswell was so badly marked up he had to be sent home for a few days. Next time we saw him, his face was still discolored and swollen, one eye still screwed up. We were afraid he might try to blow someone away.

One time Carew had screwed up a play that cost Boswell a ball game. Allison took Dave home to dinner and gave him a couple of drinks to calm him down. But after he took him back to the hotel, Dave went to a room Carew shared with Oliva and kicked the door down in an effort to get at Rod before calmer heads got him away from there.

Poor Allison was always playing good guy and getting burned by Boswell. Martin figured the only way to handle a Boswell was physically, and maybe he was right. Billy proudly showed us his swollen knuckles the next day. He's like the tough kid on the block. But Billy the Kid isn't a kid any longer. He's an adult, and supposed to act like it.

Martin might have been fired right then and there. The story broke in headlines and made Martin and the team look bad. The Twins shouldn't have been in a bar, much less brawling, and with their manager. Griffith was furious. But his team was in first place and he didn't have the guts to make his move.

The A's pulled to within six or seven games of us early in September and had us in their ball park for four games, but we won three of the four. Tovar won two for us with home runs in extra innings, one of them in the eighteenth inning of a marathon. We murdered them in the fourth and final game. They still had another shot at us, two games in our ball park, but we won both behind Boswell and Perry. That finished them.

We drew well over a million fans to the Met that season and Twin City fans were wild. That was before the Twins went on the skids, attendance dropped, and Griffith started to talk about pulling out.

In the playoff for the pennant in 1969 we ran into a well-balanced Baltimore ball club that beat us in two tough games that opened the Series in Baltimore. Perry faced Mike Cuellar in the opener. Oliva hit a two-run home run and we took a 3–2 lead into the ninth. Boog Powell hit a home run to tie it. Perranoski came in as we went into extra innings. Ron didn't allow a hit out of the infield, but they wound up winning it in the twelfth on a two-out, suicide-squeeze bunt. Boswell faced Dave McNally in the second game. They pitched shut-out ball into extra innings, until Curt Motton singled in the only run of a 1–0 game in the eleventh. McNally stopped us on three hits.

We went back to Minnesota without the bounce I had come to expect from my teams. Short of starters, Martin gambled on Miller, the reliever, and we were knocked out early. We got ten hits. I got one. They got eighteen, and Jim Palmer coasted to an embarrassing 11–2 triumph that completed the sweep.

Griffith was embarrassed, bitter. He didn't handle defeat too well. Martin hadn't handled Calvin too well and the old man went looking for reasons to fire him. Even though Billy had won a divisional title, blowing the playoffs was one reason Cal could use. And Billy's bout with Boswell was another.

I gave him one or two. Asked about Billy during the season, I said he had a chance to be a great manager but he sometimes was a little hard on players, especially young players, especially young pitchers. I said a lot of good things about him, but the story that came out said, mainly, that Martin couldn't handle young pitchers. I told Billy I'd been burned by a bad reporter and apologized. He accepted my apology.

Between games we played a lot of poker. One day when the pot had grown to about four hundred dollars, Doc Lentz, the team trainer, came by, saw all the loot on the table, and then told Griffith about it.

Martin was fired that winter. The stories said he had been axed because of his fight with one of his players and because of being swept out of the playoffs. But when I ran into Billy, at the bar at Duff's in Minneapolis, he told me the only reason Griffith had given him was that we'd been the leaders of big-money poker games, which disrupted team morale. And he quoted me as saying he couldn't handle young pitchers. I felt terrible about it, but we agreed Griffith was the kind of guy who wanted to manage his own team, who wanted a weak manager he could handle, who wouldn't take back talk from anyone, and who had been looking for excuses to let a strong guy go.

We sat around for hours, moaning and groaning about it, before Billy went on his way. He had won the division, but he could buy losing the playoff as a reason for being fired.

He went on to Detroit, where he won the division, but lost the playoff and was fired. He came close to winning in Texas, but he got fired again. Then he won the division and the playoff in New York with the Yankees, but spent the following season on the verge of being fired before winning everything. He takes over teams that have been losing and wins with them, but he argues with his bosses, fights with his players, and creates turmoil. He is a great manager and a good guy, but hard to live with.

I got fired from Minnesota too. I had caught well, handled the pitchers very well, even hit pretty well at .263. I had made the American League all-star team. I was trying to figure out how to talk Griffith into giving me my twelve-grand cut back when I found out he was about to give me my release. I got a telephone call from Dick Walsh, who was general manager of the California Angels in Anaheim at that time, and he told me I had been put on the waiver list. The Angels were interested in me, and would offer me forty-five thousand. He wanted to know if I was interested. I said I was because I'd be happy to get back to southern California, but I said I was surprised I was available. I'd done a good job for the Twins and I was shocked that Griffith was going to give me away. I hung up unhappy, cursing Griffith. I knew he'd never been too happy with me. I should have seen the signs when they started to use a young guy behind the plate at times, George Mitterwald, who started two playoff games.

Then I got a call from Bob Short, who lived in Minnesota but owned the Senators in Washington. Short said he was interested in me for the Senators and asked me to come see him at his office in the hotel he owned, the Leamington. When I got there, he asked me if I wanted to play awhile yet. I said I did. Then he asked me what I wanted to do when I was finished playing and I said I wanted to go into broadcasting, or maybe law enforcement, having worked a little while with the sheriff's office in Pomona.

He said, "Look, I think you can still play. We need a catcher. We also could use a name player who's black. We've got a big black population in Washington. We need a drawing card. We'll pay you forty-five grand. We also may need a manager. I have a manager now, Ted Williams, who may get a hair up his ass at any time and decide to go fishing and forget the game. If he does, you're my manager. Either way, when the time comes I can get you on our broadcasting team. Or even one of the federal law-enforcement agencies. I have a lot of political pull in Washington."

Well, he was a charmer. I thought if just one of those things came through, I'd be set for life. I said, "I think you may have yourself a man. I have a loose end to tie up, but if you'll give me a day or so I'll get right back to you." He told me to take all the time I wanted. It didn't take long.

I called Dick Walsh and told him about Bob Short's offer. He said, "I hate to talk against another man, but Bob talks a better game than he plays. He's a supersalesman, but he's not known for coming through. It's your choice, but he's made a lot of promises to people he hasn't kept." I said, "I'm sorry to hear that, but I have to hope for the best. The money's the same, and if any one of the opportunities he's offered develops, I'll be in good shape." I thanked Walsh, and he wished me well. I went back to Bob and signed with the Senators.

The Senators trained in Pompano Beach, Florida. They stayed in a small hotel and played in a small park. Short was as short of cash as Griffith, and just as cheap. He'd paid a lot to land Williams, but Ted was a star, not a manager; he was supposed to be a drawing card, but no one goes out to see a man manage. They played in a new, big ball park in Washington but couldn't fill the first deck, much less even open the top deck.

The political people, the people with money, left town every evening for Maryland or Virginia. The people who stayed in town, mostly black, couldn't afford the tickets. I suggested they'd make a little money by selling the seats upstairs for fifty cents each, but the Bob Shorts and Calvin Griffiths of this world don't want to listen to anything that sounds like they'll be giving anything away.

I was anxious to meet Williams, one of the greatest hitters of all. I was interested in the science of hitting, though I didn't have the tools to be a great hitter myself.

The first question he asked was, "Hello, John, how many home runs did you hit last year?" I said, "I don't know—three or four." He said, "You should know. Who did you hit them off?" I said, "I don't remember." He said, "A good hitter remembers every home run he hit, every hit, the pitcher, and the pitch he hit. If you're going to play for me, you're going to be able to tell me everything about every pitcher on both sides, every pitch, and every hit."

From that moment on, he taught me more about hitting in a few months than I had learned in my lifetime. He taught me how batters swing and what works and what doesn't work and how a batter can set up a pitcher instead of the other way around, which is the way I'd always looked at it. He showed me how to take bad pitches and go for good pitches, how to wait for the pitch you want. He had it down to a science. Ted Williams knew more about hitting than any man I ever met, and I have become a good batting instructor because I use a lot of what he taught me. Baseball has missed a mark by not using him as a roving batting teacher, working with players on all teams.

Unfortunately, hitting was all he talked about, all he cared about. He didn't care about baseball beyond the bat. I don't know if he knew the entire game. He let his coaches run the games. He gave his signals only to his hitters.

However, he couldn't help me. I was beyond help. I don't know when it happened, but it had happened—I had lost it. I had been struggling a few seasons with weight, with a shoulder, with a knee. I had bounced back the year before. But suddenly, in 1970, I had slowed down. My hands were slow, and my arm, my legs, and my eyes were gone. It was horrible. I used to kid him, "Where were you when I needed you, twenty years ago when you could have helped me?" He'd laugh a little. He knew what it was.

I think I hit .230. I'd hit that before, but before I'd hit the ball hard in bad luck, and now I wasn't hitting hard, I needed luck to get a hit. I was thirty-seven years old and had to face the fact that I was just about finished. I hated to admit it even to myself, but I had to go home to my family, to the fine place we'd found in the country, and pretend I was slumping temporarily. I figured I could still catch. But Ted took that away from me.

One night we were pitching a kid named Joe Coleman in Anaheim. He had a live fast ball but couldn't get his curve across the plate. I had to work with his fast ball, but they got a run off him in the first inning on a couple of cheap hits. When I got to the dugout Ted said, "Rosey, I want that goddamn fast-ball pitcher out there to start working with his curve ball." I said, "Okay, Skip, we'll start working in some curves." He said, "I don't want you to work in curves. I want him to throw only curves."

I couldn't believe it. I said, "Skip, he can't get by with his curve. He'll get killed." Ted said, "He can't get by with his fast ball. He's got to learn the curve." I said, "Okay, but you can't ask that poor fucking kid to learn in front of all those people in the stands." Ted said, "Fuck the people. It's time the goddamn fast-ball pitcher learned." I said, "I can't catch that way." He said, "Then you can't catch."

After that I didn't catch for fifty games. The players, who can be cruel, called Coleman "the goddamn fast-ball pitcher" and me "the goddamn fast-ball catcher." And then I was called into a conference with Williams and Short and was told there was no longer any point to keeping me on the active list. They were bringing up another catcher. They said that I could coach and travel with the team the last part of the season and draw the rest of my salary, or quit and try to catch on with another team. I wanted to quit and walk away with my head held high, but I knew I couldn't catch on anywhere at that point and I needed my salary. I talked it over with my wife and we decided maybe if I coached there the rest of the year I could catch on as a coach somewhere else next year.

I stuffed my pride and stayed. It was sad. I was no kind of coach. They had me in the bullpen warming up relief pitchers, but I wasn't coaching them. An old guy named George Susce was the bullpen coach. He was making sixteen thousand for the season and I was still making my forty-five. He couldn't see that that was just the way it worked out. He hated it. He was on my ass about it all the time. The other players loved it. They'd make up signs like ROSEBORO'S BULL-PEN and stick them up just to get George's goat. He'd tear the signs down and snarl that I was stealing my money.

Maybe I was. My pride fell apart in pieces all around me. I became more of a loner than ever. I was among strangers who didn't know me when I could play this game and didn't respect me as a man who earned his keep.

Early in my career with the Dodgers I was making less than twenty grand for playing full time, while late in his career Duke Snider was making more than forty sitting on the bench. I remember complaining to Bavasi about the injustice. He said, "The justice of it is that if you play a long time, and play well, the time will come when you can continue to make the pay you've built up while sitting out your last season or two." I said, "I don't think it will ever happen." It didn't. I don't want to rail about race. But if you look around you'll see that they don't pay many black players as subs once they've lost their ability to play regularly.

It's funny, but I really liked Ted Williams. He was an agreeable guy a lot of the time and he could be good company. I loved to listen to him talk about baseball and I learned a lot from him about hitting. But he was one of those fellows who feels he knows everything, who can't stand anyone disagreeing with him, and has to be the boss. I think he knew a lot more about some things than I did, but I think he was wrong about the one thing.

He was a little like Koufax, but tougher. He was an artist at his specialty and he didn't care about anything else. He hated the attention he attracted and he despised publicity. He had a bad ball club and he had no interest in it. Our only outstanding player was Frank Howard, who hit a ton. Our only outstanding pitcher was Darold Knowles, a reliever. We had players like Mike Epstein, Ed Brinkman, Aurelio Rodriguez, and Del Unser, and pitchers like Dick Bosman, Jim Hannan, and George Brunet, some of whom were fairly good, but none of whom were good enough.

I made a few friends—Bosman, Dick Allen's brother, Hank, and the kid who took over as catcher, Paul Casanova—but I have few good feelings about that team. There was a lot of racial hatred in that town and on that team. It was a losing team and losing teams always fall apart, blaming one another for their failures. Williams didn't even try to hold the team together. He didn't try to inspire his players. He never complimented anyone for a good play or chewed anyone out for a bad one. He seldom had a word to say after games, win or lose. He showered, dressed, and went on his way. We usually lost. We lost twenty games more than we won and finished last.

It was the longest and worst season of my life. I remember that meeting with Short. He never said a word about doing anything for me. I waited for him to come to me with something, but he never did. All he gave me was my release at the end of the season. I never went to see him. What was the point? I had been warned this was a man who made promises he did not keep. Short and Griffith are the only two men I have hated in my life.

But maybe baseball is that way. As long as they need you, they're good to you. When you're no longer any good to them, they have no need for you. Better ballplayers than I was have had a hard time finding a decent place in the game once they no longer could play.

I had to admit I could no longer play and it was the hardest thing I have had to do in my life. I spent many melancholy moments, lonely, feeling lost, wondering what I could do with myself, wishing I could go back twenty years to start all over again. Hot, stinging tears came to my eyes.

23.

THE NEXT year, 1971, turned out to be a tough one because I was out of baseball. I contacted a lot of clubs but couldn't come up with a coaching job. A few things fell through that would have kept me in the game. I was lucky to land a job with a bank at eighteen thousand a year back in LA.

That was quite a comedown from the money I had been making and it created quite a few problems. It was just the start of my money problems.

I was happy when I was contacted for a coaching job with the Angels for the 1972 season. The Angels had been having racial trouble. Alex Johnson had won a batting title for them, but he was a bad apple. He was surly and wouldn't talk to anyone. He had pulled a gun. He'd had an argument with Dick Miller, a rough reporter. They were going to get rid of Alex, but they wanted a black coach to keep the black players in line. I didn't like the idea of being just a black cop but I wanted to get back in baseball.

Del Rice, who had just become manager, called me first, then Harry Dalton, who had just become general manager. I talked to them and told them I wanted to treat all the ball-players alike. They said that would be all right and that my mere presence there would be helpful to the team and maybe give blacks one of their own to turn to. A few did, and I think I helped, but as it turned out I didn't get involved in any big situations.

I said I wanted to be a working coach, but they said the

bullpen job was the only one they had open. I told them I didn't have the highest opinion of bullpen coaching. You answer the phone and warm up the relievers. You tell the manager or the pitching coach whether the pitcher is ready or not. And that's it. I wanted to be the pitching coach, but that was taken. I said I'd give the bullpen a try, but if it didn't lead to something better in time I might not stay with it. They said that was all right. They thought I could do the job they needed at that time and if I did a good job they'd think of me for a better job.

Dalton offered me sixteen thousand. Well, I already had dropped to the other side of the salary scale. I told him I was making eighteen thousand at the bank. We settled on seventeen thousand. I took a cut to get back in baseball.

I considered southern California my home by then and it was good to get back in baseball there. The Angels even trained in southern California—in Holtville and Palm Springs. They played in Anaheim. But the Angels were not the Dodgers and life with them was not what it had been with the Dodgers.

The Angels had been in baseball ten years and hadn't had a winner. I looked it up and they'd only won more games than they'd lost two or three years in that time. They were used to losing and expected to lose. There was little spirit on the team. The ball park was new and attendance was better than it should have been, but they didn't promote the product at all.

The owner, the old cowboy Gene Autry, was a nice man who kept coming around to wish us well. He was a good drinker, but a good guy. Dalton had been brought in from Baltimore, where he had been very successful, and he was expected to build a winner in Anaheim. As it has turned out, he didn't, but I don't know why. Dalton is a dedicated man who knows the game and is serious about his work. He had a terrible team when he took over, but he did turn it into a pretty good team in time, but it still didn't pay off in the standings.

It's almost as though fate has it in for the Angels. Nothing they try seems to work out for them. Good players go bad. They have suffered several serious injuries. A couple of prospects even got killed in off-field accidents. They seem jinxed.

Dalton brought up Del Rice from the farm system to manage that season. Del was a decent man who knew his sport and worked hard. Bobby Winkles, one of the smartest men I've known in this sport, had been brought in from a successful college-coaching career at Arizona State and was coaching at first. Peanuts Lowery, an old outfielder, was coaching at third. Tom Morgan was the pitching coach, one of the best.

As I said, they had a very bad ball club. They had some good pitchers, but few good players.

In his first deal Dalton had traded for Nolan Ryan from the Mets. He threw harder than anyone and always was known as a comer, but he never really got the chance to get it together in New York. He got his chance and he got it together that first year in Anaheim. He came very fast and became if not the best the most spectacular pitcher in the game during my years with the team.

Nolan was like Koufax in that he might do something spectacular anytime he took the mound—strike out eighteen in a game, throw a no-hitter. He was like Koufax in that he was a nice, clean kid who didn't care about publicity. Nollie and Dave Chalk and Tom McCraw and I played a lot of cards and kept to ourselves a lot. Ryan was unlike Koufax in that he was mean on the mound. He'd spin a hitter in a second. He never mastered control and never became consistent. He'd walk himself into losses.

Off the field, Nolan had his head screwed on straight. He was a fine family man. On the field, he was all screwed up upstairs. He was always worried about being in rhythm. He was always worried about striding too soon or too late, too far or too short, about having his arms close enough to his body, about following though right. The hitters were scared half to death of him and struck out half the time, but he was always trying to outsmart them. I don't think it's ever been proved anyone could hit his fast ball, but he was always getting cute with the curve. Even though he hasn't been the pitcher he could have been, he has been a great pitcher.

Another who had a lot of ability, but a lot of troubles, too, was Andy Messersmith. They also had Rudy May, who could throw better than most pitchers, but was scared to death of throwing. He was another mental case, scared of the manager and the pitching coach, always looking into the dugout to see if someone was upset with him. He went to a psychiatrist, but it didn't help. He went to other teams later, but that didn't help. He just never became the pitcher he should have been. Then they had another pitcher, Clyde Wright, a redneck who couldn't throw well but was smart enough to make the most of a lot of junk and got the big outs with a spitter.

Sometimes the starters were really effective, but they had no one behind them, and when they got in trouble there wasn't a good relief pitcher in the entire bullpen.

When I got there the Angels had Gene Oliver on first, Sandy Alomar on second, Leo Cardenas at short, Ken McMullen on third, Jeff Torborg behind the plate, and Lee Stanton, Ken Berry, and Vada Pinson in the outfield. Pinson was past his peak. Berry could go get them but couldn't hit. The only hitter was Oliver, and he was inconsistent. Cardenas had slowed. The team was slow. Mickey Rivers had speed but wasn't being played.

Despite pitching, the Angels lost five games more than they won in '72 and finished fifth in their division.

There were some wild men on and around that team that year and the other years I was there.

When I was with the Dodgers, the broadcasters and the writers were mostly veterans and pretty straight. Vince Scully did as much to popularize the team as anyone. He was a pleasure to listen to. Walked like an athlete, I remember. Didn't mix much on the road. Jerry Doggett was good. Frank Finch, Bob Hunter, and other writers were among the best. There were some hard drinkers, but they kept in control.

Dick Enberg of the Angels was an excellent announcer and some of the young writers had talent, but there were some hard drinkers who were always out of control and some who really ran on the road. Dick Miller was a good reporter, but he was the leader of a pack of wise guys who were always trying to top each other, who covered up for the players who got in trouble, then wrote sarcastically about their playing.

There was a lot of bad feeling in the clubhouse There was one Southerner, a pitcher, who was always bitching about blacks, except he called them "goddamn niggers" when he thought no one was looking. Other whites told us about it, but I never caught him. Baseball has come a long way in its black-white relationships, but a lot of it is out front. Behind the scenes, when the whites are together, there are things said about blacks that they wouldn't want blacks to hear. It was that way in Anaheim.

This white pitcher buddied with one of the black guys on the ball club, but it was all out front. The black guy started to go with a white girl, one of those groupies who are always around. The guys on the team would have parties with the girls, black and white all mixed, and this white girl would sit on this black pitcher's lap, and you could see her boyfriend's buddy tense up. The white guy got her alone one time and beat the girl badly. She didn't come around any more and her boyfriend couldn't figure it.

Maybe Rice should have kept better control of the ball club. Maybe he shouldn't have had some of the parties he had. Not parties exactly, but meetings with the coaches, especially on the road in his hotel suite, to talk about the team. They drank a little and they always kidded me about my Cokes, as if I wasn't a man for not hitting the booze.

Maybe they should have won with a bad ball club. I don't know, but I don't think Rice should have been fired. He was fired that winter before he really got a chance to take hold. I think he would have wound up doing a good job. He had a little to learn, but he had the ability to become a real good manager. He waited a long time for his chance in the big time, then didn't get enough time to make the most of it. I felt real bad when he was bounced.

They moved Bobby Winkles in as manager, but Dalton didn't give him much time, either. If Dalton had a fault it was that he was impatient with his managers, but maybe management put so much pressure on him it caused his impatience. Maybe it comes down to the men they picked to manage. Later, management would say they lacked experience, but hell, they had a lot less experience when they were picked. If they give a man a job they should give him a chance to do the job.

Winks moved me out of the bullpen and made me his first-base coach. He replaced Lowery with Salty Parker as his third-base coach. From the start of spring training in 1973 we could see Winks was well organized. He was smart and imaginative, came up with good ideas, and was a good teacher. He ran a good game. He had the making of a good manager, maybe a great one, but he had his faults.

He was a little too much rah-rah, maybe. He insisted the guys run on and off the field, and wear jackets and ties off the field. Long hair, a lot of it, was in style, but he insisted they keep their hair short and keep hair off their faces. It was all right with me, but it rubbed some of the players wrong. You can't treat big-league ballplayers like college kids. He was out of step with the times.

These things have nothing to do with winning or losing games anyway. Winks had the old-fashioned feeling that rules like that give a team discipline, but they do just the opposite, they put the players in revolt. The things he might have done for discipline, he didn't do. He wasn't tough and didn't chew guys out when they got out of line. He let them make mental mistakes. He was a little guy and he had to build himself up by being strong. When he didn't, the players started to laugh at him.

One plane flight the guys were raising hell. The traveling secretary went to Winks to ask him to restore order, but Winks came to me to ask me to do it. Some of the guys were drunk and chasing the stews up and down the aisle. I had been waiting for Winks to lay the law down. Instead, he came to me and said, "Rosey, go back and see if you can calm them down." I said, "Hey, Winks, that's not my job, that's your job. I'll go back with you and back you up, and if I have to land on someone I will, but I'm not the manager."

He got mad about it and I think we fell out then and there. Winks got the traveling secretary to do what he was supposed to do. And at the end of the year he put me back in the bullpen, like I was exiled. I never had the same kind of close relationship with Winks I'd had with Rice.

The team hadn't made many changes. Rudy Meoli moved in at short and Al Gallagher at third, but neither was any help.

At my suggestion, the Angels acquired Mike Epstein and put him at first and that gave them another bat. They also acquired Richie Scheinblum and he was a good hitter, but they mostly pinch-hit him and didn't play him much. The big deal was a trade of Messersmith and McMullen for Frank Robinson, Bill Singer, Bobby Valentine, and others. Robinson was designated hitter and part-time player. It looked like they really beefed up their batting, but they didn't take much advantage of it.

I knew Epstein from Washington. Mike was a moody but marvelous man, very bright. He was another gun freak and we became good friends. He was a big guy and a big hitter. He had to be handled right. I warned Dalton and Winks that he was hard to handle, but I said, "If you treat him right, he'll do right by you." They took a chance on him.

He warned Winks when he came in, "I get down on myself at times and when I do I don't talk to anyone, not even my managers, but it's not because I'm mad at you, and if you leave me alone I'll come out of it on my own." Winks said that was fine with him. But then the time came when Mike was slumping, Winks said something to him, Mike didn't answer him, walked right by him, and Winks went into a rage, swearing he would never play for him again. He did, but he was in the doghouse from then on. It made him mad and he had a bad year. He was his own worst enemy.

Robinson was slowed down, but produced power for us. He hit thirty or so homers, drove in almost a hundred runs. But he was bodacious, a braggart, loud and crude, and disrupted the team. He was strong and a lot of the guys on the team turned to him and away from Winks. Mostly black players, but others, too. That was Winks's fault because he wasn't strong enough. Guys have to have someone to turn to, someone to look to for leadership. Maybe Robby should have turned them back to Winks, but there was a lot of talk Frank would become the manager. There wasn't any doubt he wanted it, and the more respect the players showed for him, the better his chances. I don't blame him. But it tore the team apart.

Ryan had a sensational season. He pitched two no-hitters and broke Koufax's records by striking out nineteen batters in one game and 383 for the season. Singer had a strong season. Ryan won twenty-one games and Singer won twenty. They won more between them than the rest of the staff put together. With all that pitching and added power, we had about the same season as the season before, lost four or five more than we won, and wound up fourth.

Dalton brought me back as coach in 1974 and even gave me a fat thousand-dollar raise, to eighteen grand. As a coach you have no bargaining power. You take what they want to give you or you go. And I was back in that goddamn bullpen. But I took the job.

I didn't lie to Harry about the bullpen. "That is it, answering the fucking phone?" I said. I'm sure he wanted me to make more of it. He said the man coaching third wasn't doing the job so he was going to be moved to first, which closed that out to me. I said I could coach third, then, which is the key coaching job. He said Winks had someone else in mind for third. He didn't have to tell me Winks didn't want me. Well, I'd popped off once too often. I paid the price. But I took the bullpen because I thought there might still be a future for me with the ball club.

Winks was brought back, but it was understood that he had to get a better job done or he would go. There was a lot of talk Robby would become manager and even a little talk I might. Naturally, we said we wanted to become managers but didn't want to take the job from our manager. Shit, we'd have shot him for it. Most would, whatever else they say. Most who have played think they can manage. I did. Still do.

Denny Doyle and Dave Chalk came in to give us a pretty good double-play combination. Mickey Rivers moved in at center and gave us speed. Ryan threw another no-hitter and had another big year. Frank Tanana turned up to give us another great arm. Singer fell off with a sore arm, but Tanana filled in. But what they didn't win, no one won. Robinson fell off. We didn't hit and we didn't win.

There was a meeting with Winkles and Dalton in which they decided that getting rid of Epstein would solve their problems. It was ridiculous. It was at dinner at an Italian restaurant in Oakland. I listened to them talk about Mike as if he was the worst guy in the world. Dalton said, "He's not doing the job."

I said, "If you get rid of all the guys that aren't doing the job, you won't have anyone left to play." Winks said, "You can't handle him." I didn't say anything because I was thinking it was the manager's job to handle players.

I walked back to the motel with Dalton. Harry said, "Epstein upsets the team. He's a bad influence." I said, "The only one he upsets, influences badly, is himself. He's hard on himself but he never has a hard thing to say about anyone else. He stays to himself, but he'll stick up for his teammates. He's a good guy to have on a team." Harry said, "He's a bad apple in the barrel. We'll be better off without him." He was mad. He wanted me to say it would be good to get rid of the guy, but I wouldn't say it. I couldn't be a yes man. It turned Dalton against me the way Winks had gone against me.

I couldn't betray a player who was getting a bum rap. He was just another player, He went. But he didn't deserve to go any more than others did. Richie Scheinblum went too. And he didn't deserve to go. He couldn't play but he could hit. If God was pitching Richie would get his hits. But Richie wasn't played much.

I have to say this: I heard Mike and Richie referred to as "goddamn Jews" several times by important people on the team, in management as well as players. Some of the same people who didn't like blacks didn't like Jews. They'll deny it, but it's true. "Jew bastard" this and "black bastard" that. Bigotry doesn't come in only one color and it tears a team apart.

Winks was ten to fifteen games under .500 at mid-season and was fired. Robinson didn't get the job. I didn't get it. Whitey Herzog got it, but only for a few games while they were dealing with Charlie Finley to get Dick Williams, who held Williams under contract and prevented him from taking the Yankees' job he wanted. By the time Autry and Dalton got to him, Williams would have taken any job. He had won in Boston and Oakland, but he couldn't win in Anaheim. We lost ten or eleven in a row when he took over. He was ten to fifteen games under .500 in his halfseason. We landed in last place.

Herzog went on to manage Kansas City successfully and I'm sure Autry regrets not keeping him. Robinson ran games real well in Cleveland, but had problems with players, black and white. Both might have been better than Williams.

Right off, Williams took Tom Morgan and me up to the press room after a game for a bull session about baseball. The next day he stopped by our lockers to tell us that he hired his coaches on ability, not for friendship, and it looked like we were doing good jobs, so we could relax and feel comfortable because we'd be back with him the next season.

We knew that new managers brought in their buddies as coaches because they didn't want strangers sticking knives in their backs, but sometimes when they took over at mid-season they waited until the next season to make changes. Tom was worried until Williams talked to us, but I warned him not to believe what anyone said in such a situation. I had learned not to trust stuff like that.

I turned out right. You couldn't trust Williams.

He showed the press one side of himself and the players another. He was easygoing in public and hard-assed in private. He ran a good game. He was smart and quick. He had the guts to gamble. But he had bad players and was frustrated by them. He had won with top players and was impatient with poor players. He angered the old guys and scared the young guys.

Williams screamed, cursed, chewed players out constantly, seldom had a good word to say to a guy, never gave anyone anything for a good play. He never did anything for anyone and never developed any rapport with his players. The team was ready to riot. Guys defied him and had awful arguments with him.

Williams had trouble with players in Boston and it led to his being fired a year or so after he had won a pennant there. I think he learned from it because he didn't have trouble with the players in Oakland and won championships with them, but they were so good he had nothing to bitch about. Here, they weren't so good and they began to bitch plenty about his hard ways.

He may have learned a lesson here. It looks like he's been better with the young guys and ordinary talent he's had in Montreal.

Before his first Angels season ended he announced he was

going to bring his own coaches in for the following season. Well, that was his right, except that he had told us something else earlier. The two faces of Dick Williams. I wasn't surprised, but I lost a lot of respect for him.

The Alstons are few and far between.

Near the end of the season he did come to me to tell me he was bringing in Norm Sherry to be his bullpen coach. I told him that was his privilege and turned away from him. I thought that was funny, though, because I knew Norm was an Angels' man, not one of Dick's buddies, a guy who had been managing in the Angels' farm system and might be the next Angels' manager.

That's the way it worked out. Norm must have been forced on Dick and before the next season was over he had replaced Dick as manager. Another Angels' guy, Dave Garcia, was brought in to back up Sherry, and before another season was over he had replaced Norm. That's the way it goes in baseball. They sneak up behind you. You turned around and good old Buzzy Bavasi turned up in Anaheim and Dalton moved on to Milwaukee.

Williams moved on to Montreal. There's always another job for these guys. They belong to a private, restricted club. They get hired, they get fired, they get hired again. It doesn't matter how mediocre you are. If you're a white Christian, welcome to the club. The good guys get the good jobs up front while blacks like Larry Doby, Willie Mays, Monty Irvin, Jim Gilliam, Jackie Robinson, Henry Aaron, Ernie Banks, and many more get paid off to stay on the sidelines, in the shadows, and do as they're told. If you're white you can be in baseball all your life, but if you're black the time comes when you're just an ex-ballplayer.

My time came at the end of the 1974 season. I could have tried for another coaching job, but at less than twenty grand a year, what was that? And there was only one to a team, none on some teams. After leaving the Dodgers, baseball had not been good to me. I was soured on the sport. I didn't think I'd miss it the way it turned out I did. And I thought I could make it in civilian life a lot better than I did.

24.

Ten to twenty years ago, ballplayers weren't making the money they make today. I made sixty thousand at my all-star peak but today bench warmers make a hundred grand, regulars make two hundred, stars make three or four hundred, and superstars make five or six hundred grand. It's crazy and it's going to break baseball.

I was born twenty years too soon. I signed for a bonus of five grand and had to give half that to the scout. I made less than a thousand dollars a season my first season in pro ball. I made less than five grand my last season in the minors. I made the minimum, seventy-five hundred, my first season in the majors.

I worked my way up—ten grand, twenty, thirty, forty, fifty, and finally, after fifteen years, sixty grand for a couple of years. Then I started back down—forty-eight, forty-five, then nothing. An accountant once figured out I'd earned three hundred fifty grand in my playing career, and I blew it all. Every cent. Players like me earn that much in two, three years today. Players a little better do it in one.

Actually, I made a little more and blew a little more. My teams earned bonus money. Four years I made ten to twelve grand in World Series shares. And I worked every winter, averaging four or five grand a year. Uncle Sam took a lot. I lived simply but it costs to live. I had a wife and three kids. It wasn't all blown.

A lot of athletes have made and blown a lot more. Ballplayers, boxers, jockeys. They've blown it on women, booze, big houses, big cars, fast horses, gambling. They had more fun than I did, I guess. I didn't go down those roads. Agents and business managers have taken some for big money. They didn't even have agents in my day. I needed advice like a man needs air, but I never had a business manager.

Like a lot of athletes, I blew it in business. Bad business. I don't think business was a bad idea to begin with. The more I made, the more we spent. We didn't have a lot left in savings at the end of each year. I knew I wouldn't have too many years at the top. I could see I wasn't going to get fifty or a hundred grand in savings for the future. I wanted to use the money I was making to make money for the future. I should have put it in savings.

The accountant couldn't even account for fifty grand. I don't know where it all went.

I went into a lot of things and everything went wrong. I kept going into different things. I kept thinking that if just one thing hit big, I'd have it made for life. Otherwise, I didn't know what I was going to do in life. All I knew was baseball. I think I could have done something else with my life, but this is what I had done. I was naïve and sweettalked into bad deals, led astray by bad guys. I can't blame them. I have only myself to blame.

In the beginning I had the idea that if eight or ten or twelve of my buddies among the black ballplayers put in a thousand dollars each every season we could form a corporation to invest in real estate or buy apartment houses. We blew a grand each on the road without knowing where it went every year anyway, but this way it would be working for us. And you could buy apartment houses for that kind of cash in those days. Earl Robinson and Bill White were interested, but others weren't. I went into it on my own and lost most of the money I put into an apartment house in Compten. The area ran down and no one wanted it. I dumped it.

Later on along the way, on the advice of friends, I passed the tests for insurance and real estate licenses. A friend who was a million-dollar salesman for an insurance firm, got me into the business of rehabilitating old houses for resale. We'd buy them, fix them up, and put them on the market. Sometimes we'd buy them in bad neighborhoods, raise them off their foundations, and move them to better neighborhoods. One time one failed to pass the inspection because the blocks beneath the house were not solid. I was into the sale of a type of coating paint that covered twenty times thicker than ordinary paint. So I simply sprayed those blocks so they looked solid. They passed.

However, all kinds of problems came up. For one thing, I always wound up doing most of the physical labor while the others did the brainwork or the paperwork. I worked like hell. And very often we couldn't get the cash for the houses we had hoped for. Sometimes we found out we had bought houses the sellers didn't have the legal right to sell. And sometimes the buyers didn't come up with the money.

I sold one to Lou Johnson. We even put in carpets, drapes, and a refrigerator and stove for him, painted the interior, and took a note back from him on the cost. He split with his wife, they moved away, and we never got our money. We wound up losing this one and others on foreclosures. I lost a lot of money in real estate.

Frequently I borrowed dough from Bavasi on my salary to invest in promising prospects. I borrowed five thousand from him to start a travel agency with four fellows. Our feeling was that members of the black community were coming up in money and starting to take trips. We would give them the same advantages of a travel agency in their own community that the whites had in theirs. Unfortunately, they thought they were paying us extra for the service. We never could educate them to understand that the airlines and others paid us our ten percent.

I thought we had the background because one of my partners was an ex-redcap. When I told this to my co-author he almost fell to the floor laughing. He says that that in a nutshell is a perfect example of how ballplayers go broke in business. But he was a smart cat, who made good money and invested it in good-paying propositions. However, it turned out I was the only one who invested my money in this proposition. Instead of operating with twenty-five grand we opened with my five grand, while the others said their shares came in expertise. We didn't have the dough to keep up. And a lot of the dough that did come in disappeared. We also got a lot of bad checks from clients.

We had an office staff, but began to go under because we couldn't keep up with the paperwork, the forms, the running around and collecting tickets. A couple of lawyers next door and Ray Charles's business manager, Joe Adams, invested and tried to help, but it wasn't enough. I put in another five thousand, then another, before we folded. I wound up losing fifteen grand on that deal.

One of our clients at the travel agency must have made me as a mark. He was a rah-rah cat who had a lot of hustle. He had worked hard to put together a television shop, putting up paneling, shelves, display cases. But he couldn't get the credit to stock the store. I could get the credit because I was a name ballplayer, despite my bad business record. I put out three grand to get TVs, hi-fis, and other stuff from RCA.

It looked good. We got the goods wholesale, but they were worth ten to twelve grand retail. The markup is three to four-hundred percent. But when I returned from a road trip to see how the store was doing, it was stripped and shut tight. I peered in the windows and there was nothing in there. I went to my partner's house and he was gone.

I found out later he had said his mother was sick and had to head home, and had taken everything out of the store, sold it all, and took off. He came back and I sued him for my money but never collected a nickel. He's still sprinting around town, cooking up one new deal after another, promising to pay me back my money, offering to get me in on good things.

Then, a security guard at the ballpark told me about a Union 76 station he could get cheap and asked me to go in with him. Union 76 sponsored Dodgers' games on radio and television. Strange as it may sound, I always liked the smell of gas and working around gas stations. I also thought it would be a good deal for my dad. I always was trying to get my mom and dad to move out here, buying houses they could have and things like that. Eventually they did, but not that time.

I did go in on the station. I put some money in so we could

buy the place and stock it on consignment. I worked there whenever I could, pumping gas, wiping windshields. My partner did the oil and lube jobs and some repairs. We tried to sell tires and batteries and those things where the profit is in this business. We might have made a go of it, except for a few things.

For one thing, the supplier regularly dropped gas on you whether you needed it or not. You had to pay for it promptly, and you had to keep money on hand for this purpose. My partner got in the habit of dipping into the gas money. We wouldn't have any when we needed it. He'd buy old cars he thought he could build back up to sell or use for parts he might need. We wound up with a lot of old cars sitting around and no dough.

He had nothing. It turned out I went into business with quite a few fellows who had no dough. I thought they did, but it turned out all they had to offer was expertise. Whatever that was, it wasn't enough to make money for us. I put in bad money after bad. We fell so far behind on our gas bill I finally gave up and closed down the place. My partner never had anything to lose. I lost a lot of money.

There's big money in the record business. If you know what you're doing. I went in with a guy who had been in the business, but he didn't know what he was doing. We started up Cenco Records. I put in money for equipment. Then I was raped to pay for recording sessions. We recorded Ike and Tina Turner before they were big. We had a pretty big record with them. But it turned out we had to turn out another record, called a "cover record" for the dealers before we could get our dough from the first record. We folded before we got a cover record out. We never got our money out of the first record. I finished $7,500 in the red on that deal.

You might wonder if I ever got into a bar and grill. Of course. Traditionally, ballplayers blow dough on saloons and restaurants. I wasn't about to be any different. All my other investments had been in the LA area, but after I moved to West Covina, east of LA, a group of guys came to me with the idea of a nightclub in a big, busy shopping center in nearby Pomona. Naturally, they had no dough.

A pool hall had folded in the center and they wanted to put the club there. They had done their paperwork and figured out they needed eighty-eight grand. They had gone to the Bank of America and interested them in making a loan, but needed twenty percent up front and a statement of financial stability. Believe it or not, I provided both. I went in for twenty grand.

My partners were classy. One was a college instructor. All were black, and the black community was on the black-is-beautiful kick at that time. They wanted to put together the place in an African motif and call it The African Palace. I went along with it. There was a big black community in that area and no first-class nightclub. We gave it to them.

Nothing was too good for my partners, but I went along with them. It looked like an African compound by the time we were finished. We had our own waterfall and out of it came a canal that ran through the joint and a pool with real live fish. It was bordered by rocks, many of which I put in myself because my partners didn't like to get dirty. We had jungle murals painted on the walls and papier-mâché animals around. We had electrodes installed in the ceiling so it looked like you were sitting under stars shaped in the astrological signs of the zodiac.

The tables and chairs were made of giant telephone-cable spools. Hand made. There were special elevated sections for VIPs. The people sat on puffed pillows. The bar stools were hand-made from barrels. We plastic-coated the natural-wood bar to a fantastic finish. A lot of bartenders had robbed saloon owners so at the last minute we installed a computer bar which automatically measured out the right drinks. It only cost fourteen grand. Instead of paying it out I signed a check for the full amount in the rush of opening night.

On top of that, we opened without liquor. We were near a high school and there was some opposition to a bar. One lady in particular led the fight against us. Eventually we got our liquor license, but not in time for opening night or our first few weeks. We had a fifteen-grand sound system so performers could record live there if they wanted. We had a big-name singer on our opening night, we were packed wall-to-wall, and we sold five hundred dollars worth of Cokes.

We did do good business for a while, but we had problems. A lot of people sat around nursing drinks. We were supposed to turn over our customers twice a night for the two shows a night, but we couldn't get those who came in for the first show to leave so we could let others in for the second show. We tried charging admission at the door, but that turned customers away. We put on a cover charge for each show, but that turned customers off.

Everyone wanted to sit in the choice locations and the waitresses started to argue over who served the big spenders. We had to bring in a gal to run the waitresses and put them on a rotation, but the gals were always squawking and squabbling.

We started to see some of the same faces all the time. There were some gals there I knew never paid. Turned out one of our people was letting them in the back door and they were working the club, hustling, and he was taking a cut. Then there were some bad dudes who always sat up front—mobsters, pushers, and so forth. They sat where they wanted. They were bad for our reputation. No one threw them out. No one dared.

I was still in baseball and away a lot. My two top partners supposedly were running the club, but they couldn't agree on anything. We started out with a jazz policy, but some of our customers called for rock or soul music. We started to mix it up and never settled on a sound the customers could count on. We brought in some big names, but wound up bringing in buddies of my partners who couldn't make it in LA and were paid seven or eight hundred a week to play our place.

The bank was all over us because our books weren't being kept properly. My partners hired someone who was studying for his master's in business to serve as our accountant and manager. I was on a road trip in Kansas City when I read a newspaper item where three dudes were killed in a narcotics bust in Detroit and the Tigers' general manager just missed being bumped off when bullets went through the wall into his apartment. I got back to my club, asked about our new manager, and was told he was killed in that narcotics bust in Detroit. It turned out he was a bag man, delivering dope and dough between LA and Detroit.

On top of everything we were always worried we were going to get knocked over. We had to have security, but I didn't want a lot of guys with guns around. I was into karate and we hired some of the cats from my class to stand around. They were bouncers, really, and had a few brawls with bad guys that didn't do us any good. I wound up sitting at the cash register with a big gun in my pocket and one eye on the door.

I always hated being around drinking and drunks, but I wound up doing it in an effort to make a buck and to protect my interests. I never had a chance. One of my partners wound up as some sort of superfly with the fancy clothes, the fancy cars, and the fancy chicks. A lot more money was going out than was coming in.

We had $120,000 invested before we even opened and blew another bundle before we closed. I wound up in bankruptcy.

All this time I was always working at one thing or another. Between baseball seasons, between business ventures, I worked at whatever I could find.

When the Watts riot came in 1965 and the blacks burned down, broke up, or looted a lot of what was in this LA ghetto, I got out of it okay, although I lived in the general area. I drove down the freeway through the heart of the riot area without incident. I got home, got my guns, and sat by my front door prepared to protect my property, but no one threatened me.

After the season, I got a call from a member of the Los Angeles Police Department. They needed someone in their community relations department to work with the blacks in the troubled parts of town. They were interested in me, as a name ballplayer with a decent reputation. I had done some youth work for the Dodgers and I think I was recommended by them.

There was some hassle over the appointment before the mayor and the city council confirmed me as the first civilian on the LA police department. I was paid a thousand dollars a month to work with two black officers and one Chicano officer. Our job was to improve relationships between the police and the public in the minority communities. We were not given guidelines, just told to tell the people we wanted to help them in any way. We spoke to all sorts of groups, mostly youth groups.

Essentially, we told the people that we knew there had been misconduct on the part of many of our officers, even police brutality, and that members of the minority community often were considered suspect and often were treated unfairly in cases where crimes were committed. We were aware of this now, were seeking to correct it, and would do right by anyone who came to us with a complaint. I told students that I knew their lives had been hard and they had little hope for the future, but if they stayed with their studies, things were changing, they might have a chance. And any chance was worth taking. I even recruited a couple for the cops.

The program was well received and the general reaction was that I had done a good job and done some good. I wanted to stay with it. However, the police department had its problems like any other group. A majority of officers felt their job was to enforce the law and that the social work should be left to social workers. There were many who felt we were wrong for bending over backwards to make it with blacks and were romancing the same people who created the riots and committed crimes.

Many didn't want blacks or Latins moved into the community-relations department ahead of whites. They started to move whites with seniority into our roles. We all felt there was no way they could be effective dealing with blacks or Latins. All but one of us resigned.

I was sorry to do so. If I had been out of baseball I might have stayed and fought for the sort of program I thought would work. But I was still in baseball, only a part-timer in this sort of police work, and there was no way I could deal with the full-time regulars.

I have some newspaper clips covering my work with the LA police. At the end of one there are some quotes from me which haunt me. I was asked at a high-school session what I planned to do when I left baseball. I said, "I plan to become a bum." There was a lot of laughter. Then I said I'd like to do what I was doing right now and enjoyed it as much as I did playing ball. But, I said, "I'm not ready to retire from playing ball. When you make twenty-five grand a year, you don't retire. You play until they don't want you anymore."

When I was on my last legs in baseball, one off-season in Minnesota I worked for Computer Data, recruiting college kids, traveling all across the country. I guess I did well with that, picking the prospects that fitted in with their organization. They offered me a full-time position. However, they wanted to pull me in to the office to work in personnel. I would have been way out in the sticks. Because of the snow, travel would have been tough. And essentially I would have been used as a black to work with the blacks they employed. It was really limited and I didn't go for it. Maybe, in view of what happened, it was a mistake. But I don't think I would have been happy there.

When I was out of baseball in 1971, looking for work, not finding any, not being able to pay my insurance, my insurance man got me appointments with personnel people at two banks. Security Pacific Bank hired me in public relations at eighteen thousand a year. I even got a title—I was a public relations officer. And I had a secretary. My job was simply to get around the black community, keep up with the businessmen who banked with us, try to spot problems before they became problems for us, and encourage other businessmen to bank with us. It was all right, but there really wasn't much to do. After a while I was making appointments with people just to keep looking like I was busy. Again, I was being used strictly as a black to deal with other blacks. I didn't think there was a future for me there. Maybe I was wrong, but when I got the chance to get back in baseball with the Angels, I took it.

When I was with the Senators, and knew I was done at the end of the season, Bowie Kuhn, the commissioner, came to our clubhouse and asked me about my future. I said I thought I might like to get into some sort of police work. He said he thought he might have something for me in his office. I had been good for the game and he'd like to see me stay in it now that my career was coming to an end. He suggested I stop by his office to talk about it next time the team was in New York.

I did, and met a former FBI agent, Henry Fitzgibbon, who thought I could help police baseball. The commissioner said the salary would be between twenty and twenty-five thousand. It sounded ideal. However, he added that he'd have to contact me after the season to confirm it.

I thought it was set. I had even arranged with agencies in New York to find houses to look at. But the commissioner didn't contact me after the season. Finally, I got to him. He said it would have to wait until the owners' meeting at the end of the year. So I went back to LA and waited, while my family waited in Washington. Even after the meetings, I didn't hear from him. Finally, I called and he told me he couldn't hire me because the owners thought he was spending too much money on his office already. He said each team put fifty grand a year into the commissioner's office and had a say on how they money was spent. At that point, I had to wonder how much of a say the commissioner himself had on how his office was run. I was really let down.

When I was with the Angels, Bill White suggested I try for the sports announcer's job on the NBC-TV "Today Show" in New York. Joe Garagiola was leaving. I had been told I had an above-average speaking voice. I never was slow to speak my piece. A lot of athletes were into broadcasting and I always thought I could do better than most. Of course, it was nice that it was the same sort of big dough ballplayers make.

I arranged to cut a tape at a station in Cleveland and got Dick Williams to be my guest. Off the tape the guy at Cleveland said they might be interested in me. And he called a pal at the ABC affiliate in Washington, which wanted a sports man, and recommended me. When we got to Baltimore, I went over to Washington and did an audition tape there. One of my rivals for the "Today Show" was Bryant Gumbel, a black guy with NBC-TV in LA, and there was talk that if he got the "Today Show," I might get his LA spot.

At one time there were four stations supposedly very interested. But it took a long time to get any results. I was starving in LA that winter, waiting, calling, getting put off.

At one point one or two of my tapes were lost, which wasn't surprising since they were flying all around the country. I had to take time to track them down and send them on to where they were supposed to go. Weeks went by, months. I couldn't find out anything, and kept getting the runaround. There are a hundred people at each station you can call without finding out who's in charge, who has a final say, who even knows what's happening.

Finally, NBC-TV decided to keep Gumbel in LA, so that was that. He's one of the good ones and later did double up with a co-hosting job on "Grandstand" out of New York, flying back and forth weekends. Bill White, to his surprise, got the "Today" job. He hadn't even auditioned, said he didn't want to leave the Yankees' job to take it, but he took it. It didn't last too long. The retiring Redskins' quarterback Sonny Jurgensen got the Washington job. He was a big name in that town. And they moved some guy out of news into the Cleveland job.

White turned me on to an opening at WPHL in Philadelphia, but the guy there, like all the others, said I didn't have enough experience. I'm not sure where I was supposed to get it. The only job I was offered out of all this was at Channel 7 in Boston, strictly a weekend job for forty dollars an hour. Since my work would only consist of a couple of hours a week and I had no other work to do there, there was no way I could move there and take that. I'd still like a crack at a broadcasting job, but one hasn't opened up to me.

Monte Irvin, who worked in the commissioner's office, tipped me off that Princeton was looking for a baseball coach and told me who to call. I set up an appointment and flew to New Jersey. I had flown all over the country with ball clubs paying the bills, but now I had to pay my own way and it came at a time when I had been out of work and didn't have any money. I was even collecting unemployment. I used that money and a couple hundred I borrowed from a buddy and flew East.

It was winter, raining and cold. I rented a car, drove through desolate countryside to the college, and put up at a nearby motel. I hung up my suit carefully, hoping the creases would smooth out, and went to sleep. In the morning I met with the assistant athletic director and he gave me the guided tour. Before we left, I looked down at my feet and noticed I had on brown socks with my blue suit. He seemed like a good dude so I mentioned I wasn't dressed right to meet important people. He said no one would notice. I said maybe, but I'd know. He took me to a campus store where I could buy dark socks and off we went. The buildings were beautiful, the facilities were fine, and the people were nice, but I soon realized everyone and his uncle were interviewing me and passing judgment on me.

I wound up with the athletic director, Royce Flippin, a former football star, and he said he thought I could do the job. I asked him what the job was and he said I would recruit players for the team, coach the team, teach physical education, and do public relations for the school. That seemed like a lot to me. I asked him what the job paid. He asked me what I wanted. I figured fast and said twenty thousand. He said it was too much, more than even the football coach was getting. I said I didn't care what others were making, but I'd do my darnedest to earn my money. However, he had already lost interest. I guess I asked for too much.

I went home and waited. Flippin called to tell me all the Ivy League teams were having hard times financially and cutting back. They were just going to let an assistant football coach or someone like that take over the baseball team. So I was out of baseball again before I even got back into it on the college level.

I tried some teams on the big-league level, without any luck. I contacted Dick Tracewski, an ex-Dodger coaching at Detroit. He put me on to the general manager, Jim Campbell. He said their coaching staff was full. I said I was looking for a position in baseball, in administration, anywhere, not necessarily on the field. He said, "All our minor-league coaching positions are full too." All he would even consider me for was coaching. I was beating a dead horse.

From the time I left baseball after the 1974 season I looked for work in a methodical manner. My wife and I had split by then, and I was living alone. I was lonely, but there were no distractions and I was free to look for work. I had contacted the Purcell Employment Agency, which worked with the Players' Association, and they were looking for leads. I went through my memory and my phonebook. I went through the want ads in the newspaper every day. I tracked down everything that looked promising. I kept a ledger in which I listed the companies I contacted, the people I talked to, their comments, anything I had to do to follow up, and the final results. Little came of it.

Through friends, I made contact with the governor's office, the mayor's office, the attorney general's office, senators, congressmen, councilmen. From time to time it looked like I might be appointed to one program or another, but every time it fell through. I applied to the CIA twice. I applied to detective agencies, protective agencies, and so forth, without a nibble. I couldn't even get a job as a security guard at two-fifty or three-fifty an hour, and I couldn't have lived on that. I applied to automotive firms and supermarket chains. I heard Kentucky Fried Chicken wanted a black to work with Colonel Sanders so I went after that and didn't get it. I heard they weren't hiring blacks.

I applied at all the airlines. Nothing. A friend who'd attached himself to me when I was a big ballplayer tipped me that United needed to replace a black dude. I got an appointment with an executive who told me they needed a black man to do public relations in the black community for them. It was what I had done with the LA police and Security Pacific Bank, so I thought it would fit me fine.

I did everything but point out to him that he had hit on the perfect nigger. What I did do was admit that I had been down and out for a while, was going through a difficult divorce, and was about to file bankruptcy. Maybe it was stupid, but he asked me about my situation, I knew he'd check on me, and I didn't want to get caught conning him. I didn't get the job.

I was down and out. A year went by before I knew it. What money I had had gone home to my wife and the kids. It wasn't enough for them. She bitched about it. But I was reduced to eating cookies for dinner. I went to interview after interview, keeping my clothes together somehow. I submitted to embarrassing questions. I filled out forms that asked the most intimate details. Nothing came of it. I applied for unemployment, stood in those long lines, submitted to those embarrassing questions, filled out those forms, did whatever they told me to do. Whatever money came of it, some went home and the rest stayed with me as long as I could stretch it. I'm not the first man to have been humbled, but I was humbled for sure.

After a while, I couldn't even afford my $195 a month apartment, but I didn't have the dough to pay the first and last month's rent on a cheaper one. My salvation came when a friend of mine who'd just left his wife found a two-bedroom house in Inglewood he wanted to rent if he could find someone to go in with him for a hundred a month. That was half what I'd been paying, so I jumped at it. But I still had to get up my half. I didn't know how. Before I hocked my guns, I considered sticking someone or someplace up. I was an honest man, but I was desperate. I found out then why some men do what they do. What you have to do, you do. I couldn't bring myself to it, but I thought about it. And if someone had offered me money to knock over someone, I might have done it. It's terrible, but true. A lot of men have been humbled. I was.

I'd always made money at poker. I tried it, but found out that when I had to win I couldn't win. The pressure ruined my play. I went around trying to collect bad debts. I had no luck at all. When I'd had dough I'd loaned it to guys who needed it. Most of it I never got back. Now I needed it. Whenever I remembered an old debt, I asked to be paid back. It was embarrassing, but I did it, and got nothing. One cat was into me for a hundred. He came by to tell me he couldn't come through for me just then. He saw a yachting cap I liked and asked if he could have it. I couldn't believe it. Here I was broke and begging and he was asking to take a cap from me. He got the cap. I got nothing.

A lot of guys offered to lend me money over this stretch. At first I was too proud to take them up on it. When my pride disappeared and I went to them and reminded them of their offer, most of them got tongue-tied and begged off one way or another. A few cats came through for me. But how much could I hit them for? One more month's rent, maybe. A couple of meals. Some cats invited me over to dinner, but I seldom did it because I couldn't repay them. I'd rather eat my cookies.

Cats invited me to play cards, but I couldn't afford to get in the game. Cats invited me to play golf, but I couldn't afford to pay green fees. When you have been at the top, it is terrible to find yourself at the bottom. Guys still think you're something when you know you're nothing.

Some people were super. There was a beautiful lady at my bank who went with me when I was overdrawn. I promised not to write any more checks until I could cover them and promised to repay the debt and she went with me. There was a good guy at another bank whose job it was to see that my car payments came in or they took my car. He went with me as long as he could. He even turned me on to a car dealer in Pomona who might hire me as a salesman. The guy did hire me and even trained me, but I couldn't sell cars. All I got out of it was a car to drive so I could turn my own car back to the bank and get that debt off my back.

The worst thing about being out of work is being in debt. You can't even starve in peace. The people I owed dough to kept coming after me and hired collection agencies to come after me. I can't complain. I owed the dough. But they made my life hell, coming around and calling and threatening me with all sorts of things. When the phone rang I had to answer it because it might be an answer to an application for a job, but I hated to answer it because it also might be a bill collector.

My last year with the Angels I worked with LaRue Harcourt's organization, Athletes' Financial Services, which worked at helping athletes and other professional people handle their money. He did a good job for the guys, but he was too good a guy for his own good. He brought in ball players like me for a thousand a month salary. A lot of his athletes started to complain that they'd be better off working on commission because of some of the big deals they arranged. Guys started to leave him to go on their own and each of them would take a couple of players with them. They hurt him so bad he had to cut back and stop employing people. I couldn't go back to him.

Some of the guys got together to form their own outfit to

represent athletes and entertainers and they wanted me to go in it with them. I was so desperate I was ready to do anything. I figured I'd learned some lessons I could apply to other athletes and could steer them clear of the holes I'd fallen through. We worked like hell to get it going, then it fell through.

One young guy who'd been in business for himself for a few years representing athletes wanted to help me, but couldn't afford to hire me. I did bring him some players and he has done right by them. He did right by me. Charlie Dye is his name and I owe him for the help he gave, but he just didn't have a job to give. Some guys who would give didn't have it to give.

One day I ran into an outfit called Professional Budget Service. They were supposed to get the bill collectors off your back and set up a program so when you were working and earning money you could systematically pay off your debts. That sounded better than bankruptcy to me, so I went in to see them. Right off, it cost me fifty bucks to enroll. I had to dig up the fifty. The young guy who ran the operation knew me by my name because of baseball. He said he was opening an office in Anaheim and wanted me to run it for him. He offered to pay me a hundred dollars a week while he fixed a place up and I fixed myself up with an insurance license. It turned out I worked my butt off. I fixed up a place and I studied and passed an exam to get my license. I was in business, right? Wrong.

I was set to take over the place. Then he told me the terms. He was going to take seventy percent of my commissions to one point, fifty percent to another, thirty percent of the rest from then on. I could see repaying him the salary he'd advanced me, but beyond that I could see I'd be working for him for less than enough to live on. I asked him if he thought I was crazy. He said I'd be crazy not to take anything I could get. Maybe. I didn't take it.

He even had the gall to come up with an idea to put tennis courts on top of a big building and operate it as a club if I could get some ballplayers to back us on it. He said we'd be partners. I knew what kind of partner I'd be.

Meanwhile, I had met another man, a Dodgers' fan, Dick

Takata, who said he would take me ino his insurance agency.
I went with him. He put me on an allowance while I learned
the business and that got me by. But when I went out to sell
insurance I didn't sell any.

At this point the son of the fellow for whom I'd tried to
sell cars called me up and asked me to sell insurance for him.
I told him I couldn't sell insurance. But I went out to talk to
him anyway. And I cooked up a deal where his firm would
deal the insurance for another friend of mine who was
handling athletes. Only, the deal fell through. And I didn't
sell any insurance for him, either.

Don Newcombe, who was a consultant with a savings and
loan company and with other firms, helping them handle their
businesses in the black community, turned me on to Founders
Savings and Loan. I went to them and was offered the same
sort of consultant job. I was supposed to bring in big deposi-
tors. I brought in one. I went to a hundred others, but since
Watts they'd all been nailed by one bank or another and
were committed. They all wanted to talk baseball with me, but
not business. After a while the company thanked me for my
efforts but told me they had to let me go.

So I was on my outs again.

It gets so complicated. One lead leads to another and they
all run out. One job busts, another opens up, but then it busts,
too. I was trying to do things I didn't know how to do and
wasn't suited to do.

I was a catcher, and there wasn't any call for over-the-hill
catchers.

I went into bankruptcy. It wasn't so bad. Sitting in court,
testifying, getting stripped, that was bad. I had no dough to
repay anyone. I had to dissolve any assets I had to pay off a
few pennies on every dollar I owed. I didn't have much to
dissolve. Things like the nightclub were all debts. At least it
left me in the clear.

I dreaded the announcement that came out in the newspaper, but nobody made much of it. I didn't have much pride
left. I was still broke, still down and out. I needed a helping
hand, but I didn't think I'd get any. There were times when
I thought I might as well kill myself.

25.

I HAVE told how we went into marriage young, without thinking too much about it, without knowing each other real well. Jeri and I didn't have a bad marriage, it just wasn't very good. The kids were the best part of it.

The sporting life is a hard life for a marriage. The athlete and his wife are apart a lot. That wasn't too hard on us. We were just as happy apart, doing our own things. I always liked life on the road, where I could be by myself.

A lot of ballplayers run around. This has to be hard on their wives and their marriages. The wives suspect their husbands all the time. Sometimes they're right. Only a few wives run around, as far as I can tell.

There's a lot of bitching between ballplayers and their wives because of this. But a lot of their wives put up with it because they like being married to a big ballplayer making big money. They like living good lives.

More athletes' marriages end after they stop being big ballplayers making big money. Not so many break up during guys' careers.

I remember when Willie Davis and his wife were having hard times, his wife told my wife, "Whatever he does, I'm still Mrs. Willie Davis."

My wife was always into it with the other wives, talking about other wives and their husbands. She was always trying to tell me about this player or that wife, this or that marriage. I'd tell her I didn't want to hear any of that stuff; I didn't want to get mixed up in any part of it.

I never told my wife anything about any of my teammates. Some players told their wives things in private and the gals went right out and told the other wives. Wives have wrecked careers. They can complicate the life of a player who has to produce on the field.

A lot of time the wives are jealous of one another or of their husbands. A sub's wife is jealous of a regular's wife. The wife of a pitcher gets pissed off at the shortstop's wife because the shortstop made an error that cost her husband a game.

I was a regular with the Dodgers all the time we lived in LA. I wasn't the star of the team, but I won some all-star honors and was a key man. I liked that, but I think my wife liked it better than I did.

I liked playing, I liked playing well, I liked winning. I liked the life of a ballplayer. My wife liked it better than I did. She never watched me play. She spent her time sitting in celebrities' boxes, talking to bigwigs. It used to make me mad.

The glamour got to her much more than it did me.

She tried to catch me running around but never did. I didn't run around much, not as much as many others. Which didn't excuse me, of course. There was a lot laying around to be picked up, but I didn't bend down much. I was scared and not at ease with it. Mostly I went to movies and laid around my room watching television and eating.

Which is not to say I was a saint. But in my ten years with the Dodgers in LA I had only one affair, with that lady in Chicago, and it didn't develop into anything serious. I did develop a real relationship later with a lady in Atlanta, it did become serious, and she has become most important in my life, but there wasn't much to it while I was still living with my wife and still in baseball.

Aside from our kids, my wife and I didn't have too much in common and didn't have a lot to talk about. We were interested in different things in life. She wanted to play an active social part around big-league baseball, while I wanted to relax and stay to myself anytime I could get away.

To kill time on road trips, I used to shop for presents for her. When the kids came along I put the money I used to spend on her into them and started to shop for them. She resented it when I brought them presents and none for her, and she let me know about it in no uncertain terms. I guess I was wrong, but I resented her doing it, and it spoiled the shopping for me.

I never was one to count presents under the Christmas tree, but she did.

Not that I was tight. I was making good money and gave most of it to her. I turned my paychecks over to her and she cashed them at the bank. She did our banking. She took what she wanted from our money and I never looked to see what she took. She bought clothes, whatever she wanted, and I couldn't have cared less. I didn't take much money myself. I didn't spend a lot. The per diem the team paid covered my expenses on the road. I never carried a roll around.

I made good money and we lived a good life, if nothing ultraluxurious. We had a two-bedroom house in Compton before the kids came. It was a good house, but the neighborhood was beginning to go bad. We had three robberies there. I gave her a gun, not to shoot anyone, but to fire into the ceiling to scare robbers away. One night somebody threw a milk crate through a back window and broke in while she was in the front bedroom. She called the cops, but was so scared she never fired the gun. The police had to pry it from her hands. Two World Series rings, watches, portable televisions, and other stuff was stolen.

It's hard on a wife who has to live alone a lot. It has to be scary. I felt for her.

After the Watts riot nearby, we moved into south Los Angeles. We had five bedrooms, room for the kids, a pool. It was super. There was grass and a lot of trees. We liked it a lot. We stayed until I was traded to Minnesota, then sold it. Later, after I landed the coaching job with the Angels back in southern California, we moved into a nice house in West Covina.

My folks finally came out in 1965 and I gave them a house I had picked up in Pomona, which is near Covina. I carried the payments on that until I couldn't. By then Mom had died and Dad had moved into an apartment. He was sick and almost died from an embolism one time, but came out of it. He is one of the most beautiful men you'd ever want to know. In his seventies, he plays golf, has buddies, a lady friend. He goes back to Ohio from time to time to visit my brother, Jim.

Jim lives in Columbus. He is an executive with Borden, a director of special markets, concentrating on minorities. He's divorced, but has an arrangement with his ex-wife. She has their son, Tony, a smart teen-ager, but Jim gets to spend as much time with Tony as he wants. Jim hasn't remarried. He remains a father to his son.

It wasn't traumatic for Jeri when we went to Minnesota. I was still a ballplayer making good money. We found a nice house to rent in the suburbs, on a lake. It was great for the kids. They had excellent schools and they got into ice-skating and sledding and even skiing. But the snow was up to here all the time and it was bitter cold. Then in the summer it got horribly humid. Bugs as big as dive bombers came out, and it rained so hard you couldn't see your hand in front of your face. It was a long drive in to work, so we moved into an apartment nearer town, made friends, and enjoyed it.

When I wound up in Washington I lived in an apartment up the street from the Watergate Hotel until the kids got out of school and could come. The way Short had talked, I thought we would be there awhile. We were looking to buy, but we rented a place in Ashton, Maryland, about thirty-five miles from the ball park. It was laid back, very rural, with about twenty-five acres of wooded land around the house and a creek than ran nearby. The house was three stories high, set on a little rise, a sort of knoll, with a great view. The house was old but well built, with hardwood floors and fireplaces in almost every room. The furnishings were old-fashioned but fine.

It took us a while to get used to country life. One of the kids came running in to tell me there was a snake outside. I took a baseball bat and went out and fungoed it to death. When neighbors heard about it, they were bugged because they never bothered the snakes, the snakes never bothered them, and they were regarded practically as pets. Eventually, Jeri and the kids made friends with other families that lived in the area. They used to have barbecue picnics and parties on the lawn by the stream and the woods.

It was sometimes jumpy at night because there wasn't any other house real close to us. It would get black some nights and you'd hear the old house creak like there were ghosts. The wind made sounds blowing through the trees outside like someone was there. Storms would strike up and the house would rattle, the lights would flicker, sometimes go out, and you'd be left with candlelight in that creaking old house.

But Jeri and the kids just loved it there and I wish we could have stayed there.

Our troubles started when we had to leave and I had nowhere to go and nothing to do. We waited month after month for the commissioner to come through with the job he had mentioned. Our money was going out, nothing was coming in, and we were getting into hot water. I thought of moving back to Minnesota to try to get back with the computer firm, but I thought I'd be better off going back to LA where I was best known. So I went back to LA, moved in with my father, and started to look around for work. When I landed the position at Security Pacific Bank, I brought Jeri and the kids back to LA.

I was making eighteen thousand, which isn't bad, but it was a lot less than I had been making. If you work your way up to sixteen or eighteen or twenty grand, good, you can live pretty good on that. But when you get up to sixty you live a lifestyle that's a lot better. It's hard to adjust when you drop back to forty-eight, then forty-five. It's real rough when you drop way down to eighteen. When you're used to living in big houses, it's hard to drop down to small places. You can't just throw away what you've accumulated over the years. The kids can't understand why they can't do what they always could do. Jeri didn't try. She lived the same way she had when I was making three or four times as much. It was my job to make the money, that's all.

Of course, I had blown a lot of our money, no doubt about that. Whatever I went into, she was against. When it failed, she could say "I told you so," and did. She was right. But I was trying to put together something that would last our lives,

and I never could have managed that on my baseball money.
I just wasn't any good at it. I don't think you can blame me
for trying. She did.

The funny thing is that whenever I got something going,
she wanted to run it. She was always advising me. It created
trouble with my partners. When we went into the nightclub in
Pomona, my partners and I agreed our wives would have no
say. We wanted to avoid the friction it could cause. But just
putting them out of it created trouble.

Well, it was her money too, so I guess she had a right to
bitch when I blew it. But she never brought a dime in. She
never worked a minute. She was too busy socializing. She
was deep into school things and way over her head into Girl
Scouting. It took up all her time. She didn't have time for me,
but it *was* time she spent with the girls. She was a good
mother to our kids. I want to make that clear. And she kept
the house nice, made nice meals, did a lot with our children,
especially our daughters.

I was close to the kids. I played ball with the boy, Jaime,
and taught the girls, Shelley and Stacy, judo to protect themselves. I taught the whole family to play poker and we had
good times with card games for hours on end. The girls were
bright and beautiful and I really loved watching them grow
into independent young ladies. But I had to be away from
them a lot and it was Jeri who took care of them and really
raised them. She did a terrific job with them.

But big bills had built up because of our past way of life.
I had to fight like hell just to keep our heads above water. I
needed help and I wasn't getting any. I used to be an old-
fashioned fellow who figured the man went out and earned
the money and the woman stayed home and cared for the
kids and the house, but I have changed with the times. It is
hard for a man to make it on his own today. If a wife can help
financially, fine.

Jeri was attractive and had a college education. I asked her
if she might take a job, but she said she didn't want one. When
I landed with the Angels, she helped the wives get together to
form an auxiliary, The Supporters, which put on parties and
did shows for charity. It was social and she loved it. She got

good publicity for it. But charity begins at home. She was out raising money for needy people when her own family was in need.

I was making seventeen, eighteen grand a year and falling further and further behind every year. The last straw was when I set her up for a job at my old bank, Security Pacific. I found out they were looking for attractive, educated black ladies to train in management positions. I told her about it and talked her into trying for it. I set up an appointment for her. She was to be interviewed by buddies of mine. It was a lock.

The morning she was to go for the interview, she decided she couldn't be bothered. She said she didn't want to dress up every day and drive the freeway to work downtown. She didn't want to work. I couldn't believe it. She wasn't willing to help. I threw up my hands in disgust.

I want to make it plain that I was probably more to blame for our problems than she was. I blew all that loot in bad business investments. It was my job to work, not hers. But when I begged her for help, she didn't give it. It looked like all I was there for was to make the money so she could lead the life she wanted. I had a life to lead, too.

We wanted to lead different lives. That was the real problem. We had reached the point where we were doing our own things and weren't doing anything together. We had nothing to say to each other and weren't even talking, or even touching. We had become strangers, merely living in the same house, sharing the children. Money problems didn't destroy our marriage, but they were the last hurdle we couldn't clear. If you've got money, you may think it's not important. But if you don't have it, it's important. If you can't pay your bills, it's as important as anything can be. Some couples can work it out together and get through it. But if you fall out of love and don't have dough, you're doomed.

For a year I thought about leaving home. I wanted to leave my wife, but not my kids. It wasn't that I hated her, I just didn't love her and didn't want to live with her anymore. I don't think she loved me, but she wanted our life to go on as it had before. It just couldn't. It wasn't the same anymore.

I wasn't a big ballplayer making big money anymore. I love my kids like I love air, maybe more. I'd die for them. But I'd rather live for them. I was dying little by little in that house and I was looking to start living again.

It was tough. I took my walk the morning she refused to go downtown for the job interview. I packed a few things, grabbed some clothes, and threw them in the car. She asked what I was doing and I said I was leaving. She said I was kidding. I said I was serious. She said, well, if I went, she wouldn't be alone long. I said that would be fine with me and wished her well.

It didn't happen. It hasn't happened. I wish it had. I wish she had what I have. It would be easier on both of us. But she didn't mean it when she said it. When you're mad, you say things you don't mean.

We had two cars, a Camaro and a Mercedes. I'd been driving the big car, but I left it to her and took the little one. I said I'd be back to talk to the kids. She said I didn't have to bother, but I said I was going to. I went, and then didn't know where to go.

I went to a buddy who was a big wheel at a hotel, figuring he'd get me a room I could use until I could pick a place. As luck would have it, he was off for the day. I picked up a paper and found an ad for a furnished apartment in Anaheim. I went over there and took the place almost without looking at it. It was all right, but it was a singles' place with a lot of recreational facilities I didn't care about. I just wanted a place to stay. It was $190 a month and I only had $90 on me, but the manager agreed I could bring him the rest in a day or so. I threw my clothes in the apartment and I had a home. I had no sheets or blankets or anything, but I had a home.

That night I headed back to the house. I took the kids in a back room and talked to them. I told them I loved them but I had left home because I no longer loved their mother. I said I wanted to be home with them but I couldn't take it anymore in that house. I said they knew their mother and I didn't hate each other because we didn't argue or fight all the time, but we just didn't have any feeling for each other. You can't fake the feeling, and if you don't have it, you don't have anything. I said I hated to hurt them but I thought I would hurt them more if I stayed and let a bad marriage get worse. This way, maybe their mother and I could make new lives for ourselves.

I said they would always have a father as well as a mother, and that I hoped to see them a lot and spend a lot of time with them. I wanted to stay an important part of their lives and would help them with anything they wanted. I would do anything for them and would always be there if they needed me. I said sometimes marriages just didn't last, but the love of a parent for his children never ended and the hardest part of moving out was I'd miss them so much.

They were crying. I started to cry, and we cried together. I was so choked up I could hardly get the words out. Then I couldn't talk anymore and I just held them and hugged them.

It was by far the hardest thing I have ever had to do, and it hurt me more than anything else. I felt like I wasn't worth a thing and I thought about just staying with them, but it had taken me a long time to make the move and I felt like it was the thing to do and I had to go through with it. I knew I'd hurt their mother and I hated that, too. But she'd hurt me, we were hurting each other, and I thought it best that we be through living with each other.

The kids seemed to understand, though they were young. I told them I'd taken an apartment in Anaheim near the ball park and they told me they'd come over on the weekend to help me make a home of it. I thought things would be all right, but I should have known better when they never got there. I found out later that their mother said if they came it would be like condoning what I'd done.

That was in January 1974. I had a month to go before spring training started and my baseball paychecks would start to come in. I was still working with Larue Harcourt at that time and had some money due me there. I got together about three hundred dollars to give to Jeri. And I signed my Angels' paychecks over to her most of the season. I gave her as much money as I could. Every time I came into any cash, I gave most of it to them. The problem was, I didn't come into much.

I went to see the kids at least twice a week until I went to training camp. After that, I called them a couple of times a week and wrote them every week, but I didn't get any calls or letters back. When I got back, I went back to visiting them as often as I could. As time went on, I felt less and less welcome.

At first they seemed glad to see me when I came and kept asking me why I couldn't come home to stay, but I guess I hurt them when I said I just couldn't do that. Jeri kept saying I should think of the kids and come home to stay, but I guess I hurt her when I told her the same thing. After a while she gave up and started to talk against me to the kids. I guess I can't blame her, because she was bitter.

She called me one time to come over to see something Shelley had written, titled "Reflections." In it she wrote about how good her life had been before it changed, how much they enjoyed the ball park and the ball games and the trips they took with me and how much it meant to have me at home. It touched me a lot. I thought about it all the way back to the Valley, where I was working. But the more I thought about it, the more I realized she was saying that she couldn't enjoy life anymore because I wasn't at home anymore. I drove back to the house that night just to tell her the best part of life lay ahead, whatever I had done, and I still would do things for her if she'd let me.

But my kids were beginning to turn against me. They came to stay with me one night. I didn't have any dough to do anything with them or for them, but I was happy just to be with them and I hoped they were happy just to be with me, watching TV, playing cards, eating pizza, rapping. When I got up the next morning, they were packed up and ready to be taken home. I had expected them to stay with me that day. They acted like they couldn't get away fast enough. When I said I wanted to be with them, they said if I wanted to be with them I'd never have left them. It sounded like words that had been put in their mouth. It made me mad and sad. I took them home. I felt like trash.

That was the only time they ever stayed with me. They came to my place one other time, with Jeri. They came without calling first and found me taking tennis lessons. I wasn't working at that time, had nothing to do much of the time, and took the lessons because they were free at this place I was staying at. It must have looked to them like I was having a high old time, which I wasn't. I was having the worst time of my life. When I told them it wasn't what it looked like, they just snickered at me and made me feel like two cents. They left and I was alone again, feeling like I was losing my kids.

The worst time of my life was from the end of the season, the end of September 1974, when I left the Angels, to the middle of the next year, July 1975. I was looking for work and getting turned down everywhere. I was out of work and out of money, living on Cokes and cookies. I was having a hard time making apartment and car payments, but I was sending four hundred dollars a month home, which I was scraping up here and there. My wife said it wasn't enough, and I knew it wasn't, but what could I do? I was doing the best I could, but it wasn't good enough.

Shelley has beautiful eyes but weak. She has to wear thick glasses, which hurt her appearance. She wanted contact lenses. She was babysitting and working here and there to save some money. She wanted her father to help her but he couldn't. How can you tell your kid her dad is down on his ass and can't give her what she wants? I felt terrible about it and figured I had to understand if she hated me for it.

Soon, Jeri said I couldn't see the kids unless she was with them. It always was a bad scene, uncomfortable. I'd tell them I loved them and they'd laugh at me and ask me why I had left them if I loved them. I'd ask them to call me but they never would. I'd wait for their calls but they never came. After a while I'd call and ask if I could come see them, but they were always too busy to be with me. It's tough to lay your feelings out like that to your kids and have them laugh. It hurt like hell. After a while, I stopped.

Christmas came, with no money to get them much. I scraped together the cash for a couple of presents and sent them around with brother Jim and his son, Tony, in town visiting. They told me the girls wouldn't even open the presents until Tony, who had a good relationship with his divorced parents, talked them into it. That hurt too.

When the calls came they weren't from the kids or about jobs; the calls came from bill collectors. When Jeri had a bill she couldn't pay, she simply put the people onto me. I'd sit there in that little room dreading the phone ringing, hating what happened when I answered it, having to tell people I couldn't pay them what I owed.

A pal had offered me a thousand-dollar loan anytime I needed it. I called him on it. Right off he started to back down. I let it go. Later I found out he went to my house and told my wife "the nigger" was going to borrow a grand from him but he didn't know if she'd ever see any of it, so he wouldn't give it to me.

Another buddy said he'd help me anytime I was hard up. I went to him and he told me he didn't have anything. What could I say? It turns out his wife and my wife were friends and his wife had told him he couldn't help me because I had hurt my wife. Wherever my wife and I had friends, it seemed like they were for my wife and against me.

Well, I was the one who had left.

And I was the one not working and not making any money and not sending much home.

So I sat in that lonely little room, with no job, no prospects, no money, no food, few friends, practically no family, my kids turned against me and not talking to me, my wife bitter toward me, and I thought about killing myself. There were a couple of times when I took a .357 magnum from my collection and sat down with it and thought how easy it would be to put the gun to my head. All I had to do was pull the trigger and put a bullet in my brain and blow my troubles away.

I think it would have been easier to do it than not. I had to force myself to face another day.

Sometimes it seems suicide is the simplest solution. It's terrible, but I can sympathize with those who turn to it. You reach what looks to be the end of the road and you have nothing. Why go on?

It's not that I had been a big baseball star. I'd been that, but I could live without that. It's not even that I'd been an important person and on top and now I had hit rock bottom. I'd been on the bottom before. It wasn't that I had made big

money and now wouldn't. The money didn't mean that much
to me. It wasn't that I'd been a flop in business. I didn't have
to be a big businessman. Maybe all of these things were
mixed into it, but what it really was was that I had no job,
nothing to do, no money, no way to pay my bills or support
my family, nothing going for me at all.

I think I would have blown my brains out if it hadn't been
for Barbara. I don't know if it will work out for us the way I
want it to, but, whatever comes of us, this one thing has
come out of our relationship—she saved my life. Aside from
a few friends who tried to help, who did help, but who
couldn't do as much as they wanted to do, she was the only
one who really helped, who held out and held up for me.

She was far from me, in Atlanta, but she'd write me and
stick twenty bucks or fifty bucks in the envelope and I wasn't
too proud to take it because it would pay a bill, buy me a
meal, get me gas for my car, get me through another day or
two. I'd be in the deepest depression and the only good calls
I ever got came from her. The phone would ring and I'd pick
it up and hear her telling me to hold on, not to let it all go.
I could pick up the phone anytime to talk to her and tell her
my troubles and she'd advise me to hold on.

I met Barbara at a restaurant in Atlanta while I was still
playing ball. She was married. Her maiden name was Walker
and her married name was Fouch. I thought, "God, what a
pretty woman." She was that. Tall and slender. Talking to her,
I realized she was just plain nice as well as smart. I had to do
a tape for the Office of Economic Opportunity, encouraging
youngsters to stay in school and she was supposed to distribute
it and publicize it.

She had her own public relations firm and also a modeling
agency in Atlanta. She had been a model all during her college
days, in fact she had been the first black cover girl in the
South, and she had gone North for a while and modeled in
New York.

Carl Fouch was a major real estate developer in Atlanta.
He was about six years older than she. They had known
each other since she was a teen-ager and she married him after
she graduated from college. For a while there they were real

prominent in black society in Atlanta. They were prominent, politically active, progressive. They had a mansion, servants, and cars. But, as she has told me, she sort of just let the marriage happen, she was never sure of it, but it was generally a good marriage. She says they were so much in the public eye it was scary to think of divorce.

She worked with me on the OEO tape that time and we got along well. Too well, I thought. She invited me to a party but I passed on it. I was flattering myself that she might see something in me, and I didn't want to get involved. We were both married and as long as she was with her husband and I was with my wife, we didn't.

After I left Atlanta that time, I didn't see her or talk to her on the telephone or write for almost a year. She was just someone nice I had met, but we both had marriages. But I couldn't help thinking about her all that year. And the next time I got to Atlanta I got in touch with her and we had lunch and talked. After that, every time I got to Atlanta, we'd have a bite and a little chitchat. But that's all.

She had a daughter, Morgan Nicole, called Nikki, born in November 1972. As I get it, they thought it might hold the marriage together. It didn't work. It usually doesn't. After about eight years of marriage, they separated. About a year later I separated from my wife. Barbara and I hadn't seen each other in a long time, but I started to telephone her to talk about my troubles. And she'd telephone me to talk about hers.

The big thing was that we could talk to each other. We had a feeling for each other. I don't think what we had broke up our marriages. I do think that when our marriages broke up we were all we had.

She was successful in her work while I was out of work. When I was far down in the dumps, she would call or write me to get my spirits up. If she got a dollar and a quarter, she sent me a dollar of it. She kept me going. It got to where we were talking to each other every night. It was costing us a hundred dollars a month we couldn't afford in phone bills. We decided we were in love. She decided to give up what she had there to come out to help me here. I wanted her to come, but I had nothing to offer her. She came.

She brought Nikki with her and they moved in with me and my friend, Roy Hammork, at the house we had rented. It was an awkward situation and we were uncomfortable with it, but we put up with it for four or five months.

There came a time where we had to move out anyway. We found a house to rent in the Crenshaw area of LA, a fairly nice black area of old homes. We lived there awhile, then moved into another house in the area. We want to be together and build something for ourselves.

She's a working woman. Right away she wanted to go out to make some money to help us make ends meet. She did some modeling, and she landed her own radio show. She helped pull me out of my depression and get me moving again.

Another who helped was Don Newcombe. I knew he'd pulled himself out of a hole. I talked to him. I was bitching about baseball having betrayed me. He made me see no one owed me anything. He said, "You have to make your own way in life. You're trying to grab hold of someone's coattails for a free ride. You've got to go out and make it on your own."

I decided to use what I had, which was a name, an ability to talk, a lot of contacts, and a desire to do well. Barbara had done well in public relations and we decided to try to do as well with our own public relations firm. A lot of action I'd been involved in had been with the groups representing athletes, operating in a building at 9000 Sunset Boulevard. Through our friends there we were able to get a small suite in which to start the Fouch-Roseboro Agency. So I was back in business.

This time I had someone with me who knew the business I was in. But it was tough to get started. We often stayed up half the night putting together proposals. Barbara is a stickler for the spelling and grammar, for putting them together in the proper sentence and paragraph structure, for doing neat work. We came close to getting a contract to represent the Las Vegas Convention Center in southern California, but lost it at the last minute. We did wind up with the Miss Black America Contest. We did develop deals with Ralph's Markets, the May Company, and a few others.

For a while we got together with an advertising agency, and

we moved out of our offices and into one on the Sunset Strip together, but that didn't work out. We were trying to run each other's businesses. We decided we could work together without being merged. Then we got together with Emmett Cash and my old baseball buddy Earl Robinson, who are into movie and television production, moved into a five-room suite at 6430 Sunset, and started to pick up a little steam. We got some film deals going. We now have good deals going with Ameron Corporation, a major pipe producer; Sare, a group seeking recognition for Latins; and the Mutual Black Radio Network; we are close to closing one with a major brewery.

It has been a hard haul with a lot going out and a little coming in for a long time, but things started to break for us in '76. We landed accounts we could do good work with, like Alex Haley of the book *Roots,* Andrew Young of the United Nations, and Benjamin Brown and others of the Democratic Party. Young and Brown are old friends of Barbara's from Georgia. We got to the point where I could take a few days off from week to week during the summer to work for the Dodgers as a minor-league hitting instructor when that opportunity opened up to me.

The bankruptcy did not hurt too much. The business is in Barbara's name and she is president. She makes sure we operate in a businesslike manner, with the books and all.

There is little stigma attached to bankruptcy today but I am going to see that I never have to go through it again. I am going to see that I do not ever make the same mistakes. I will never again go over my head in any deal. I feel bad about my failures, but I guess a man is entitled to a second chance and a fresh start, and I'm going to try to take advantage of it. I travel around, meet people, tell them what we have to offer, set up deals Barbara can close.

Going through our divorces has posed problems for us and hung heavy over our heads. Barbara's husband has had business reversals. She has not taken any money from him and he is not paying her any alimony. He may want to provide child support. Although they are far apart right now, he is kept as close to Nikki as time and money will allow. He is her father and Barbara takes their daughter back to Atlanta so he can be with her as much as possible. She is a doll and I love her like one of my own, but he is her father and Barbara and I will not come between them any more than we have to. Her divorce is not final, but mine is.

I live a lot closer to my kids, but in a way are a lot further apart from them. Jeri is bitter about Barbara and it has set up another barrier between me and my kids. I would like Barbara and my kids to get to know one another, but Jeri and they make it clear the kids don't want or need another mother. I don't want her to be their mother. They have a perfectly good mother. I just want them to be friends. So I can be their friend, too, as well as their father. My girls are both bright and good students. I would like my company to expand to the point where they could come work with us. I'd like my brother's boy, Tony, an Einstein, to come help us someday soon. Maybe my boy, and Nikki, too, when they get old enough.

My divorce has been bad business. I guess it's been my fault. I agreed to pay Jeri four hundred dollars a month but fell far behind in the payments. If I didn't have the money, I couldn't manufacture it, but she needed dough to live on too. She couldn't keep up payments on the Mercedes. I offered to swap her the Camaro, with its smaller payments, but she preferred to let the bank take the big car, which was worth a lot, and get her own small car. So that was down the drain. She complained I was driving a Caddy, but that was provided me for free at that time by the car company I was trying to sell cars for. She complained I couldn't afford to keep up payments to her but could afford a maid. Nikki was so young we had to hire someone to stay with her while Barbara and I were working. We are just all messed up in misunderstandings.

At Christmas 1976 I gave presents to the kids. And their mother. Since I was apart from them I never got a present from them. But when I got to court to have a hearing on our divorce, Jeri had the kids there and when I went to them to say hello she pulled out the present I had given her and gave it back to me.

My lawyer went ape. The kids had to leave the room. It was set that I was to pay $204 a month child support. At first it was set that I was to continue to pay my ex the $400 a month we'd agreed on, but I got that cut to $100 because it was all I could carry, along with the payments I had to meet for her. She was awarded half of my baseball pension for life. I'll get that when I turn forty-five, in 1978, but I don't know how much it will be. Several hundred a month, I guess.

The judge thought we should sell the house. I didn't want to do that. I didn't want them to have to move into an apartment, but as it turned out they were able to move into a smaller house. And we couldn't sell the old one until I had made arrangements with the bank to pay off what I owed them at four hundred a month. All this stuff adds up, of course. You're already bent over and you wind up with a monthly nut that can break your back.

So the house was sold and I wasn't even told where my kids had moved. I had to find out on my own. I was in the neighborhood on business with Barbara and decided to drive down to their school by myself to see if I could catch them coming out the door, just to see them. It was lunchtime and I waited. Sure enough, I saw Shelley come out. I called to her and she came to me. She sat in the car with me and we talked. I felt like it'd been so long since I'd seen her that I didn't know her.

She told me it was tough for them and how mad Mom got when money didn't come from me. I told her how tough it had been for me, how much I wanted them to have money, how much I wished I could do for them. It wasn't too bad a talk and when she had to leave I had tears in my eyes. I went and got Barbara and brought her back so she could meet the kids when they got out of school. Jaime wasn't there, but she got to meet Shelley and Stacy. They seemed to hit it off. I got my girls to say they'd see me, visit me, and try to stay close.

But when I called their house later, Jeri raised hell with me for cornering the kids at school and bringing *that woman* to meet them. She said she was the only fan I had in that house. She said the kids were down on me and that when Shelley went back into the school, she almost came apart at her locker she was so upset from my visit, and friends had to console her. Well, that was that.

When our firm put on a fancy affair at the inaugural in Washington on behalf of Benjamin Brown and Andrew Young, backed by the Arco Oil Company of Los Angeles, Coca-Cola of Atlanta, and "Roots" producer David Wolper, I had Barbara send the kids an invitation as a souvenir. I got it back with a note signed by Shelley and Stacy that they didn't need invitations to Washington parties, they needed money.

I remember one time when I called and asked to speak to Jaime and one of the girls said he was at practice for his first game of the Little League that season. I said, hey, wow, I love to watch him play ball and I'd love to see it, when is it, where is it? She said she didn't know. I asked who knew. She said Jaime did. I asked when he'd be home. She said about six. I said I'd call back then. When I did, I got Jeri and she said she wished I wouldn't come to the game. I went anyway, and with Barbara. It's a long drive, but we took a chance.

We got to the Little League field and there they were. Jeri was there and I saw my girls there but they didn't come to me or speak to me. I watched Jaime play and loved it because he can play. I decided to go by the dugout to talk to him. He was sitting on the edge of the dugout when I got there. I said, "Hi." He looked at me, looked over at his mother, looked back at me, said, "Hi," and looked away. That was it. We left to go to my father's. I could hardly see to drive because my eyes were so wet.

At the end of the school year I learned from my father that Shelley was to graduate high school with honors, had won a scholarship to UCLA, and was going to take a trip to Europe before starting college. She'd asked my brother Jim for the money, not me, but when I found out, I got her the money. Jeri is kind enough to let my father stay in touch with his grandchildren, but I hate having to hear about them second-hand. I wasn't sent an invitation, but I found out about it in time to go to Shelley's graduation and it was a thrill. I've seen her a few times since. I even let her read the manuscript of this book. There were things in it I knew she wouldn't like, but everything in it was me, as honest as I could be. She was moved by it and said she understood me better because of it and felt for me in a way she hadn't before. I think we can be closer now. I hope to God I can be closer to all three of my kids than I have been.

I don't blame my kids for our problems because they got caught in the middle of something beyond them at their age. Maybe in time they will see things differently. If I have been a bad father it has not been because I lacked love. I am told I should demand my rights with my kids, but I can't take them to court and order them to visit with me and expect it to be any good. They have to want it as much as I do. So I do without. I don't want to do without forever.

I can only hope it will work out between Barbara and me. We have been through bad times but it has been good between us. But it has all been for me and nothing for her. She has helped me more than I could ever help her. She has given up a good life. I hope the business works out because it is something we are in together. The money is still short and I have learned that the lack of money can ruin relationships quicker than anything else. I worry that if we can't make money together, we can't make it together. Worries like this can come between the love we feel for each other. We all need to be loved. I worry about being left alone, without love.

I have learned that a lot of my love of life lay in baseball. I will build up my business as best I can and try to get to where I have paid off my debts and can pay my bills and lead as peaceful a life as possible, but I don't think anything will ever take the place of baseball. It is the simplest and best part of life for me.

When I heard the Dodgers had an opening for a hitting instructor, I applied for it. I was interviewed by Al Campanis, now general manager of the team, Bill Schweppe, vice-president in charge of minor-league operations, and Lee Scott, the traveling secretary. We got to know one another, really, for the first time. I had said so little to management in my time with the team, no one in the front office really knew me. Now they said I had more on the ball than they had believed. Peter Malley, Walter's son, now president of the club, approved my appointment. I was offered $1,250 a month and took it.

I didn't realize how much baseball meant until I went back. Just getting on the Dodgers' plane again and going back to Vero Beach for spring training for the first time in ten years was a thrill. Getting off the plane, I was greeted like a long-lost hero. It moved me. The base had been modernized, but it was still a place to play baseball. I found out how much I had missed the camaraderie of the clubhouse, playing poker and chess with the guys, shooting the bull with them. I think you miss that fraternity of friendship more than anything.

Through the season, as I took my trips across the country to teams in the organization, I was always one of the first to get to the ball park and one of the last to leave. I taught catching as well as hitting, enjoyed it, and I think I helped a few players. The reaction has been good, but I don't know if the job will last or if another will open up. But I know I want it to last. I want my business to work out, but I want to be in baseball too.

After I left baseball I stayed away from ball parks for a few years. I had bad feelings about how the game had gone for me and I hated the thought of going back as a has-been. There is nothing sadder than a washed-up player visiting a clubhouse, walking around shaking hands with the guys who are doing what he wishes he could still do, talking about times that aren't anymore. I was afraid I'd feel bad that I wasn't in it anymore.

But once I had a job back in baseball it wasn't so bad going back. I agreed to take part in one old-timers' game, then another. I saw guys I hadn't seen for years. I hadn't realized how much I missed them. I saw guys I really love. We talked about days gone by, but they had been good days, and it was good to reminisce about them. If they were good days, why not remember them? Why dwell on the bad days of today?

Baseball sure made today's days a lot better for me. I'm young yet, in my forties but far from fifty. I can't play anymore, but I can still play a part in the game. I hope they let me.

I've been a ballplayer. It's been my life. It's the life I like. There's a lot that's bad about it, but more that's good. For me, anyway. Maybe it's a kids' game, but maybe I'm just a kid who can't grow up. It's my game and I'm a kid at heart. I've learned a lot about life—about being a good guy and a bad guy, about making money and blowing it, about trying to make it in business and the outside world, about love and how much you need it and how much it can hurt you. And one thing I've learned about myself is that whether or not there is a place for me in the game, there will always be a place in my heart for baseball.

There's only so much the average guy can do. A guy has to do what he does best.